Professionalization of Teachers and Institutions

Richard Hay

SHIPRA

Rs. 1250

ISBN: 978-81-7541-801-1

First Published in India in 2015

Professionalization of Teachers and Institutions

Published by:

SHIPRA PUBLICATIONS
LG 18-19, Pankaj Central Market,
I.P. Ext., Patparganj, Delhi 110092, India
Ph.: 011- 2223 5152, 2223 6152
Email: info@shiprapublication.com
www.shiprapublication.com

Foreword

India's higher education system is one of the largest in the world, occupying the third position in size and diversity, next only to that of the United States and China. With more than 500 universities and 25000 colleges, academic and professional, and a staggering number of 3+lakh teachers, the structural basis of our educational edifice is indeed colossal. Yet the system is not able to serve more than about 15 per cent of the eligible college going segment of the nation's population. What is more worrying is the fact that the standard and quality of these educational institutions simply does not match its size. This is a genuine concern of everyone interested in the progress of higher education in the country.

Teaching is universally accepted and approved as a noble profession. But in India it is hardly perceived or practised as such. The peculiar pattern of the evolution of higher education in the country, particularly its affiliation system, is often blamed for this sorry state of affairs. In India, colleges preceded the university. Starting from the early decades of the nineteenth century, colleges were started both by government and by private agencies. Teachers with prescribed qualifications were appointed to these institutions on the basis of guidelines laid down by the colonial rulers. They were considered employees of the government or of the management. Non-teaching staff appointed to colleges to assist the teaching process were also dubbed as employees, but without teaching duties. This early labeling of teachers as 'employees', stuck and had a profound effect on the psycho-social niche of the educational culture of the times. When India's first universities came into existence in 1857 in Calcutta (Kolkota), Madras (Chennai) and Bombay (Mumbai) to regulate higher education in the country in general and the affairs of affiliated colleges in particular, they took up the job of defining the duties of teachers, keeping their professional nature in view. This included various aspects of teaching, drawing up of syllabi for various courses, preparing and prescribing teaching materials, methods of teaching, working hours, higher dimensions of learning-teaching process, etc. Though the universities' statutes and directives were general guidelines for the development of the professional life of teachers, it was the external profile of the new set of rules that prevailed rather than their inner essence. Teachers were contented with the routine profiles of their given duties and tasks, rather than propelled by their professional demands. A great majority of them were hardly concerned with professional improvements at all and showed a tendency to fall in line with external requirements of the institutions since they were privileged 'employees' with comfortable service conditions and security of employment.

This early setting of limiting the academic space of teachers, though brought about not by design but accident, was to the detriment of developing teaching as a profession. The affiliating pattern further added to the woe. College teachers found little scope for playing any direct or significant role in the academic life or progress of their institutions which were regulated and controlled by a sort of remote-controlled scheme. As a result, the teachers in colleges found themselves as employees of the Government or of the managements rather than as free-thinking educational professionals who could genuinely participate in and contribute to the advancement of higher education. In their capacity as employees, they did as good a job as other employees in Government or private services did. They attended colleges in time, took classes regularly, conducted class examinations, helped the authorities when it was sought for and left the campus, like other employees, when the evening bell was struck. Most of them became uninterested in any academic activities beyond the classrooms. Also outside office hours, hardly any teacher remained in the campus to follow up any meaningful academic pursuits or research activities. Even conceptually, professional development of teachers remained a remote possibility, even an illusion. I am aware that there were exceptions to the general pattern described above. It was these exception that kept the affiliation system alive and kicking.

The author of the present volume, *Professionalization of Teachers and Institutions*, belongs to this rare breed. Prof. Richard Hay spent nearly three and a half decades within the affiliating institutions, but refused to remain a mere cog in the wheel. Most of the time he was in the Government service where the general lethargy and employee-mentality are maximal. He served as lecturer and principal in several colleges, including the prestigious century-old Government Brennen College, Tellicherry which was the alma mater of a whole galaxy of many eminent men and women in the erstwhile Malabar region. While serving these tradition-bound, habit-enslaved institutions, Prof. Hay strove to make his teaching career a meaningful sojourn for the development of his vocation. The present volume is the outcome of the professor's patient, persistent, well-poised enterprise. It is indeed a laudable effort.

There are many factors that contribute to the deterioration of standards in higher education. The *Professionalization of Teachers and Institutions* opens our eyes to the rarity of written professional contributions by the teaching community towards enlightening the general public about the inner nuances of the higher educational system, highlighting its strengths and weaknesses or enriching their own craft from within. The basic urge and challenge for improvement and for consequent operational practices of any profession should come from within by its own practitioners. But in the case of higher education, such efforts happened only on the fringes. Bulk of the faculty in the colleges and universities remained innocent of any such serious effort. Many highly qualified teachers spent their entire life in the campuses of colleges or university departments without even writing an article, leave alone books, on their long experience in pedagogy or on enhancing the standard of the subject they were handling for so long. In fact, it is the teachers who observe and absorb the dynamics of the learning-teaching process in the given milieu. It is they who know the aspirations and feelings of the growing generation which has been placed under their charge. Teachers alone would be able to judge whether what was taught in the classrooms was adequate to the needs of the young knowledge seekers and prepared them sufficiently to meet the complex demands of adult life. Teachers alone were best suited to assess whether the courses offered in the institution are life-related or will help students to find some jobs after completing their study. Yet college teachers leave behind precious little by way of recording their findings, observations or experiences on any such vital matters that determine the relevance of higher education in the country or the future of the bright young people who have pinned their high hopes on college education. Just as the doctors are the leaders of medical profession and medical education, college and university teachers are the leaders of higher education system. It is therefore the duty of teachers to enrich their profession by critically assessing what they have been doing and expressing their views on improving and modernizing their craft. Such considered views and suggestions by the practising teachers would have greatly helped higher authorities, policy makers and social leaders to make higher education more relevant to the times and to evolve it as a powerful instrument of social progress. But it is most disappointing to note that the published literature on higher education in India is the least refurbished among all the different professional writings. The situation seems to be worst in Kerala where books or monographs on any aspect of higher education are extremely scarce.

It is in this context that the publication of *Professionalization of Teachers and Institutions* is to be welcomed. It is a valuable addition in the field of college and university education, particularly on the leadership role of teachers in the system. I wish that every college and university teacher in the state and the country reads this valuable volume at least once during their professional career.

Dr. A.N.P. Ummerkutty Thalassery
Former Vice Chancellor,
Calicut University

Preface

From the beginning of my career as a teacher in higher education, I was keen to develop my professional qualities. The first step, I took up to fulfill my ambition in this regard was to acquire another post-graduate degree in Higher Education and attend many training programmes to hone my skills as a teacher through the arduous method on a continual basis.

The areas covered in this book, I think, are very critical for the success and, especially for the professional development, of a teacher and an institution. While writing this book, I have depended more on my long-standing experience in the profession in key positions in different institutions in higher education both in the public and private sectors. The reader would appreciate that the practical ideas elucidated on the subject are expressed in a lucid style in this book so that a novice in the teaching profession finds it easy to assimilate them and improve upon his/her skills and abilities to become a proficient teacher. Similarly, an education administrator in higher education can get better insights into the complex task of development of institutions and implement and evaluate various educational programmes at the higher level of administration.

My exposure to this noble profession in prestigious institutions in higher education for thirty five years has given me the inner strength to embark on this veritable task. I have been involved at the higher echelons of administration of several higher education institutions in India and abroad and was instrumental in developing the core competencies of most of the institutions which I served with pride and contentment. I look back over three and half decades of success and failure, trials and triumphs, ecstasy and anguish while writing this book. My current respite from academe is proving timely and satisfying.

The purpose of writing this book is to help develop competent and exemplary teachers who would be assets to this noble and rewarding profession and to the respective institutions and provide essential support and guidance to education administrators to upgrade the quality of institutions of higher education. My long experience as a teacher and administrator has inspired me to think aloud about different facets of teaching which play a decisive role in the making of a good teacher and about the importance of administration in the molding of an institution. This book offers practicing teachers as well as teacher-trainees and administrators of educational institutions very useful guidance based on hands-on experience rather than theory.

Teaching profession, by and large, attracts the intelligentsia of a country. It has become more challenging now as high-quality institutions are setting higher and higher standards by either developing or adopting innovative teaching practices. The twenty-first century has witnessed a paradigm-shift in the methodology of teaching, copiously supported by technology which has resulted in enhancing the efficiency and proficiency of the teacher. This noblest of all professions is quite possibly the most demanding of all professions too, considering its superior status, onerous responsibilities and remarkable service. The administration of educational institutions has undergone rapid changes demanding the service of highly professional administrators with solid academic background who have been exposed to the best administrative practices at the helm of affairs.

Professional development is crucial to enhance the teacher's abilities and skills to carry out his/her tasks diligently and efficiently. A teacher has to achieve an acclaimed level of proficiency, without which he/she will not be able to fulfill the basic duties and responsibilities. This book, which presents a no-holds barred look at the nuances of the teaching profession and administration, is expected to provide the much-needed guidance in developing quality-conscious and self-motivated crop of competent teachers and administrators. The very raison d'être—to ensure quality enhancement—will go a long way to encourage teachers to attain a prime place in the sphere of education and administrators to excel in their performance.

The pace of technological advances has accelerated in all fields, especially in the field of education. Simultaneously, development of knowledge-societies has become the order of the day. Obviously, this generation of students is more exposed to the source of information than their predecessors. This, in turn, helps them to access knowledge much swifter and with greater ease. In such a demanding scenario, both teachers and administrators will have to seriously apply their minds to ensure professional development strategies so as to build appropriate competence to meet the challenges. This book addresses such issues positively.

The book is discursive, gently proceeding logically, from one theme to another. It is hoped that it provides good insights into teaching and administration which can be used by teachers and administrators for their professional development both in the early stages of their career and as senior personnel. The practical state-of-the-art approach followed helps the reader to understand and appreciate the different approaches to teaching and the methods by which teaching could be made effective in different classroom situations. Whether it is the art or practice of teaching, every attempt has been made to clarify the role of a teacher to bring about positive changes in educational institutions both in schools and colleges. The book also provides fundamentals of the practice of teaching and elucidates on the tools and techniques of teaching. It is expected that it will help many teachers to redefine their own teaching philosophies and enable them to develop their own strategies for effective teaching. A number of cases with questions for discussion are added to facilitate practical application. The case study takes the reader through what actually occurs in an educational institution. It will also serve the needs of administrators in the field of education to understand the complex situations, and find solutions by adhering to modern concepts and practices.

This book is an attempt to explore a plethora of possibilities, both structured and unstructured, to make headway in the teaching profession and facilitate the grooming of exceptionally good teachers, and administrators in the field of higher education to set higher goals and excel in their performance. It is also intended to offer practical guidance to teachers and administrators in higher education, on how to navigate many of the common challenges they are likely to come across in their career. It will pave the way for a life-time of educational leadership for the teachers and administrators who read it.

You need not read this book from front to back. You can select a chapter and read it and then flip on to other chapters of your interest. The first eleven chapters focus on pedagogical issues and the rest presents an overview of institutional development. The author looks forward to valuable suggestions from readers to augment the usefulness of this book.

Prof. Richard Hay

Acknowledgements

What made me work with zeal to write this book on professional development of teachers and institutions has been my commitment to this noble profession for more than three and half decades. During this long period, I had ample opportunities to see for myself renowned teachers at work, who literally transformed their classes into live, exciting and memorable moments, to be cherished by their students throughout their life. Many of my teachers have influenced me both as mentors and facilitators. I owe a deep debt of gratitude to them.

In the course of my career as a teacher and an administrator, I have been inspired by many of my colleagues. When I took up the reins of administration in several illustrious centers of higher education, I started closely observing the style of teaching, the tools used and methodology followed, which in the end was instrumental in deciding the quality of teaching to a great extent. Without the timely contemplations on them this book would have not become a reality. I am ever grateful to my colleagues belonging to different disciplines for providing me insights into the art and practice of teaching.

Three professors have played significant roles in shaping my destiny. These ace teachers are: Prof. E.G.L. Papali, Prof. Dr. Mohammed Mohsin, and Prof. Dr. C.L. Anand who were all heads of departments of the institutions where I had studied. I place on record my deep debt of gratitude to those stalwarts in education.

I am ever indebted to Dr. A.N.P. Ummerkutty, former Vice Chancellor, Calicut University, who had served as chairman of several NAAC Peer Teams and as chairman of UGC Visiting Teams, for being kind enough to write the foreword. His keen insights into the working of the affiliating pattern had helped me a lot to understand the ramifications of this traditional system.

I profusely thank Dr. P.M. Sankarankutty, Dept. of Placement and Training, Karunya University, Coimbatore and Dr. Bhaskaran P. Nair, Dept. of English, Pondicherry University who went through the draft and helped me to make it perfect. I sincerely thank Dr. K.P. Suresh, Dept. of Education, Mahatma Gandhi University who was kind enough to go through the draft and suggest some changes and Dr. C.N. Balakrishnan Nambiar for his valuable insights.

It is difficult to write a book which contains the varied facets of higher education without making reference to the works of the great thinkers in the field of education. I am particularly indebted to those enlightened minds.

I am deeply indebted to the University of Maryland, Theodore R McKeldin Library, Toronto Reference Library and the York University, Scott Library which opened their doors wholeheartedly to me as a researcher. I place on record my deep appreciation of the services rendered by their staff and their magnanimous attitude in providing assistance to me. I owe to all those institutions of which I was a part of and to my country, a deep sense of gratitude for all that I have gained.

My deepest gratitude goes to my sons-in-law, Ajay Cattungal and Shawn Joy who took lots of pain in enabling me to visit universities and libraries in the US and Canada to engage in research on several areas of higher education.

To many students, whom I taught and led with confidence at the various institutions, I express my thanks for the support. I am also most grateful to Shipra Publications, Delhi for their patience in editing the book and for their friendly advice.

Thanks to my wife, Shakila, for her constant support and motivation and to my children, Romola Joy and Rowina Cattungal for their prayers.

Prof. Richard Hay

Contents

PART I

1
The Art of Teaching

I have no special gift. I am only passionately curious.

—Albert Einstein

In a completely rational society, the best of us would be teachers and the rest of us would have to settle for something less, because passing civilization along from one generation to the next ought to be the highest honour and the highest responsibility anyone could have.

—Lee Iacocca

Introduction

In this world, there is no profession as sacred and noble as teaching. The future of a nation depends on the quality of teachers that the nation can feel proud of. It is in the classrooms of a nation that teachers prepare the young minds to bring equality, freedom, growth, development and dignity to its citizens. The future of mankind is dependent on creative, forward looking and humane teachers. The role of teachers is to inspire, empower and enable the younger generation to think positively to build a peaceful, harmonious, prosperous and environment-friendly world. One of the key goals of education is to inculcate tolerance for other cultures, ethnicities, religions and nationalities. Teachers have to work towards creating a world where everyone becomes compassionate and empathetic, and lead others by example. It is the teachers who can empower generations with the knowledge which would enable them to build the future of their nation.

In the words of Jawaharlal Nehru, all over the world people realize that only through right education can a better order of society be built up. As the new system of education aims at developing a cohesive society, which will eliminate inequalities and imbalances and ensure equal access to quality education, teachers must respond positively to the impact of drastic changes taking place around them and assist the new generation of learners to possess the knowledge and appropriate skills to adapt to the changes. I am reminded of the words of Nelson Mandela: Education is the most powerful weapon which you can use to change the world. According to G.K. Chesterton, education is the soul of a society as it passes from one generation to another.

John Dewey described education as a social process for achieving growth and that education is not a preparation for life; it is life itself. Therefore, the teacher must become more responsible and accountable. In fact, the success of any educational endeavor depends on the quality of performance of the teacher. As teachers occupy a prime place in the educational process and are leaders of the system, their accountability is of elemental nature. Donald Kennedy states that institutions of higher education have a responsibility to the society that sponsors and nurtures them as well as to their students and the people who work with them. The university is about opportunity: the opportunity to give others the personal and intellectual platform they need to advance culture, to preserve life, and to generate a sustainable human future. It is teaching that provides endless challenges and opportunities for the growth of a nation.

Teachers of the twenty-first century have to possess technology and research skills, apart from the usual pedagogical skills. They have to become lifelong learners and keep on upgrading their professional skills so that they are able to bridge theory and practice and create a high quality, learning environment in the classroom. Advanced nations have been built with the support of accomplished professional teachers who are knowledgeable, resourceful and technologically-oriented. It is the hallowed centers of learning of the world which have guided mankind as beacons of light, and brought in progress and prosperity to humanity. In modern times, only those teachers who are empowered with knowledge and technological skills would be able to deliver effectively. If the teacher holds on to the outdated teaching practices and style, he would lose his credentials as a capable teacher.

It is high time that the institutions shed their outdated practices, perceptions and methods, and adapt to the needs of the modern era which has been characterized by new potentials for growth and development. Institutional administration must seek effective methods of administration to establish new goals by expanding their vision, put themselves in strategic positions and proactively capitalize on the demands of existing and emerging markets and newer societal goals and needs by offering new programmes and enhancing the quality of all existing programmes. If education does not fulfill the needs and dreams of the young people, who are the beneficiaries of higher education, it becomes a sheer waste of time and resources. Zachary Karabell (1998) tells us how students perceive contemporary higher education:

Students are not passive recipients of their education. More than ever, they shape what goes on in the classroom, what is taught, and how much they will spend on their schooling. In their efforts, individually and collectively, intentionally and inadvertently, to mould the classrooms and the university to meet their needs, they often encounter professors who have rather different goals. Professors believe that a college diploma represents the culmination of education. Students, however, increasingly see the diploma as a credential that will lead to a better job. In an ideal world, education and credentializing would be compatible, but in the world of higher education today, they are often at odds.

The basic question we will have to put to ourselves is whether the contemporary higher education system provides the required educational support for young individuals to make a meaningful and decent living in a competitive world.

Clayton M. Christensen and Henry J. Eyring (2011), in their futuristic vision of higher education institutions, observe that in future the most successful institutions will be those that lift their students furthest and fastest and that share their scholarship most broadly. Universities will be recognized for the learning they impart rather than for admitting the smartest students. The impact of their scholarship will be judged by not only those who cite but those who integrate, apply, and teach what they have learnt.

We should think about how knowledge would accelerate growth and development and become a deciding factor of competitiveness in the global environment. Jenny Rogers (2007) states that knowledge and people with knowledge are the key factors of development, the main drivers of growth, and the major determinants of competitiveness in the global knowledge economy. In his seminal work on competitive advantage, M. Porter (1990) has pointed out that a nation could no longer rely on abundant natural resources and cheap labour, and that competitive advantage would increasingly be based on combinations of technical innovation and creative use of knowledge.

The achievements of higher education percolate in the society, and touch the lives of its citizens and perhaps, all humanity. Talking about the social benefits of higher education, Walter W. McMahon (2009) observes: What is probably the largest and most important social benefit of higher education is the benefit to the broader society from the dissemination of new knowledge. This includes adapting the newly created knowledge and new technologies in all academic fields. New knowledge is created by research at the research universities but also by R&D within firms, government agencies, and universities worldwide. This becomes known to faculty actively engaged in these fields.

Technology, added to a pedagogical approach that is unsound cannot produce good instruction. Computer-based technology or any other kind of technology cannot in and of itself improve instructional practice (Eileen M. Coppola, 2004). Even though technology is so valuable in the modern world, by itself it cannot improve education. However, it can drastically change it. It is the teachers with their knowledge, right attitude and professional skills who can improve the quality of education. It is the teacher who through the depth of knowledge possessed and the dexterity of using technological skills will be able to create indelible impressions in the minds of the students, and make teaching and learning productive and effective.

In the present world, subjects like mathematics, science, management and technology are given priority. However, even in this new era, the role played by humanities in creating socially-conscious citizens cannot be ignored. Humanities at best teach students how to think critically, says Zachary Karabell (1998). The winner of the 1976 Nobel Peace Prize, Betty Williams says, "it is time to start teaching humanity in classrooms. We can produce doctors or mechanics or whatever but we need to start producing the whole human being." In this context, the words of Dalai Lama echoes in my mind: It is vital that, when educating our children's brains, we do not neglect to educate their hearts.

We must understand the humanities in two ways. The humanities are a set of educational disciplines—literature, history, classics, philosophy; but the humanities also represent a world-view—a view in which human values—justice, freedoms, rights, compassion, respect, equality, inclusion, responsibility,—are the measure of progress and development. In this new millennium, serious and sustained study of the humanities and social sciences would only add more value to education. The seven social sins, according to Mahatma Gandhi are: politics without principles, wealth without work, pleasure without conscience, knowledge without character, commerce without morality, science without humanity, and worship without sacrifice. These are some of the sins which are the canker worms that devour the sap of a nation. These sins are the critical pointers which warn us about the degradation of a society and remind us of the significance of human values which help in building societies that follow a righteous and ethical life. Graham Haydon (2006) states that some of the values of life are: self-respect, self-discipline, care (care for others), goodwill, respect (for others), loyalty, trust, cooperation, love, commitment, truth, integrity, honesty, balance, diversity, beauty, and a sense of security, comfort, cheerfulness, convenience, intelligence, efficiency, cost-effectiveness, neatness, reasonableness. N.R. Narayana Murthy, the co-founder of Infosys, asserts that human values drive progress and define quality of life.

It must be appreciated that only value-driven resourceful teachers would be able to develop compassionate and humane people all over the world. Similarly, only the creative teachers would develop a crop of students to transform and discover their own future. Talking about the role of parents, teachers and the society in the upbringing of children, John Adams says an effort should be made to elevate the minds of our children and exalt their courage, to accelerate and animate their industry and activity, to excite in them an habitual contempt for meanness, abhorrence of injustice and inhumanity, and an ambition to excel in every capacity, faculty and virtue.

The key to inspiring teaching lies in sustaining an intellectually vital and engaged classroom. This, in turn, requires nourishing the inner lives of the Inspired faculty—faculty who are not dispirited and whose morale is high. They can build the relationships, forge the connections, bind together the pluralistic global learning communities that will provide undergraduates with models to carry throughout their lives, models that inspire lives of purpose and commitment to causes larger than themselves. (Diana Chapman Walsh, 2000).

It is the teachers with exalted minds who are able to play a decisive role in carving out a wholesome and rewarding future for the younger generation. Of course, the path to be followed to reach such goals is filled with challenges and obstacles, which have to be overcome with tenacity and strong will. Similarly, administration must act as a catalyst to develop and manage a talented group of teachers so that the institution derives value from education. Administrators must have a clear vision as to how to develop the institution to meet its current and future goals. University and college administrators are responsible to introduce the best practices in education which ensure qualitative improvement and excellence at all levels. Managing academic change in an era of worldwide value-shift in education has become a top priority for academic administrators. It facilitates the creation of an institution culture and climate based on high expectations of students, teachers, other stake holders and society at large.

The new global environment which has brought in a sea of change in the goals and functioning of universities and colleges has been opening up new opportunities to students. If they have to benefit from these opportunities, universities and colleges will have to reshape and remodel their structure and functioning. The suggestions given by Werner Z Hirsch and Luc E Weber in this context are enlightening: Globalization and, in particular, the rapid growth and development of the "knowledge industry"—will profoundly change the educational system as the ability to move information more quickly and economically becomes greater and more wide spread. These developments require a repositioning of the university. Because universities have traditionally dispensed courses only regionally to their students, they have benefited from a regional monopoly. However, monopolies based on regional proximity cannot survive the globalization movement. Universities will experience competition, worldwide and regionally. For some, it is a threat, for others, it is a new opportunity offering universities the possibility to go beyond their regional role. To act globally and in a competitive environment, the university must consider students as its clients by adapting programmes to meet their needs and wishes. Universities should listen more carefully to society to learn and understand its changing needs and expectations, as well as its perceptions of higher education, especially in the light of the forces driving change.

Universities should be more responsive to needs when offering new study programmes or starting new research. They should also show a greater willingness, or even take the lead while cooperating with industry and the state. Universities and their units should be reliable partners of companies and institutions. They should sharpen their sense of responsibility towards society. More than ever, they are the only independent tenants of collective values and culture and the best placed to express constructive criticism and suggest new ideas. They have been able to play this role more or less freely for centuries. This responsibility is as important in the present globalized world dominated by the power of the market and short-sighted politicians, as it was in the periods of obscurantism or totalitarian regimes. The greatest threat is that knowledge, which is traditionally a public good available to all those seeking it, might become private good reserved only for those who can pay for it.

Rationale

It is pertinent that the administrators and teachers take into account the UNESCO Report on Education, which is considered to be the most important document on education. (The Report of the Delors Commission on Education for the Twenty-first Century, 1996) I quote below the quintessence of this report which has brought in worldwide value shift with respect to education, and it is used as a frame of reference to develop the contents of the topics in this book.

"Learning: the Treasure Within" suggests the need to redefine the scope of learning with focus on four kinds of learning, described as the "four pillars of learning". They are the following:

- *Learning to know*: acquiring the instruments of understanding; acquiring validated knowledge using scientific methods; developing a cognitive-rational framework for interpreting the events and phenomena of the world around; learning to learn from opportunities.
- *Learning to do*: developing competencies to act creatively in the social environment; acquiring the competence to deal effectively with work situations and improve the existing set-up; developing the capacity to cope effectively with uncertainty and play a meaningful role in creating the future.
- *Learning to live together*: acquiring the competence to deal effectively with human beings in one's own and other cultures and live with them; acquiring the ability to co-operate with others in common tasks; proficiency to act as member of multi-cultural society with diverse needs and perceptions; ability to understand the importance of others and use this understanding to develop a new social order; dealing

with tensions in the complex new social order; using the concept of interdependence of humans to work for common causes.

- *Learning to be*: an essential summation and progression of the three types of learning described earlier; learning which stands for the moralistic or value-strand of education; developing a human being who can act with greater autonomy, judgement and personal responsibility; learning which develops a person who understands himself; learning which develops an individual with the ability to visualize the unforeseen needs of the future and has the capacity to act appropriately in new situations; preparedness for future changes.
- The four categories of expected outcomes of learning, as outlined above, necessitate the development and use of new conceptions of education and learning.
- Teachers have to possess new skills and abilities to meet the demands of the twenty-first century. In this context it is advisable to appreciate the other salient points of UNESCO report on education which pinpoints the "New Goals for Education" in terms of new skills and abilities to be developed, which are given below:
- *Understand the new century*: All the learners should be able to make a correct assessment of past events—a historic perspective of what has gone before and an objective perception of the negative and positive aspects of human actions of the past to be used as a guideline for future action.
- *Managing change in a rapidly changing society*: This has to be done through a discriminating use of the scientific principles of human behaviour and also treating education as an art which involves the ability to deal with other human beings using human judgement, adaptability and understanding.
- *Learn to keep on learning*: Changes in society will demand the learning of new skills and unlearning of outdated skills. This indicates the need for lifelong learning, especially in developing countries which will have to develop special facilities for providing the new kind of learning.
- *Develop skills for self-employment*: The fact that many jobs are becoming redundant in the labour market has to be taken into account and adjustments will have to be made to fit the new generation learner to the new employment scenario where skills of self-employment and entrepreneurship will become more important. The youth will have to be equipped to take risks in the new economic environment.

- *Skills for improved management of information*: The new generation youth have to be trained to select and prioritize information in the new world which is suffering from information overload, a world inundated with surfeit of information. The youth should be given intense training to develop the skills to select worthwhile information and use this for creating usable and productive knowledge.
- *Ability to cope with stress*: The new generation learners will be exposed to a wide variety of stress situations which are created by the inexorable march of technology and the resulting uncertainty in the world. The new world scenario forces on us the need to redefine the system of education to provide lifelong training and retraining to help the learners to work in the multi-cultural and ever-changing society of the future.

In the new world, which has been characterized by the deep impact of the 'Information Age', 'Knowledge Economy' and 'Knowledge Society' in which knowledge has become the central theme and the real power, teachers will have to acquire adequate relevant knowledge and develop appropriate skills to make the new generation learner face the challenges of the twenty-first century with confidence. Administration will have to provide the right leadership, support, and the infrastructure to build the institution to meet new challenges and to maintain excellent standards of education. In the words of Francis Bacon, 1597, "Knowledge is power," the significance of knowledge is expressed with a deep insight. In the modern times, as new knowledge is created faster, the old knowledge becomes irrelevant in many contexts. James J. Duderstadt, (1999) suggests that powerful forces are driving an increasing societal demand for higher education products and services. In today's world, knowledge determines the wealth of nations. One's education, knowledge, and skills have become primary determinants of one's personal standard of living, the quality of one's life. We are at the dawn of an Age of Knowledge, in which intellectual capital–brainpower–is replacing financial and physical capital as the key to our strength, prosperity, and well-being. As knowledge and education become key strategic priorities, our societies have become more dependent upon those social institutions that create these critical resources, our colleges and universities. There is growing concern about the capacity of our existing institutions to serve these changing social needs–indeed, even about their ability to survive in the face of the extraordinary changes occurring in our world. Rune Krumsvik (2009) has stated that the shelf life of knowledge is becoming shorter. On the one hand, human knowledge is evolving very fast as, our societies, and technology keeps changing. Students are not likely to have a simple trajectory or a single career, as human trajectories move fast and go through rapid transformations (McCracken, 2008). As a result, much of what we learn will be relevant only for a limited time.

Education and Teaching

All over the world, people recognize the significance of investing in intellectual capital as only education would bring about positive and long-lasting changes in a society. To reform, to change and to develop a capable and resourceful individual is the only pragmatic way to provide quality education. It is also a proven fact that it improves considerably only in an open system. The words of Cardinal Newman are of great relevance to understand the purpose of university education: "A university training is the great ordinary means to a great but ordinary end; it aims at raising the intellectual tone of a society....It is education which gives a man a clear conscious view of his own opinions and judgements, a truth in developing them, an eloquence in expressing them and a force in urging them."

In "Academic Duty", Donald Kennedy elucidates the duties of a teacher as follows: "Responsibility suggests the duty one owes to the institution—and first and foremost, to one's students. It means meeting one's classes well-prepared and maintaining one's standard of scholarship. It means giving a student the time he or she needs to work out a problem.... In essence, it means delivering full support to a set of institutional objectives.... Thus much of academic duty resolves itself into a set of obligation that professors owe to others: to their undergraduate students, to the more advanced scholars they train, to their colleagues, to the institution with which they are affiliated, and to the larger society, that society has high expectations of the professoriate and is especially impatient with its shortcomings."

It has been accepted world over that human faculty is the key for a vibrant knowledge-based economy and, education is the positive and definitive method that nourishes and nurtures the development of the citizens of a country. It is the bounden duty of the government to take steps to ensure enhancement in the quality of education at all levels for which they have to facilitate reforms and provide adequate budgetary support to implement such policy decisions. For the democratically elected governments the responsibility is still higher: They must always share the responsibility to establish excellent centers of higher education, and guarantee standards at all levels of education for all the people. It is in a macro environment that the policymakers must have a clear view of the bold initiatives to be introduced in the education sector so that the current teaching environment is adapted to a more knowledge-based system, which encourages a passion for learning through fostering interactivity and creativity. An education policy which considers the ground realities would yield better results. Therefore, education must be the top priority of all governments, and no government can leave behind an educational system in deep crisis for want of their attention and patronage.

In the book, *Tomorrow's Professor*, Richard M. Reis emphatically states that the teaching, "both educates and entices future scholars. It means not only transmitting knowledge, but transforming and extending it as well." Luc E. Weber (1999) remarks: Teachers will have to accept that their role is changing; they will be decreasingly information providers and increasingly animators and commentators in charge of giving context and in-depth understanding of an area. Moreover, as is already the case for research, they will be confronted with growing competition in their teaching assignments, thanks to increasing transparency on the type and quality of courses available elsewhere and through multimedia.

Education does not take place in the proper sense if freedom of speech is curtailed or not guaranteed. The essence of education is freedom of expression. This is the corner-stone of an educational philosophy, which fosters a profusion of ideas from all corners without any restriction. If there is no space for debate in a classroom, education becomes senseless and sometimes, worthless. Unfettered thinking can produce valuable and quality ideas and make students more creative. Indeed, education acts as a powerful tool to actuate reforms, ensure progress and prosperity. Besides, educational institutions are a vital part of the economic infrastructure of a country, and are a prominent and inescapable social engine for growth. A country's future depends on their success, and educational institutions are expected to initiate positive change and progress incessantly in a society. It should be understood that the teachers and administration can jointly play a pivotal role in accelerating the process of societal growth and development, and shape the destiny of a nation. I quote Thomas Jefferson about the purpose of education: "I look to the diffusion of light and education as the resource to be relied on for ameliorating the condition, promoting the virtue, and advancing the happiness of man."

Teaching involves personal responsibilities, sacrifices and an inner urge to constantly improve one's quality, keeping always in mind the exalted mission and goals of education. The teaching profession is by all means a prestigious one as teachers are the key constituents in creating a student-centered approach in any model of educational process that guarantees the development and prosperity of the people. Teachers are obliged to be fully prepared to make the learning process as simple and effective as possible and foster the development of the innate potentials of students. To achieve this, first of all, teachers are required to be wholly devoted to the profession and be enthusiastic and keen on his/her presentation. Robert Frost's classification of teachers is thought-provoking: "There are two kinds of teachers—the kind that fill you with so much quail shot that you can't move and the kind that just gives you a little prod behind and you jump to the skies."

What makes an educational institution a much sought after institution? This is an often repeated question in any forum that discusses the methods to empower and strengthen its core competence. The best method to achieve excellence and empowerment for any institution is by obtaining the selfless service of a team of efficient, dedicated, conscientious and resourceful teachers who are highly focused in pursuing the educational goals with fervor and zeal. As an organization is known by the quality of its products, an educational institution is known by the quality of students who are molded by committed and distinguished teachers. It is quality that matters in every field of human endeavour. In this sense, teachers can make or mar an institution.

Some universities will seize the opportunity to rebuild a more integrated community of scholars as they participate in rigorous consultations and make hard decisions about what they most want to be, about how they can improve teaching and research and the quality of citizenship and ethical conduct within the confines of more constrained resources (Clark Kerr, 1995). It is the reputation of the teachers in an educational institution, apart from the facilities provided, that ultimately defines the level of education. It is quite important that the educational institution must have a sedulous group of teachers, and proper facilities which always make them distinctive and enable them to stand apart. In addition, an educational institution has to provide an ideal learning environment through its academic research, co-curricular and extra-curricular facilities which have been planned and developed according to apprcciable standards of excellence. More important, educational institutions are unquestionably the character-building institutions of hundreds of students who pass through its portals every year. In all these crucial areas of human development, it is the teachers who make the institution stand out as a great pillar of strength of a nation. The importance of standards in education is reflected in the words of William J. Bennet: "Education is, after all, a serious business. Its lifeblood is standards. If there are no standards, how do we call something higher education?"

The college or university is precious like the umbilical cord which gives us life, and when it is cut off, it etches in our minds indelible impressions by way of knowledge to lead a worthy life. We always remember with reverence and gratitude the college or the university where we have studied. Indeed, it is our Alma Mater for life. Jaroslav Pelikan (1992), has brought out the essence of the Alma Mater by invoking Newman, after describing the purpose of the university:

> "For if the vocation of the university is not only the one it shares with the college, the extension of knowledge to undergraduates through teaching, but the preparation of professionals through training, the advancement of knowledge through research, and the

> diffusion of knowledge through publication, together with the creation of a free and responsible community in which such advancement and diffusion of knowledge are an ongoing and unending process, then it functions much as we may, if we have been blessed, remember our parents functioning—and as perhaps we also may, if we have been twice blessed, function as parents ourselves, at least from time to time. Because the university is where in Newman's phrase, "a habit of mind is formed which lasts through life", the university is the Alma Mater for life, with whom her children have, in Newman's language, perpetual residence, intellectually and spiritually if not always physically, even unto death."

Teaching is "above all", Michael Sandel, a Harvard political theorist, argues, "about commanding attention and holding it." That means not just generally motivating students' interest in the subject but capturing and keeping their attention for each class (Ken Bain, 2004). When does a teacher himself become a barrier to learning for students? Of course, there are such instances too which cannot be overlooked. Look at the following three obnoxious ways of handling classes. In the first situation, instead of facing the class, the teacher looks up on the ceiling, in the process, the eye contact being cut off. In the second situation, the teacher goes on speaking while writing on the board. And, in the third situation, the teacher sticks on with the conventional style of teaching depending fully on the lecturing and note dictating method, that too with a poor command of language. It has been found that some teachers are not at all interested in using modern aids and technologies of teaching. The teachers must kindle the minds of their students and not simply dictate notes to prove themselves to be unproductive in a creative and dynamic environment. The very style of such outdated and repugnant teaching distracts the attention of students. It has been found that even some seasoned teachers become inaudible while lecturing in the classrooms, thereby making the class uninteresting and dull. The results of such haphazard teaching affect the image of the institution as well. Teaching involves application of a variety of professional skills which are applied with care, dexterity and precision. It is essentially a creative activity wherein the teacher must continuously hone the skills to excel in his performance. Teachers' contributions count heavily in the making of an institution. Indeed, collectively the teachers of an institution set the academic standards and produce encouraging results and progress for the entire institution.

To be a passionate teacher is to be someone in love with a field of knowledge, deeply stirred by issues and ideas that challenge our world, drawn to the dilemmas and potentials of the young people who come into class each day—or captivated by all these. A passionate teacher is a teacher who breaks out of the isolation of a classroom, who refuses to submit to apathy or cynicism (Seymour B. Sarason, 1999). Edward G. Bulwer-Lytton declares that the best teacher is the one who suggests rather than dogmatizes, and inspires his listener with the wish to teach himself.

The Mechanics of Teaching

Voice: Teaching, being an art, the personal skills of a teacher is of great significance. Certainly, the voice of a teacher, apart from the content value of instruction and the style of teaching, decides the quality of delivery. The teacher has to decide the appropriate volume and sound after considering the number of students in the class and the size of the classroom. Voice is the most useful instrument for a teacher. It can attract students to the class, and make them attentive; it plays a big role in not only conveying the idea effectively but also in maintaining the attention of the students. It is certainly one of the deciding factors in a teacher's success. The pitch, timbre, volume, speed and cadence of the sounds and words are all matters of utmost importance in teaching. The teacher must make his voice reflect enthusiasm and a certain amount of excitement so as to draw the attention of students throughout the session. One of the easiest ways to judge the quality of one's voice is by listening to one's own voice on a recorder and evaluate the effect of the varying pitch, tone and expression on oneself. A combination of many factors, like the pitch, volume, diction, pause, pacing, rate of speaking, expression, pronunciation and breathing decides the effectiveness of teaching, apart from the value of the content and relevant tools and methodology used. Some verbal mechanics of teaching are outlined below.

The Pitch: Voice may be pitched very high or too low depending on how one uses the vocal chord and the throat muscles. To be an effective teacher one has to realize the effect of a normal and healthy range which would match one's vocal tones as required in a particular classroom with a given number of students. A delivery in perfect cadence is highly appreciated by all students. The rhythmic flow of language in harmony and proportion is a cherished quality of a good teacher.

Pitch refers to the highness or lowness of tone or sound. A teacher whose pitch is too high or too low and sounds monotonous transmits a negative impression and certainly distracts the attention of the students. Inflection is the lowering and rising of pitch and it has great impact in a classroom setting. In general, the size of the room and the number of students in the class determines the vocal volume of the teacher. The teacher can decide on a normal range which is comfortable to him. Once the normal pitch is established, listen to how it sounds and how impressive it is, and then use that pitch comfortably. By constant practice, the teacher will be able to decide the pitch required of in different classroom situations. The teacher should speak loudly and forcefully so that all the students in the classroom hear him/her properly. It needs energy and passion to make one's voice heard.

Diction: Diction or articulation refers to the clarity, intelligibility, and distinctness of the utterance. It is the manner of uttering or enunciating words and sounds. The method of producing the vowel and consonant sounds determines the quality of one's diction. If it is poor, it affects the clarity of words and students are not able to understand the ideas clearly. A teacher must make it a point to articulate sounds in the proper way. Each syllable must be uttered both clearly and carefully so as to make the entire word sound clear and comprehensible. Some teachers do not take the pain to pronounce all the sounds in a word and thereby they create doubts in the minds of the students about the intended word. Some teachers do not open their mouths properly and thereby the diction becomes hazy and sloppy. Since the mouth is not opened sufficiently, the sounds do not come out of the throat properly. It is always good to increase the duration of the vowel sounds to bring in clarity and variety in articulation.

Pause: Likewise, pauses enhance the quality of delivery. Some do not pause when it is required, and it results in overlapping of ideas, which causes difficulties to the learners. A pause helps the teacher to signify the importance of words, ideas and the main points. It is used as if we use punctuation while writing a sentence. Pauses at the appropriate time bring dramatic effect to the delivery. A pause automatically brings back the attention of the students if they have gone into wool-gathering or day dreaming. A long pause is a must when the teacher completes a subtopic. This practice will always have a good impact on the entire class. Silent pauses are preferred to vocalized pauses. When we were students, some of us used to count the number of vocalized pauses, viz., you see, OK, do you follow me, etc., and declare from time to time the scores in a hushed voice, resulting in giggling from certain corners of the classroom. Even now this practice is continued. The best way to learn how and when to pause is to rehearse the lecture by pausing at appropriate places, remembering that very often the purpose of pause is not only instantaneously prepare the mind for the next idea, but also to attract the attention of students.

Pacing: Pacing is very important and essential while lecturing which must be determined by the teacher well in advance. The teacher must feel comfortable while delivering a part of the lecture and ensure that students are also comfortable while listening to the lecture. Pacing must be determined after ascertaining the effectiveness of the delivery on listeners' interest. Some teachers lecture at a slow speed and some others lecture at a high speed. Both the practices lead to monotony which result in the loss of the students' interest in the topic. The teacher, for instance, while emphasizing points, must make it rather slow. Like spacing, the rate of speaking plays an important role in determining the efficacy of listening. The delivery becomes dull, dreary and monotonous if the teacher speaks each syllable, word and sentence at the same speed. Have we ever considered the rate of our speaking? I put this question to one of our senior teachers and the reply given by him startled me and so I made enquiries on this count from his students and found that due to his fast rate of speaking they were not able to follow his classes. In a particular class, the majority of students were dosing while the lecture was going on. What a pitiable condition is that! I was chagrined to observe that the teacher concerned was speaking at a slow pace throughout the session. Then, the question is what would be the comfortable rate of speaking to be followed by a teacher. From my long experience, I can recommend between 130 and 150 words per minute. The moment the teacher notes that a student starts yawning or whispering to the student sitting next to him, it is an indicator that he has lost interest in the lecture. If the teacher is slow in the rate of speaking, it can also be an indicator of lack of preparedness on his part. If the teacher speaks fast, the student will not be able to keep up with the pace and tend to lose interest. A teacher who has a monotonic delivery can, within a few minutes of his class put his students to sleep. The best way out is to deliver the lecture at a rate comfortable to both the teacher and the taught.

Expressions: Expressions of the teacher signify the enthusiasm and keenness in the presentation of the subject and the effectiveness of its delivery. His body language matters much in demonstrating his devotion and earnestness in doing his best. The body language, with reference to teaching, includes facial expressions and what the teachers do with their eyes, feet, hands, and posture in a classroom. Even the teacher's dress can become important with reference to body language. The physical attractiveness and personal magnetism are also important qualities in determining the success of a presentation.

Always speaking in the same tone of voice, never moving or gesturing, using monotonous grammatical structure, an overly predictable pattern of speech, and lots of clichés—all these are ways to lose audience's attention. Variety has motivational effects. Rosenshine (1971) found that a lecturer's changes in the form of movement and gesturing correlate positively with student achievement (N L. Gage, David C. Berliner, 1991).

Besides dimensions of body language, time—being punctual, late or early—or space—being close to the students while engaging the class, have their impact on students. Apart from these, the quality of voice, volume, diction, pitch, rate of speech and clarity affect the body language projections.

From the facial expression of the teacher the students are able to form an opinion about his sincerity and commitment. Body movements continuously convey meanings and messages. If the teacher lectures without the courage of conviction and without proper preparation, it is reflected in his words and expressions. Expressions can be used to express the intended meaning to the students. For instance, when a question is put, the teacher has to simultaneously raise his eyebrow or while enumerating the steps in a process, show his fingers to count the number of steps.

When the appropriate expressions are spontaneously and properly shown, the class becomes live and attentive as the students feel that the teacher is handling the session with zeal and vitality. In the words of Joseph Campbell, "the job of an educator is to teach students to see the vitality in themselves." Expressions can make a world of difference in bringing out the best in a teacher. If he/she is gloomy, the students will automatically become downcast and disappointed whereas if he/she is energetic and lively, the class will naturally be highly motivated. Positive vibrations at one end would necessarily generate positive vibrations at the other end. A classroom is no exception. One should learn how to sound words effectively with the proper accompaniment of the right expressions so as to enhance the quality of the delivery of ideas articulated in a classroom.

Pronunciation:Pronunciation invariably decides the quality of communication skills of the teacher. The rhythm, stress, and intonation that he uses are of critical importance in communication. If the teacher is not sure of the correct pronunciation of a word, it is better to refer to a dictionary or a book on phonetics. It is advisable to listen to good speakers or good programmes in the visual media to understand the correct pronunciation. There are numerous tapes and software which would help one to learn the correct pronunciation. The easiest way to learn it is to look up the word in the spelling and pronunciation dictionary in the internet. A teacher is expected to have a strong and basic foundation in correct pronunciation. One needs time and patience to become classy in one's pronunciation. Therefore, regular practice is required to fine-tune one's pronunciation. Once the teacher achieves this goal, it will pay rich dividends in the handling of language, which also decides the quality of delivery. One should think that a teacher's pronunciation is the biggest thing that a student notices. If the pronunciation is good it is well appreciated.

Breathing Life into Words: Most speech issues arise from incorrect breathing. Breathing is so vital to speaking effectively as oxygen helps in the smooth flow of words without gasping for breath. Teaching becomes effective when the teacher expresses the ideas with vigor and vitality. The effect of the projection of one's voice depends very much on enunciation and articulation of words. If the teacher wants to breathe life into words by making every word he/she utters meaningful and powerful, he/she has to have a smooth intake of oxygen. If breathing is affected due to cold or bronchitis, the teacher undergoes stress, which results in instant fatigue and lack of confidence.

The teachers can do breathing exercises regularly to maintain the power of the lungs and the vocal chords. Such exercises to enhance breathing capacity help the teacher to sound steady, clear and confident without running out of breath. The regular practice of yoga is one of the best ways to guarantee the proper upkeep of health. In yoga, there are very effective breathing exercises which would help considerably to improve the tone of one's voice. Teachers can follow both traditional and scientific principles and methods to achieve the right way of voice production and presentation.

Potentials of Gestures: The effectiveness of the gestures also enhances the quality of the lecture. The movement of the head, hand and arm spontaneously, and compatible with the articulation of an idea would create a better impression about the delivery. On the other hand, movement of head, hand and arm without synchronizing them with the flow of ideas would distract the attention of the students.

Why do some teachers feel jittery if lecterns are missing from the classroom? Most teachers are used to resting their arms on a lectern while lecturing or to refer their notes or other reference materials kept on the lectern. If some teachers do not lean on it, nothing comes out of their mouth. Some find it difficult to handle their gestures without this indispensable accessory. In some classrooms, instead of a lectern, a chair and table are provided. Whether there is the lectern or a table and chair, teachers are expected to learn how to use gestures properly so as to improve the quality of delivery in any situation.

Awkward gestures repeatedly made by teachers drive students to distraction. For example, some teachers are always found scratching their heads when they miss a point, some play pocket billiards when they are not prepared or otherwise, some hold on to the bridge of the nose as a doubting Thomas, some wring their hands often as if they are continuously washing away their sins and some even try to damage their buttons by turning it very often in all directions. All these mannerisms produce disastrous results. Teachers with such mannerisms are expected to obtain guidance from experienced teachers or undergo effective training programmes so that they learn how to use gestures properly. They are supposed to correct themselves in the use of gestures in the beginning of their career. Indeed, gestures are very important and are to be used effectively to enhance the quality of communication, especially to supplement verbal messages.

While handling a class, the teacher is expected occasionally to move back, forward, sideways and sometimes closer to the students, mainly, to catch their attention. When the teacher intends to emphasize certain key points, he can take a step for each point and raise and lower the pitch to get effective listening.

The Potency of Eye Contact: Eye contact is very important and necessary to ensure the effectiveness of teaching. Once it is established well, the teacher can easily gauge the interest shown and attention paid by students. It also helps the teacher to obtain visual feedback from students from time to time to be reassured that positive response is maintained throughout the class. Eyes also can do wonders: Teachers can even listen to their students with their eyes. Proper eye contact established by the teacher can send a credible message to students that he is both serious and powerful. It enables the teacher to enhance credibility and acceptance. Eye contact also personalizes the comments, encourages students to return the attentiveness to them in kind, and enables the teacher to read their faces to gauge their interest and understanding. Eyes are powerful enough to transmit emotions and control student. At times, one stare by the teacher is enough to discipline the mischievous student. With proper eye contact, the teacher would not only be able to attract the attention of the entire class but also enforce discipline, and motivate and inspire the students.

The Power of Words: Language used by the teacher is a significant factor which determines the degree of excellence of the language skills possessed by him/her. Choosing the apt or right words to explain the point requires the support of a sound vocabulary. All the C's of communication are relevant in this context: clarity, correctness, coherence, consistency, creativity, completeness, conciseness, credibility, competence, consideration, commitment, courage, confidence, concreteness, character and commonsense. The real power of words can be derived from an admirable command of language, to which a sound vocabulary makes a big difference. Vocabulary is vital to a teacher to build up a large store of words to express his ideas. By using apt words, the teacher can communicate freely and convincingly, and express feelings and emotions effectively and fruitfully. He will project confidence and power, and build self-esteem by using words which sound authoritative and most appropriate to the context. Aldous Huxley had succinctly explained the significance of words: "Words form the thread on which we string our experiences."

The instructional objectives can be fulfilled productively only if the points are conveyed effectively by using the most appropriate words. Words become tremendously powerful and meaningful when they are used in the proper context. In the words of R.W. Emerson, "words are also actions and actions are a kind of words." With the use of proper words, the teacher is in a position to inspire, energize and motivate students and persuade them to become good learners and achievers. In one of the illustrious colleges where I taught, students from other classes used to sit in the mathematics class just to listen to the fluent English of a mathematics professor. The quality of language used by eminent teachers attracts generation of students to such teachers of eminence. The credibility of successful teachers, to a great extent, depends not only on their mastery of the subjects but also on their command over language, clarity of expression and the richness of ideas. These masters exploit the profound power and impact of words and constantly enrich the quality of language as a medium of communication. As conscientious teachers, they upgrade and hone their language skills to express their ideas effectively and to the point. Such teachers maintain their iconic position in their field of knowledge through hard work, commitment and devotion to their profession. This is the secret of their success.

The Delivery: Experienced teachers always start a class by giving a short review of the previous lesson or connect the topic with the previous level of knowledge. When they conclude the session, they give a summary of the main points. This practice puts the students at ease in adapting to the teaching environment. But some do not make even the slightest attempt to connect the related topics or summarize what they have taught.

It is the duty of the teacher to announce in advance the topics he proposes to handle during a particular week so that the students not only get an idea about the topics but also an opportunity to browse through relevant books, publications and other source materials to at least obtain a kaleidoscopic view of the subject to be taught. Teachers become more effective and acceptable when they are perceived to be credible. Such perceptions are enhanced when the teacher is considered knowledgeable and trustworthy. What really matters in this context is the quality of delivery.

A sequential order of progression should always be adhered to while presenting a topic at any level of education. If the teacher by-passes this step-by-step process, learning becomes strainful. The teacher has to understand the efficacy of step-by-step delivery and plan the presentation keeping it in view.

Some teachers fail to review, update and upgrade the material used for teaching for want of initiative and preparedness. This is a grave and alarming problem which certainly saps their confidence, and makes their presentation outdated. It is distressing to pinpoint that nowadays only a few teachers venture into the much needed habit of referring to books on the related subjects.

As a consequence of the impact of internet on education, the habit of dictating notes in the class is almost dispensed with. Instead, notes are uploaded at the institution's website. Teachers post the assignments/homework also at this site. This system helps the teacher to explain in detail in the class about the topics covered and use that extra time gained for an activity-based learning method by adapting to modern methodologies of teaching. Teachers can also use the web to assess the performance of their students and provide timely feedback, apart from the usual classroom assessments. These, I consider, are some of the direct benefits of internet in modern day education.

Teaching is an Art

In essence, teaching is an art, which means that the personal skills of the teacher matter much in deciding the quality of his/her presentation. Even if the teacher has acquired an additional qualification from a Teacher Training

Institute or a doctorate in the related subject, his devotion to the profession, personal attributes and distinctive qualities as a teacher would, in the end, decide his/her success or failure as a member of this great profession. Teaching requires an indefatigable passion for the job which is not decided by financial incentives alone.

> "The mediocre teacher tells
> The good teacher explains
> The superior teacher demonstrates
> The great teacher inspires."

These words of William A Ward unambiguously point out how different types of teachers perform. It is but natural that the superior and great teachers are highly revered for the exceptional and extraordinary qualities they possess, and have the largest number of admirers. Hundreds of people remember such teachers with gratitude for the rest of their lives.

In *Anatomy of Professional Practice*, Fenwick W. English proposes an educational leadership that is aesthetically and qualitatively grounded and is, professionally, an art. It is this kind of foundation that provides access to moral judgement and social justice, knowledge and skill development as something more than routine managerial tasks, and the means to question and overcome ideology. To be a teacher is to be many things: a communicator of fact, a coach for skill development, an inspirer of creative insight or a thoughtful guide to analytical thought, a professional mentor, and many more (Donald Kennedy, 1997). Medley and Shannon (1994) identified three facets of teacher quality: 'Teacher competence, performance, and effectiveness in work.'

Horace Mann states that a teacher who attempts to teach without inspiring the student with a desire to learn is hammering on a cold iron. The job of a teacher is to constantly inspire the student to learn well. Teaching in all its fullness involves the expertise, energy, vitality, passion, synergy, flexibility, resourcefulness and adaptation, and above all, devotion, that leads to learning. As John Dewey says "The aim of education should be to teach the child to think, not what to think." What the teachers are supposed to appreciate and understand is that teaching is more than the classroom work. Only talented and extraordinary teachers are able to make students familiar with their intellectual and mental qualities, and instill in them the ability and conviction to realize their full potential and enable them to excel anywhere in the world. Only such accomplished teachers can bring about positive changes in a society by empowering the younger generation with the necessary knowledge and skills to succeed in a complex world replete with changes both in the academic and workplace environments. The words of John Steinbeck explain much: "I have come to believe that a great teacher is a great artist and that there are as few as there are any other great artists. Teaching might even be the greatest of the arts since the medium is the human mind and spirit." The 'New Goals of Education' of the UNESCO Report, succinctly states that education is an art.

"Managing change in a rapidly changing society has to be done through a discriminating use of the scientific principles of human behaviour and also treating education as an art which involves the ability to deal with other human beings using human judgement, adaptability and understanding."

All good art is an enquiry and an experiment. It is by virtue of being an artist that the teacher is a researcher. The point appears to be difficult to grasp because education facilities have been invaded by the idea that research is scientific and concerned with general laws (Stenhouse, 1984). Teaching is basically an art as it involves creativity, skills and techniques, and the imagination to create the intended outcomes of learning. Jean Piaget declares that the principal goal of education is to create men who are capable of doing new things, not repeating what other generations have done—men who are creative, inventive and discoverers. Only the creative teacher who is an artist can bring about this positive change in his students.

In this connection, I am reminded of the words of Will Durant, "educators should be chosen not merely for their special qualifications, but more for their personality and their character, because we teach more by what we are than by what we teach." A good teacher will foresee all the needs of students, both collectively and individually and plan diligently and sequentially the course of action that is required in that situation. As students look up to a teacher's guidance even in personal matters, the teacher must be perfect, upright and always uphold the cardinal values of life so that he is able to instill confidence in the minds of students to achieve life's goals. Like an efficient leader, the teacher can always inspire students with confidence in themselves and foster trust.

Swami Vivekananda said that education is the manifestation of the perfection already inherent in us. Originally, in view of its Latin origin, 'education' meant the drawing out of something already within the one who receives it (Peter Milward, 2006). It would be the task of the resourceful teacher to guide students to explore those hidden talents and lead them forward towards self-actualization. As observed by Curt Dudley-Marling and Penny A Freppon, (2001) teaching is an energetic vocation—the people who do it well bring intellectual and moral energy to bear in every dimension. Teachers can bring to their efforts knowledge, compassion, awareness, and engagement; they might bring as well a set of explicit commitments, articulate values, and dreams and goals (William Ayers). Becoming a good teacher involves just this kind of sustained search, adaptation, sacrifice, and true satisfaction. Teaching is remarkably complex; thus teaching must be highly skilled (McIntyre and Pressley, 1996). According to Mark van Doren, "the art of teaching is the art of assisting discovery."

An efficient teacher has to follow a student-centered method of teaching, which, according to Collins and O'Brien (2003), is an instructional approach in which students influence the content, activities, materials, and pace of learning. This learning model places the student in the centre of the learning process. The teacher provides students with the opportunities to learn independently and from one another, and coaches them in the skills they need to do effectively. "Recent work in education has explicated the importance of having students' participation in classroom discourses that reflect disciplinary thinking" (Leslie, R. Herrenkohl and Guerra, 1998; Lampert, 1990; Lemke, 1990; Polman and Pea, 2001; Shulman and Quinlan, 1996).

Jennifer Nias, in the book, *Curriculum and the Teacher*, elaborates that, most obviously, teaching is a personal activity because the manner in which each teacher behaves is unique. Teaching, like learning, has a perceptual basis. The minute-by-minute decisions teachers take within the shifting, unpredictable, capricious world of the classroom and the judgements they reach when they are reflecting on their work depend upon how they perceive particular events, behaviours, materials, persons. In turn, these perceptions are determined by a schemata ('persistent, deep-rooted, and well-organized classification of ways of perceiving, thinking and behaving') which are also 'living and flexible' says Vernon, (1955). Schemata and assumptions are learned, they are slowly built up, as from birth, we develop and exercise the skill of seeing (or hearing, smelling, tasting, touching). They are modified by experience and activity. Since no two persons have the same life experiences, we all learn to perceive the world and ourselves as part of it in different ways. Teachers, as people, 'see' and interpret their pupils and the latter's actions and reactions according to perceptual patterns which are unique to them.

As teaching is a challenging profession which always demands perfection, it is always embedded in a system of quality performance. It's a most demanding job as quality must be the end-result. Quality symbolizes excellence, merit, genius, acumen, caliber, ethos, standard and value. Quality, as we all know, is never an accident. It is always the result of high intention, vision, efficient planning, devotion, effective leadership, intelligent direction, skilful execution and commitment. Indeed, quality is the key to success. A teacher, to be successful and respected, must always be hundred per cent quality-conscious. To attain a higher status, a teacher has to be a self-motivated person, and be committed to bring out the best out of students. We all know it fully well that only self-motivated teachers can essentially motivate and inspire students.

Professional practice is about performance. The application of skills and learning procedures in situations of professional practice is an art. In an applied practice such as educational leadership, artful performance is about assuming a role and acting accordingly (Fenwick W. English, 2008).

In this world there are four types of people. The first type is those who make things happen. The second type is those who watch things happen. The third type is those who wonder what happened. The fourth type is those who don't know that anything ever happened. A teacher must belong to the first type and make things happen in the learning environment. A teacher must always be organized, committed to the learners and have a professional outlook.

For Christa McAuliffe, teaching is such a great profession which expands into the future—"I touch the future, I teach." Let me quote Goethe, the master spirit. "A teacher who can arouse a feeling for one single good action, for one single good poem, accomplishes more than who fills our memory with rows and rows of natural objects, classified with name and form. I feel this must be the purpose of God in creating teachers in this world." Teaching must result in transforming the student into a confident, responsible, goal-oriented, disciplined, refined, upright, trustworthy, patriotic, humane and socially conscious being. Education can promote social and economic wellbeing of the people in a country, and create job opportunities for all. No nation can guarantee sustainable development without empowering its educational institutions and teachers to deliver excellent education. We have great admiration for those teachers who have a passion for teaching and uphold quality standards, and help develop students who are value-oriented, quality-conscious and focused. In the words of Aristotle, "those who educate children well are to be more honoured than even their parents, for these only give them life, those, the art of living well."

I quote Henry Brooks Adams upon which every teacher must reflect to understand the superior quality of the teaching profession and the unlimited boundaries of teaching:

> "A teacher affects eternity;
> He can never tell where his influence stops."

In his book, *The Art of Teaching,* (1950) Gilbert Highet succinctly captures the attention of the reader by explaining in unequivocal terms that teaching is an art, not a science. He staunchly argues so due to the following reasons:

"It seems to me very dangerous to apply the aims and methods of science to human beings as individuals, although a statistical principle can often be used to explain their behaviour in large groups and a scientific diagnosis of their physical structure is always valuable. But a "scientific" relationship between human beings is bound to be inadequate and perhaps distorted. Of course it is necessary for every teacher to be orderly in planning his work and precise in his dealing with facts. But that does not make his teaching "scientific." Teaching involves emotions, which cannot be systematically appraised and employed, and human values, which are quite outside the grasp of science. A "scientifically" brought-up child would be a pitiable monster. A "scientific" marriage would be only a thin and crippled version of a true marriage. A "scientific" friendship would be as cold as a chess problem. "Scientific" teaching, even of scientific subjects, will be inadequate as long as both teachers and pupils are human beings. Teaching is not like inducing a chemical reaction: it is much more like painting a picture or making a piece of music, or, on a lower level, like planting a garden or writing a friendly letter. You must throw your heart into it, you must realize that it cannot all be done by formulas, or you will spoil your work, and your pupils, and yourself."

In their book, *Teaching Strategies*, (2010) Orlich, Harder, Callahan, Trevisan and Brown, point out that teaching is both an art and science. Like an artist, a good teacher makes decisions form both a technical and creative perspective. Great artists display a mastery of technical skills–painting, glass blowing, sculpting–that includes a grasp of science behind how these techniques work. They also know when and in what way to apply their technical skills. They make decisions. That part is art. Similarly, teachers develop their science by using carefully planned, fine-tuned lessons that reflect an understanding of many different teaching techniques. They apply each technique skillfully to gain the desired intellectual, social, affective, or kinesthetic result. They develop artistry by being aware of what they are doing and how their actions affect their learners. They are constantly aware that the choices they make affect the intellectual, attitudinal, and psychomotor skills of their students. Above all, they make decisions.

There is also a science to education, which adds method and reflectivity to the art of teaching, and is backed up by a body of specialist knowledge. This science asks and attempts to answer fundamental and searching questions. How does learning happen? How do we organize teaching? What works for learners? And when it works, how do we know it has worked? (Mary Kalantzis and Bill Cope, 2008). There is yet another view which states that "teaching is not just an art or a science; it is, or it should be, more like a design science-experimental, innovative, collaborative, iterative, creative (Cobb *et al.*, 2003). Teaching is professional artistry. Professional artistry is inherently related to human imagination and creativity and one's willingness to experiment. Teachers exhibit professional artistry in encounters with their students. When you see them teaching, you witness their imagination and creativity–at play unfolding in the classroom (Jack Hassard, 2005).

In these trying times for the distinguished members of the teaching fraternity on account of the proliferation of technology and the formidable challenges erupting in the external environment, what is going to come to their recue is the mastery of important personal skills. It is those personal skills and the kind of knowledge acquired that would make teaching both challenging and rewarding. Of course, scientific principles are abundantly used in education, but personal skills of a teacher, which we consider as the heart of the art of teaching, will make teaching worthwhile, meaningful and effective.

2
The Professional Touch

Effectiveness is the foundation of success. —Peter F. Drucker

What an opportunity it is to have the privilege of being a teacher, the greatest of all vocations, for it keeps us anchored in the world of youth, ideas, and research. —C. Roland Christensen

Teachers have to be Resourceful

Why are students always glued to the presentation of a particular teacher? Why do the same students not care much for the teaching of another teacher? What attracts students to the former teacher's class? Is it because the presentation is attractive or the teacher is a trickster or a magician? The reason for the success of a teacher can be traced back to the teacher's commitment to professionalism.

Teaching is described as a higher-level decision-making process. The act of teaching requires substantial amount of professional and practical knowledge. Teachers make professional decisions each day for which they require thinking processes of the higher-order and this professional thinking and planning goes on throughout the day, in and out of the classroom (*Educators' Handbook: A Research Perspective*, Virginia Richardson-Kochler, Senior Editor, 1987). Once the teacher realizes the importance of this noble profession and understands the fact that teaching requires systematic acquisition of knowledge on a continual basis and a professional conduct, which distinguishes it from other professions, he will come to grips with the realities of the profession, and become more responsible. Teaching means, essentially, the procedure of teaching, for it is through procedure that students are made familiar with a subject's ideas and apply its principles constructively (David A Hayes, 1992). If the procedure of teaching is flawless, it would be easier for the teacher to accomplish the instructional objectives.

What does 'professional' mean when applied to a teacher? Formally, it means a member of an occupation with recognized professional status (Brandt, 1993). Amy Gutmann (1987) identifies four rewards of professionalism—the pleasures of performance, high salary, status, and the exercise of authority over other people. Andrew Abbot (1988) defines 'profession' as an exclusive occupational group applying somewhat abstract knowledge to particular cases. Knowledge may be the fact that distinguishes these professionals from other workers. A concern with professionalism is intended to raise the status and rewards of teaching, attract more able and intelligent people to the field, and allow teachers greater control over the content and conduct of their work (Ayers, 1992). Raelin (1986) defines a profession as an "occupation requiring expert knowledge that justifies a monopoly of services granted by government licensing."

A professional, then, is supposed to be both competent and ethical by an explicit set of standards. Professionals tend to value their professions, to upgrade them, to increase the requirements for achieving the status of a professional in each field (Mathew Melko, 1998). It is these essential requirements that bring honour and glory to the teaching profession. The teachers will have to maintain these qualities throughout their career, if they cherish to belong to a professional group of practitioners.

Academe, however, may be taken to be most central profession. It is uniquely situated in society as the profession that trains people for all other professions and numerous other lines of work requiring certified education. In principle, the academic profession may be understood to guard culture by upholding cognitive and behavioural standards to ensure the competent role performance of practitioners throughout the occupational system. The profession may also be seen to functionally uphold generalized ideals: in their roles, professors seek precision and excellence and aim, ideally, to inculcate these humanistic characteristics and more advanced collective civilization (*The American Academic Profession*, 2011).

Teaching is an integral element of the profession, and effective teaching is integral to professionalism (John M. Budd, 2009). Teachers demonstrate leadership by modeling professional behaviour on the job, that is, by recognizing problems and opportunities, by considering the values of stakeholders, by calling up professional knowledge, by applying that knowledge through action, and by assessing the consequences of such action. Teaching is a profession because its members possess specialized knowledge and can apply this knowledge to increase the chances of solving educational problems. Teachers exhibit collegiality, interacting with others in a courteous, conscientious, and generally businesslike manner. Teachers are achievement-oriented and their professional history serves as a record of accomplishment (*Foundations of Education, The Challenges of Professional Practice*, Robert F. McNergney, Joanne M. Herbert, 2001).

Capturing students' interest in a classroom on an ongoing basis is not a herculean task. It only needs good preparation and an effective delivery by a resourceful teacher to capture and maintain the attention of students. To find out whether it was possible to maintain the attention of the students in a classroom throughout the conduct of the session or to evaluate one's own teaching practices or to evaluate one's presentation style, there is one best way to follow—a video recording. One of the easiest methods by which a novice teacher can improve the quality of presentation or delivery is by doing a video recording of delivery, watching the entire presentation and ascertaining whether it was effective. All the parameters of a successful presentation, viz., the sequential flow of ideas, the clarity of explanation, the sound modulation, intonation, pauses, etc., can be analyzed threadbare. Such an evaluation of the entire presentation is essentially needed to assess factors like clarity of ideas, pace, accent, sound modulation, etc. When the video recording is watched, the presenter is able to assess the strength and weakness of the delivery. It will also enable the teacher to find out whether any sign of nervousness was felt during the presentation, maybe due to lack of confidence. Similarly, the novice teachers must have an access to the pedagogical skills of veteran teachers from whom they could learn the art and practice of teaching. In this context, the faculty development programmes can provide simulated environments.

More than a degree in the respective subject and in teaching, and/or other higher degrees, the teacher must possess the requisite qualities which distinguish an ordinary teacher from a resourceful teacher. We need resourceful teachers who will constantly motivate students to transform them into vibrant personalities who will in the end serve the community and the nation with devotion and commitment. Education facilitates, to a great extent, the socialization of the individual, which by and large, takes place in the campuses of educational institutions. Indeed, an excellent teacher makes an invaluable contribution to the community by producing capable, worthy and diligent students who will become exemplary citizens possessing good character and caliber.

Each educational programme demonstrates coherence through its goals, structure, content, instructional objectives, methods and procedures, the nature, quality and extent of student learning and achievement. Learning goals include knowledge, intellectual and academic skills and methods of enquiry to be acquired. In addition to these goals, it gives importance to abilities, soft skills and values to be specifically developed by students. Only a resourceful teacher is able to do justice to the attainment of these significant goals.

The fact is that most teachers do not understand that they have vast potentials to explore, grow and develop as outstanding teachers. The story of the eaglet would be relevant here to explain the situation: It is all about an eagle which laid her egg in the nest of a chicken. The eaglet was hatched with the brood of chicks and grew up with them. All its life it lived like a chicken. It scratched, chuckled and cackled as if it were a chicken. It grew old and one day it saw an eagle and exclaimed in all awe and excitement—"What a magnificent bird!" Then, her neighbor commented, "You could never be like him." The eagle never gave a second thought that he was born an eagle and in the end died thinking as if it were a chicken. The greatest mistake one can make in life is to continually undervalue one's extraordinary qualities and live like that chicken.

A person enters the world of teaching as a profession. Despite all her/his efforts to be a good teacher, she/he remains an outsider until she/he becomes a missionary to the cause. Teaching has to become a mission. The moment it becomes so, the teacher becomes a value-creator, simple and direct. It all depends on what the teacher wants to become and how she/he is able to fit into the evolving mould. However, the mould could remain static because of the fixed notions and non-mobility of the teacher, psychologically and spiritually.

The teacher is expected to transform himself into a versatile professional, so resourceful that he could pay equal attention to activities like seminar, group discussion, debate, quiz, public speaking, sports, community service and student council activities which are all essential for the overall development of the personality of a student. In this case, the teacher has to provide an inspiring ethos to students so that they move from the curricular to the co-curricular or extracurricular activity without feeling overburdened.

In the present situation, the concepts of teaching and learning have undergone a paradigm shift as students can access knowledge at the click of a button and can come well-informed to the classroom about the topics handled by the teacher. This is, in reality, one of the greatest challenges the teacher has to face upfront in the classrooms of the twenty-first century. The teacher has to face it with utmost care, foresight and confidence. If he is not resourceful and up-to-date, perhaps the student will outsmart him in certain frontiers of knowledge, and such situations might cause unpleasant, and even shocking, experiences to the teacher. In any situation, it is a combination of the caliber, passion and resourcefulness of a teacher which determines the quality of his presentation and enable him to face any contingency with courage and confidence.

In an educational institution, human resource development and total quality management can bring about positive changes. Marmar Mukhopadhyay (2005) observes "For total quality management (TQM) and institutional building, nothing can be more important than the human resources in the organization." It can be pointed out that salary cost alone accounts for between 85 per cent (in higher education) and almost 97 per cent (in primary education) of the total institutional budget. Educational institutions are human systems. Hence, the quality of an educational institution—school, college, or university—is only as good as its people. Educational institutions are knowledge enterprises. (Mitra and Mandke, 2003), they perform the roles of knowledge creation, knowledge warehousing, and knowledge vending. And this knowledge is exploding, not just expanding. Since the objective of TQM is to strive for excellence on a continuing basis, it is necessary to develop mechanisms for need-based human resource development (HRD) on a continuing basis. No wonder, all major gurus of TQM have recommended HRD as a necessary component of TQM. What constitute HRD, particularly for educational institutions is the most important question. It probably begins with selecting the right kind of people for the institution–the right people in the right jobs. Yet, it has to move beyond this static proposition; the agendas of HRD, of TQM, and of institution building have to accommodate continuous upgradation of professional competence, commitment, motivation and inspiration.

Another matter of concern in this competitive world is that institutions are always vying with one another to be toppers in the field. At the international centers, standardized international tests are used to compare students' learning with that of their peers abroad. The results of GMAT, GRE, ESL, etc., are accepted worldwide. Consequently, many institutions take pains to ensure the quality of teachers and students so as to maintain higher standards, and thereby enable the institution to successfully compete in a challenging environment. In any situation, the quality of the institution and its capability to inspire students to compete in national and international tests are of great significance in deciding its overall performance. It is a proven fact that an institution can inculcate lasting values in the minds of students which would always stand them in good stead.

In a dynamic environment, the teachers must possess confidence, commitment and conviction to keep abreast of the changes which impact the educational process. In the real situation, many teachers may not be aware of the magnitude of changes taking place in their profession as they do not generally attempt to gather information about them. Very often, ironically, many teachers do not explore the large expanse of knowledge of their own subjects. Besides, they do not try to get better insights into the vast job opportunities available once they get out of the box and think differently. It is a known fact that a professional practice rooted in research-based scholarly knowledge can definitely result in engaging the classes effectively and keep students productively involved in the learning process. Without genuine conviction, the teacher will find it difficult to pursue real innovative practices and thereby become instruments of change in a dynamic environment. The intellectual acuity and mental preparedness to make learning a creative, fruitful, enjoyable and challenging activity, and the total involvement in the process of teaching make a teacher fully dedicated to the profession. In an educational setting, it is found that those teachers who are part of professional bodies or professional community networks take advantage, especially from the programmes conducted to improve professional skills and from the pertinent ideas circulated. At any cost, teachers are expected to join the professional bodies, both national and international, and learn more about their subjects and the modern practices followed in the teaching of their subjects. They are expected to be the real masters in their field of knowledge and engage their classes effectively, and therefore, they are duty-bound to constantly and consistently improve their quality of performance by updating their knowledge, honing their presentation skills and accomplishing the instructional objectives.

In his book, *Who Moved My Cheese*, Dr. Spencer Johnson narrates the habits of rats. If the rats discover what they are doing is not working they do something else to achieve their goals. The moral of the story is that if we want to produce different results in our life, we will have to get outside the comfort zone and do something different. The teacher who wants to create academic excellence will have to try out newer methods of teaching and make their presentation of superior quality. It is the teachers who can nurture enthusiasm and creativity in the learning environment for which they must be well-equipped both mentally and physically. We are always inspired by the message of Robert Frost which is applicable in all human endeavor:

> "Two roads diverged in a wood, and I—
> I took the one less traveled by,
> And that has made all the difference."

The Empowered Teacher Makes a Big Difference

An empowered teacher is essentially a resourceful teacher, and his greatest asset is receptiveness, i.e., the capability to receive and take or accept new ideas. Such teachers are open to suggestions, changes and innovations. They have an open mind and are adaptable to changes which constantly take place in a dynamic educational environment.

An empowered teacher is ready to accept increased demands of the job, and fulfill the newer obligations without hesitation and demur. He is profoundly confident about his qualities and capabilities to make a positive impact on the learning process and the running of the institution. Moreover, such teachers exhibit certain remarkable characteristics: setting examples, inspiring a shared vision, becoming accountable, searching for opportunities, encouraging and supporting the peer group and subordinates, experimenting, taking risks and celebrating accomplishments. They follow the transformative kind of leadership as they possess the requisite knowledge and skills to cope effectively with the emerging trends. They have immense confidence in themselves and believe in their inherent capabilities to lead.

An educational institution operates in a dynamic environment in which, among other things, it has to face the stiff competition from similar institutions. Indeed, it is the teachers with substantial scholarship and requisite qualities of empowerment who are able to meet the expectations of students and the entire stakeholders of the institution. In such an intellectually demanding situation, if the teacher is not receptive to a patently empowered environment, he/she would not be successful, as more competent persons will take that position. That is the typical nature of a society where survival of the fittest and the fastest is the dominant characteristic in every field of human endeavour. If the teacher is not empowered at the right time, he/she loses a great opportunity to be recognized whereas others in the team are recognized for their positive contributions. All successful organizations consider empowerment as the main ingredient for success, which guarantees high performance, meritorious achievements and higher satisfaction. Therefore, it is prudent on the part of the teacher to understand and learn about the efficacy of empowerment in the earlier stages of his development and steadily progress in acquiring the necessary qualities of empowerment.

Those teachers who are empowered make it a point to update their knowledge in their respective subjects on an ongoing basis and enhance their teaching competencies that lead to professional development, fully understanding the objectives, values and compulsions of teaching. The administration of the institution is prompted to seek their suggestions in the formation of its objectives and policies, and in deciding how to achieve its mission and objectives. The empowered teachers are powerful as their efficiency level is high and they always command much respect for their proficiency. They become the much sought-after teachers who are handpicked by the administration to take up still higher positions. Empowerment encourages the teacher to be creative and to take risks, which make them one up in a fast changing competitive environment. These are the teachers who are enthusiastic and committed to the profession. They perform well as they always brim with confidence while doing their job and they enjoy doing it.

Most teachers desire increased involvement and participation in the overall activities of the institution and also in the decision making process. But it is the empowered teachers who volunteer their involvement in many of the crucial areas of development, and it is such teachers who are selected to collaborate in future developmental activities of the institution. Their participation energizes better performance, produces better results and enhances the quality and inherent strengths of the institution. Empowerment is a powerful elixir. It increases the teacher's commitment to the institutional goals, and enhances their reputation and wellbeing. It has been generally found that some of the highly focused students select a particular institution because of the presence of such empowered teachers.

The empowered teacher is in a position to not only teach effectively but also constantly encourage his student to get the best out of education. Encouragement is the oxygen of the soul. Even a pat on the back by a resourceful teacher can motivate the student to achieve greater heights of glory. I believe that an empowered teacher can always give his students two lasting bequests: confidence and values.

Empowered teachers are also respected for their expertise, professionalism and leadership acumen. Their sense of efficacy is high, and thereby they are able to motivate their peer group and subordinates to improve their efficiency. They possess a strong drive to accomplish the goals set within the time frame. Only they can become the change catalysts, and prepare students to face the challenges and realities of our times courageously, and succeed in their active pursuits. To summarize this idea, let me quote the most passionate words of Robert Frost, which have inspired generations of teachers world over: "I'm not a teacher, but I am an awakener."

Does the organizational culture of an institution support empowerment of teachers which results in enhancement of the individual teacher's competencies, and thereby ensure their professional development? It is really crucial for the administration to understand the value of empowerment of teachers, and focus on developing a distinct organization culture which encourages it. As teachers empower themselves to become more efficient and resourceful, administrators have to empower themselves to become more organized, resourceful, focused, professional and innovative. They are expected to render all possible assistance and provide all resources to make education a productive endeavour. To facilitate empowerment in an educational institution, they have to first of all make themselves understand the need, purpose and ramifications of empowerment, and initiate steps to empower themselves. At the same time they must make the teachers understand the significance of empowerment and the need for change, and about the new roles they have to play. If the teachers are to be receptive to an empowered environment, they have to obtain, in the beginning, the details about the development plans for empowerment and its impact on changes occurring in the critical areas in the curriculum and in the process of teaching and learning.

In different empowered cultures, a paradigm shift is essential which demands more commitment on the part of the teachers, especially in institutions which pursue the path of excellence which is considered the holy grail of higher education. Institutions may fail if they do not act upon the changes taking place both in internal and external environments. Adapting to changes in an empowered environment is by itself a formidable challenge to many educational institutions. But, in this new era, in which globalization has affected educational practices all over, adapting to the changes has become a priority for all the world class institutions.

To be successful in this context, administration has to enable teachers to equip themselves with the right knowledge, skills and tools so as to enhance their qualities. Creative educational technologies play a key role in the process of empowerment. Administration must take into account the usefulness of technology in bringing about qualitative and quantitative changes in the use of pedagogical practices and make available such facilities to the teachers after providing them with proper training opportunities in this field. In this context, educators and administrators must think of redesigning the courses to adapt to the needs of students and the relevant technology, but, always backed by clear-cut instructional objectives, which in the end must foster effective learning. It has been proved beyond doubt that only empowered teachers are able to fulfill the ambitious goals of a modern educational institution mainly because such resourceful and quality-oriented teachers are able to meet effectively the requirements of great diversification occurring in higher education. It is encouraging to see that a large number of teachers, on their own volition, embrace empowerment and become more responsible, accountable and committed to the profession.

3

Use of Modern Aids and Equipment

It's not the strongest of the species that survives,
nor the most intelligent that survives.
It is the one that is most adaptable to change. —Charles Darwin

The intelligent use of teaching aids and equipment or the presentation technology has become an inescapable need of modern day educational practices. Institutions are striving hard to introduce more advanced and sophisticated tools which are dependent much on educational software. These presentation technologies create a great impact on methods of teaching, and considerably enhance its quality. ICT-enabled teaching has facilitated the use of a variety of equipment which are easily available in the form of educational software to primarily bring about radical changes in the art and practice of teaching.

By switching the channel of communication from oral to visual, even momentarily, a teacher brings about changes in the response patterns and attention mechanism of students. Adults seem to prefer visual information, a preference that appeared in learning a concept-discrimination task. (Lordahl, 1961).

In the *Chicago Handbook for Teachers* (2011) special emphasis is laid on visual aids in teaching as can be noticed in the following observations:

> Visual images are essential to teaching in many fields.... Students usually respond well to visual and audio material. The ready availability of such material in many forms makes their use much easier today than it was in the past.... One can also create PowerPoint presentations that provide outlines of the text of one's lecture, or incorporate graphs, charts, data sheets, cartoons, photos, sketches, diagrams, and maps. Integrating them with one's notes or outlines not only enhances the effect of one's lecture or discussion but also saves a great deal of time that one might otherwise spend in class, writing on the blackboard. PowerPoint presentation, however, is a supplement to successful teaching, not a substitute for it.

PowerPoint Presentation

Teachers generally feel very comfortable when they use the mode of PowerPoint presentation. It is considered an effective tool used worldwide by teachers. But there are certain basic rules to be followed while using the PowerPoint. It should not be put to use for the entire hour. Going on reading from the slides is a careless way of teaching. It is disastrous to see teachers whiling away their time by trying to set right a technical problem of the system. In such a situation, the teacher concerned must put to use other aids to teaching and try out another suitable tool, maybe by even shifting to a new methodology of teaching as demanded by the situation. The teacher will become adept in the widely used PowerPoint presentation as he/she will painstakingly learn much about its functions and usages while personally designing the presentation. The teachers are expected to familiarize themselves with all the special features of the PowerPoint to develop an engaging PowerPoint presentation. In a PowerPoint presentation, what matters much is the organization of material in words and images, the colours chosen, animations used with spoken words and the use of graphs and diagrams. By using this tool, the teacher can build up the concepts more effectively as relevant materials can be projected in a greater number of representations for arousing the interest of the learner. In such presentations, there is a stronger link between the concepts and a variety of images and words chosen to clearly express and delineate the ideas. Moreover, a well thought-out PowerPoint presentation, appeals straight away to the senses of students, making comprehension easier and faster, and facilitates maintaining rapt attention throughout the presentation. Teachers are advised to do a trial run of the PowerPoint presentation before the actual presentation is made so as to ensure the desired effect perfectly.

A PowerPoint presentation will become more effective if there is a balance between words and images used, a well thought-out organization of material with proper headings and clear outlines and animations presented with spoken words. Such presentations are to be limited to twenty to thirty minutes at a stretch and have to be followed by an interactive session.

Video Clips and Recordings

Another popular aid to teaching is the video clips and recordings which are used in classrooms to stimulate faster creative thinking by students. One big advantage is that the teacher can pause whenever required and direct the full attention of students to the topic as in the case of a PowerPoint presentation. Teachers can produce their own videos, the preparation of which requires specific skills. It can be downloaded from the internet or from sites, viz., You Tube or Video Yahoo, etc., depending on the requirements. The apt use of video clips would stimulate the classroom lecture or discussion and make the class lively. Videos are very effective if the teacher desires to show a live demonstration to make learning cogent, relevant, valid and productive. Before presenting a video clip, the teacher has to assess its relevance to teaching a particular topic and its content value in relation to the implications of the instructional objectives. He/she has to make sure when to put the relevant questions to students. The students can be asked to write the answers to the questions soon after the presentation. Many teachers also use computer/video games in the classrooms and adapt them for their pedagogical purposes.

Cheng Man-Wai and associates (2010) recognize teachers' own classrooms as powerful settings for learning, and argue that artifacts of videotaped lessons can bring teachers' classroom practices to other locations for collaborative analysis. Using videotapes of exemplary teacher practices, teacher educators can create an inquiry environment to challenge and mediate prospective teachers for reflective practice (*Teachers as Learners*, Edited by Ora Kwo, 2010).

Video feedback is also an important part of micro teaching process. The lesson itself is videotaped and immediately following, the participant uses the video to analyze his or her success with the selected skill. In some cases the participant watches the video together with a supervisor. Either way, the next step is for the participant to restructure the lesson as needed and reteach the lesson to a new group of students. The cycle of reteaching and video analysis continues until the participant demonstrates the mastery of the focus skill. (*Using Video in Teacher Education*, Jere Brophy).

Overhead Projectors

Another conventional aid widely used in teaching is the overhead projectors. Teachers can prepare in advance the transparencies and suitably use them on a tabletop overhead projector. Some teachers also use LCD projectors which are connected to computers to display the materials onto a screen. These projected images would attract the attention of the students far better than a presentation on a chalk board or a white board. The very purpose of using such simple gadgets is to stimulate the students' interest in the topic presented to the class. Of course, the resourcefulness, ingenuity and creativity of the teacher is reflected in the quality of such presentations. It is refreshing to note that most of the novice teachers seek the assistance of experts to learn about the effective use of these gadgets and rehearse their presentation, using the equipment that they plan to use in their classes. The key to perfect performance is methodical practice.

The advantages of using an overhead projector are:

- Teachers can easily prepare transparencies and digital images by using the appropriate software.

- Teachers can write on the transparencies as and when required.
- The projector can be switched on and off in accordance with the requirements of the presentation.
- The projected images are clearer and more effectual when compared to images on black/white boards.

Flipcharts

Flipcharts are yet another conventional aid which would be of immense value. An experienced teacher is very comfortable and imaginative while using flipcharts as an aid to teaching. Some teachers put the flipcharts on easels and as they progress on with their classes, jot down spontaneously the connected ideas. At times, they use flipcharts prepared in advance to elucidate the important points. These proficient teachers improvise this aid to teaching to such an extent that they are able to arrest the students' attention throughout the session.

The following data presented by experts in the realm of communication clearly explains why a teacher must use visual aids in teaching:

We remember about:

- 10 per cent of what we read
- 20 per cent of what we hear
- 30 per cent of what we see
- 50 per cent of what we see and hear
- 70 per cent of what we talk about with others
- 80 per cent of what we experience personally
- 95 per cent of what we teach others

In this context, a teacher can make use of Dale's "the Cone of Experience" to enhance the quality of the instruction material and thereby considerably improve the quality of teaching. From our own experience, we have noted that even the best lectures are forgotten by the students no sooner than they leave the classroom. Only 10-15 per cent of the information is retained by them. But if the teachers use the proper visual aids, the retention increases by 40-50 per cent. This is really a quantum jump in retention. Teachers are to take a cue from this fact and plan their classes by including visual aids. The big advantage derived out of their use in teaching is that they help in maintaining the attention of students and thereby facilitate reinforcement of the idea. Teachers are expected to make use of visual aids judiciously to bring out the best results in the teaching and learning-process. It needs some imagination and planning on the part of a resourceful teacher to put to use a judicious mix of visual aids, which would produce remarkable results in the art and practice of teaching.

I remember one of the English professors who loved travelling. After each tour, he would show his class photos, by using a PowerPoint presentation, of the glaring mistakes committed by people in the use of the English language which he had noticed during his travel, especially on the bill boards. The students used to laugh for long seeing the blunders committed by people in the disuse and misuse of the English language. In a way, it reminds students to be careful in writing the spellings. Since the professor used the visual aid to explain the importance of using the correct spelling, the students take to their hearts the importance of spellings and correct usage.

In another situation, a professor of English, while handling a Shakespearean drama used to come dressed like one of the characters, assisted by his students who were also dressed like the characters in the drama. It made remarkable and unforgettable impressions about the whole drama. It was etched in the minds of the students for years to come. They remembered with gratitude this presentation in which the teacher himself and a few students enacted to significantly enhance the quality of visual presentation. These are some examples of imaginativeness and ingenuity of resourceful teachers.

From the point of view of educational psychology too, the use of audio-visual aids is supported by the fact that we learn far better through two senses–hearing and seeing and that 85 per cent of what we learn comes through our eyes and only 11 per cent through our ears. All these facts reinforce the need for using audio-visual aids in teaching. The real value of using audio-visual aids is beautifully summarized in the following lines.

> What I hear, I forget.
> What I see, I remember
> What I do, I know.

There are more technology related tools which can be put to use in the classrooms. Tools like, Prezi, a cloud-based presentation software, particularly useful for zooming style presentations; Google Docs and Wiki spaces are quite helpful to promote active learning by encouraging collaboration among students and teachers; Google Forms, a cloud-based tool that allows the teachers and students to sign in and create surveys they can share; iBooks Author of Apple allow both teachers and students to create free or affordable multimedia books. These are some of the technologically oriented modern tools which can be put to use if both the teacher and student get familiarized with such applications. Google Docs and Wiki spaces allow groups of students to share ideas and work with one another and with their teachers on projects. Google Forms, Poll Everywhere, and SurveyMonkey enable teachers to swiftly collect information from their students. In fact there are lots of cloud-based tools that can be used to help students to learn faster and better. In the modern times it is easy for the teachers to develop more effective teaching strategies by using such technologies. In fact the range of technologies available for teaching and learning has become diverse. The new brand of teaching technologies provides a plethora of opportunities to the teachers to teach effectively in an educational system firmly embedded in digital technology. Moreover, the use of Tablet computing, Game based computing, Mobile apps, Learning analytics, Gesture based computing along the lines of Nintendo Wii and many more computer-based apps have made the teaching-learning environment more interactive, goal-oriented, personalized and collaborative. Publishing tools like blogging platforms, WordPress, Blogger, podcasting services like Podomatic, Learning Management Systems like Moodle, etc., are of much help in education. Video conferencing with White Board facility, PowerPoint through Google's presentation software, and on Apple machines which provide Keynote—for tech-savvy teachers and students, there are umpteen numbers of devices and facilities available. We cannot ignore the role played by the social media networks like the Twitter, Flickr, YouTube, Facebook and also iTunes created by Apple in promoting content sharing related to higher education as well. Some of them have created dedicated portals for education. The internet by itself facilitates communication in education, transcending the borders of countries, thereby creating a borderless world for the exchange of ideas. As indicated by studies conducted in this field, training teachers in ICT skills is crucial to implement ICT integrated system of teaching and learning.

4

Motivation—The Key to Success

"You can teach a student a lesson for a day;
But if you can teach him to learn by creating curiosity,
He will continue the learning process as long as he lives."

—Clay F. Bedford

Motivation is a psychological process which creates an inner urge in any human being to act in a particular way to reach his/her goals. To the psychologists, motivation is a process which starts with a need that activates a behaviour or drive to fulfill a goal. Some think both motivation and satisfaction are one and the same. It is not so. Motivation is influenced by forward looking perceptions concerning the relationship between performance and rewards. Satisfaction refers to people's feelings about the rewards they have received. Hence, motivation is a cause of their expectations about the future and satisfaction is a consequence of their past events. As administration is at all times interested in improving performance of teachers, it has to concentrate on creating the right ambience in the organization to enhance motivation.

Generally, as teachers, we are more bothered about a timely promotion, hike in salary, a posting in a preferred institution or entry into a new career. These are some of the examples of extrinsic motivators. A change, especially when it involves more challenging tasks and a higher status, is a powerful motivator. To take a doctorate, to publish in referred journals, to remedy a deficiency, like poor command of the language, to become a part of a professional body or invited as a guest speaker—are some of the examples of intrinsic motivators.

"Our chief want in life is somebody who shall make us do what we can" says R.W. Emerson. Can we call that person, the motivator? Very often, a pat on the back triggers positive action in everybody.

Motivation, as applicable to a teacher, does marvels in a student too. Keith and Cool (1992) tried to determine some of the factors that contributed most to the achievement scores of more than 25,000 students. Not surprisingly, the strongest determining factor they found was ability. But two other factors had strong effects: motivation and quality of instruction (Guy R. Lefrancois,

2000). Motivation contributes much to enable students to focus on their studies. A teacher can make a world of difference in the performance of students by constantly motivating them in all aspects of learning.

Maslow's need hierarchy has been accepted well in management circles as it is noted for its application, intuitive logic and ease of understanding. As a student of management, I am ever fascinated by five levels in his 'Hierarchy of Needs' theory. They are as follows:

1. *Physiological Needs*: These are the most basic level needs in the hierarchy, which comprise thirst, hunger, shelter, sleep, sex and other bodily needs. According to Maslow, once these basic needs are satisfied, they no longer motivate. When a person is satisfied with this level of needs, he is motivated by the next higher level needs.
2. *Safety Needs*: The second level of needs is almost equivalent to security needs. Everyone wants to study in good schools and colleges, obtain good jobs and take care of the family. For a teacher, a good institution provides the much needed feeling of security. Only well managed institutions will be able to provide the emotional and physical safety for its teachers. Institutions which provide pensionary benefits, health insurance and other service benefits are considered secure places to work. Once the teacher feels that the institution which he serves fully satisfies his safety or security needs, he is motivated by the next higher level needs.
3. *Affiliation or Acceptance Needs*: These intermediate level needs are all about social needs. They also correspond to belongingness or affection needs. The individual who succeeds in interacting with others in the group with a sense of belonging is able to generate a feeling of camaraderie, mutual respect and mutual trust. Once the teacher fulfills the need for acceptance or belongingness in the organization, he is further motivated by the next level of higher level on needs.
4. *Esteem Needs*: This need plays a pivotal role in deciding the destiny of a human being. It represents the higher needs of human beings. It comprises of needs for self respect, achievement, recognition, status and power. The teacher, who is motivated at this level of higher needs, tries to enhance constantly the quality of teaching, pursue higher studies, take up positions of leadership and become a teacher of repute. Teaching is such a noble profession that it fulfills the feelings of accomplishment, pride, higher status and dignity. Actually Maslow includes both self-esteem and esteem from others in esteem needs.
5. *Self-actualization Needs*: This need is the culmination of all other needs, so much so that it is considered the highest of all needs. The

> teacher who is motivated at this level of need becomes a true professional. His teaching and leadership potentials and research orientation are of a higher order. Such teachers become the cynosure of the student community and are ever admired for their praiseworthy achievements and exemplary qualities. Excellent teachers are always role models, and are recognized for their super performance by students. According to Orlich, Harder, Callahan, Trevisan and Brown (2010), this recognition is reflected in students' warmth, enthusiasm, and appreciation. Research in this field confirms that individuals who are motivated by self-esteem and self-actualization needs are generally highly competent, empowered and well-connected to the people in the organization. Such teachers are self-actualized often as what Maslow calls 'peak performance,' they have moments of intense joy, wonder, awe and ecstasy. After going through these exquisite experiences, they become inspired, empowered, revitalized and transformed.

If one examines the implications of the five needs referred to above, one realises that the teachers have to be continuously motivated by the higher-order needs–esteem and self-actualization needs. The higher-order needs are usually satisfied internally by the person concerned. They have a tremendous impact on the performance of efficient teachers. As employees, teachers can be motivated by money. But more than money, self-actualization and achievement needs play a dominant role in motivating him/her to do better. Similarly, a spirit of competition acts as a great drive to do one's best. To build self-esteem by being appreciated and recognized by superior performance is by itself a big motivator. All these, culminate in enhancing the personal and professional capabilities of teachers. A motivated teacher experiences energy and vitality which propels both right thinking and action in any educational setting.

In any organization, people seek security. Teachers too seek it, and those who feel insecure in an institution prefer to leave it. Likewise if the affiliation needs are not fulfilled, they would prefer to leave and find jobs in a better organization. As most efficient teachers seek personal growth, if the institution does not provide this opportunity, they would prefer to leave it.

A sound policy of any educational institution would be to retain the talented and committed teachers who are especially motivated by higher level needs. Such teachers are often motivated by a sense of personal responsibility, achievement drive and ethics too. In fact, they enjoy their peak performance and feel inspired, and immensely satisfied.

Like the Need theory of motivation, another theory which is of relevance in an educational institution too, is the Two-factor theory of motivation developed by Frederick Herzberg. He has identified certain factors which employees find satisfying or dissatisfying about their jobs. He called the first set of factors as motivators; these are internal factors that lead to employee's satisfaction and higher levels of motivation. The employee will neither be satisfied with his work in the absence of these motivators nor motivated to perform well according to their latent capabilities.

Motivators

- The work itself
- Achievement
- Recognition
- Responsibility
- Opportunities for advancement

Surprisingly, Herzberg has not included salary as a motivator in the above list. The reason being, he contends that pay belongs to the second set of factors which he calls as hygiene factors or maintenance factors. Hygiene factors are, according to him, external to the job, but they are located in the job environment. He clarifies that absence of hygiene factors leads to dissatisfaction and demotivation. These factors are as follows:

Hygiene Factors

- Organization policies
- Working conditions
- Job security
- Salary
- Employee benefits
- Relationship with supervisors and managers
- Relationship with co-workers
- Relationship with subordinates

According to Herzberg, if the administration provides the hygiene factors, employees will not be dissatisfied with their jobs, but they will not be motivated to perform well according to their capabilities. So, to motivate the employees, administration has to provide the motivators, as given above.

Herzberg promoted the idea of intrinsic and extrinsic motivators. If we compare his theory with that of Maslow's, then, it is understood that his hygiene factors relate to the first three levels of Maslow's hierarchy and his motivators relate to the upper two levels of Maslow's hierarchy. Herzberg developed the hypothesis that positive job satisfaction can occur only when the job itself makes it possible for the motivating factors to come into play. Hence, the work itself promotes achievement, recognition, responsibility and opportunities for advancement.

This theory of motivation lays emphasis on the need to provide motivators so that the employees are constantly motivated to perform well. At the same time, administration must not lose sight of the importance of hygiene factors, the absence of which can lead to dissatisfaction.

Both motivators and hygiene factors are interconnected if we look into the role played by them in deciding the performance of a teacher. If he is not motivated due to the absence of motivators like, the work itself or recognition, etc., his level of performance deteriorates. Likewise, if the institution does not provide the hygiene factors, like, good organization policies or good working conditions or job security, or good pay, etc., the level of performance of teachers deteriorates.

The greatest value of these two important theories is their practical application in academic administration. The administration has to seriously ponder over these implications so that they could introduce the salient features of these theories and reap good dividends by enabling teachers to act as high performers. The teachers who operate at the level propelled by esteem or self-actualization needs, do wonders. They function at their peak level of performance by using their maximum creative potentials and resources. On the other hand, if the administration follows a policy which does not motivate the teacher either at the higher level of needs or at the lower level, the internal environment in the institution becomes hopeless. The administration will have to guarantee financial security which is a strong determinant of job security, as explained by the "hygiene factors." A situation which portends job insecurity would have a devastating impact on the productivity of teachers. The administration must always keep their eyes and ears open to detect any warning signs regarding the deterioration of the quality of teaching. The root cause of poor performance of teachers must be identified and timely corrective measures initiated. It has been noticed that, in general, lack of motivation has been the major reason for the lackadaisical performance of teachers.

CASE STUDY

1. MOTIVATING THE TEACHERS

Gladstone School is a prominent institution which has been accepted well by the local community. Due to recession, the intake was affected, mainly because of higher rates of fees charged by the institution. The teachers were paid little above the prevailing salary in other schools. The administration took pride in this fact and thought that all the teachers were highly motivated due to their higher emoluments. But, in fact, the truth was something different.

The teachers were discussing one day during the lunch interval: "We are at a loss since we are working in a wrong place. We should have joined Edmond School as they get almost the same salary after putting in five years of service. The big attraction in Edmond's is not the salary or working conditions alone, but the novel system of appreciation by which the outstanding performers get bonuses. Also, they recognize the achievers at the annual day ceremony, which by itself gives a moral boost to the teachers."

This is only a part of what Edmond school does to appreciate the achievers. They reimburse the cost of laptops bought for their professional use and meet their commuting expenses. Moreover, they provide excellent training opportunities as and when required. Their policy is: The better the teachers perform, the better the organization takes care of them. Being highly motivated, teachers themselves bring in a large number of students by way of admission. They volunteer to spend more time with the weak students to improve their studies and coach them for arts festival, inter-school competitions and in literary events to come out with flying colours.

One wonders whether incentive schemes would work in all the situations to motivate teachers and recognition is an integral part of motivation in an educational institution.

Based on the Maslow's Need Hierarchy theory, what specific recommendations can be given to enhance teacher-motivation?

One also wonders whether monetary incentives is preferred to non-monetary incentives.

A Letter which would Open the Minds of All Teachers

Here is a letter which Abraham Lincoln wrote to his son's teacher; it speaks of the need to acquire proper values.

"My son starts school today. It is going to be strange and new to him for a while and I wish you would treat him gently. It is an adventure that might take him across continents, all adventures that probably include wars, tragedy and sorrow. To live this life will require faith, love and courage.

So dear Teacher, will you please take him by his hand and teach him things he will have to know, teaching him gently, if you can. Teach him that for every enemy, there is a friend. He will have to know that all men are not just, that all men are not true. But teach him also that for every scoundrel there is a hero; that for every crooked politician, there is a dedicated leader.

Teach him if you can that 10 cents earned is of far more value than a dollar found. In school, teacher, it is far more honourable to fail than to cheat. Teach him to learn how to gracefully lose, and enjoy winning when he does win.

Teach him to be gentle with people, tough with tough people. Steer him away from envy if you can teach him the secret of quiet laughter. Teach if you can—how to laugh when he is sad, teach him there is no shame in tears. Teach him there can be glory in failure and despair in success. Teach him to scoff at cynics.

Teach him if you can the wonders of nature, but also give time to ponder the extreme mystery of birds in the sky, bees in the sun and flowers on a green hill. Teach him to have faith in his own ideas, even if everyone tells him he is wrong.

Try to give my son the strength not to follow a crowd when everyone else is doing it. Teach him to listen to everyone, but teach him also to filter all he hears on a screen of truth and take only the good that comes through.

Teach him to sell his talents and brains to the highest bidder but never to put a price tag on his heart and soul. Let him have the courage to be impatient, let him have the patience to be brave. Teach him to have sublime faith in himself, because then he will always have sublime faith in mankind, in God.

This is a big order, but see, what you can do. He is such a fine little fellow, my son!"

Status of the Teacher

Status, in simple terms, is a socially defined position or rank given to groups or group members by others. Status tends to be derived from the following:

1. An individual's personal characteristics;
2. The power an individual wields over other members of the group;
3. An individual's ability to contribute to the goals of the group.

In the teaching profession, the teacher who is talented and resourceful, and known for his outstanding performance has definitely a higher status than someone who is mediocre and poor in performance. The teacher who controls the outcome of a group through his leadership competence and power enjoys a higher status. The teacher whose contributions are critical to the group's success also tends to have a higher status.

The higher the ranking of a teacher in his/her status in a group, the more is the recognition given to him/her by the other groups in the institution. Due to their inherent strength, the high-status teachers easily become leaders in the society as well, as they are able to attract the attention of members of a larger group, influence them and lead them effectively. Indeed, a teacher who is highly valued by the community can easily occupy key positions in the realms of public service and contribute much to the development of a nation. An accomplished teacher who is also an ace administrator is the right candidate to occupy public offices, mainly due to the high status he occupies in a society.

Emotion and Teaching

Emotion of the teacher plays a dominant role in the whole process of teaching. Emotional part of teaching includes the enthusiasm and passion with which he/she delivers the lecture and conducts the class. Again, it is the passion for the subject that enables him/her to be enthusiastic about making the presentation lively and vibrant. Enthusiasm is contagious. When the teacher expresses the ideas with enthusiasm and passion, students become more attentive and receptive in the classroom.

Emotions are of primary practical importance in education. They affect students' and teachers' interest, engagement and achievement, as well as their personality, development, health and well-being. By "implication," they profoundly influence the productivity and quality of life in educational institutions, and in society at large (Paul A Schutz, Reinhard Pekrun, 2007). This observation serves the teaching fraternity well to apply their minds seriously to the significance of emotions in educational institutions.

Teaching becomes more humane when teachers use emotions like, warmth, care and love. Students feel elated and satisfied when they attend classes of those teachers who exude with confidence and energy, and are caring and thoughtful. Teachers, who possess one of the most desired qualities in a teacher—positive emotional stability—are better placed to handle classes more effectively. This quality ensures the teacher to be calm, composed and self confident. Those teachers with negative emotional stability tend to be nervous, depressed and insecure. Teachers who possess abundance of passion and enthusiasm for teaching really enjoy the profession and become more productive and creative. Such teachers can easily cope with the challenges and occasional criticisms which a teacher has to face. The influence of positive emotions could produce a lot of confidence in a teacher, which in turn could empower him/her to try newer methods of teaching, use various tools and explore and use newer educational technologies.

Researches by Janet Collins (1996) and Joe Harkin (1998a) Harkin *et al.* (2000) have shown how important emotions are in the way young adult learners construct their perceptions of effective teaching. If education does not hold a proper balance between cognition and emotion, both are impoverished. Human beings should be viewed holistically, as complex and creative users of both IQ and what Goleman refers to as Emotional Quotient (EQ). Teachers and learners need to be emotionally engaged in the process of teaching and learning, not least because 'we remember things better when we are emotionally involved'(Chamberlain *et al.*, 1996). More importantly, thinking cannot be separated from feeling, and the emotional climate of the classroom is vital to good learning (*Manifesto for Learning*, Janet Collins, Joe Harkin and Melanie Nind, 2002).

Daniel Goleman's ideas on emotional intelligence do have some relevance in this context. He states that emotional intelligence is a different way of being smart. It includes knowing one's feelings and using them to take good decisions; managing feelings well; motivating oneself with zeal and persistence; maintaining hope in the face of frustration; exhibiting empathy and compassion; interacting smoothly; and managing one's relationships smoothly. He adds that persons having EQ (Emotional Quotient) exhibit the following common attributes. In essence, the panorama of skills found in the context of emotional intelligence help individuals manage both themselves and others in the following areas:

1. Impulse Control
2. Self-esteem
3. Self motivation
4. Mood management
5. People skills

CASE STUDY

2. A PROFESSOR WITH PASSION TO TEACH

If you go to the Green Valley College, you will meet the man behind the success of the Mathematics department. He is Professor Raj, the head of the department of Mathematics. More than being the head of the department, he has been a teacher there for 25 years, whose dedication brought in name and fame to the department and the college. Parents insisted that their children should undergo his coaching as it was sure that their wards would become achievers in life. Such is the quality of the scholarly teaching of that revered professor who has taught with integrity, compassion and attentiveness.

Teaching is his passion, and he has no hesitation to spend more hours in his job than anyone of his colleagues at that college. He comes daily to his department much earlier than his colleagues and leaves the department much later than others. His approach to teaching has been very methodical and he has been successful in developing critical thinking skills and stimulating interest in the subject. He takes extra pains to teach the subject thoroughly and spends extra time to value the test papers and assignments on a regular basis. Every week end, tests are conducted. This routine has been continued with alacrity and a sense of commitment throughout the year. He makes it a point to extend his help to the weak students by engaging extra classes for them. Their parents are called to give them special advice to change the habits of their wards so as to improve their learning skills and concentrate on their studies. During his leisure time he concentrates on publication of articles in professional journals and publish books on his subject.

Professor Raj has a large number of students who appreciate his hard work, and are grateful to him for his service and devotion. He has written a number of books, and is held in high esteem by his fraternity. He has been able to train and inspire a group of teachers in his department to be proactive and maintain the high quality of performance of the department. He also spends quality time to offer guidance to the research scholars assigned to him by the university. Moreover, due to his selfless service and dedication, his department stands no. 1 in the overall performance in the institution.

Not resting on his laurels, he leads his department as a mentor to his colleagues and students. As an exemplary teacher, he is adored by one and all. One day a parent put a question to him at a parent-teacher meeting: "Professor, we have never seen you taking rest. You are always fully engaged in academic matters, and you give so much importance to teaching and research. So, what advice would you like to give to the younger generation?" He replied, "Do one's duty meticulously—to your heart's content—and give the credit to the team."

☞

- According to you why many of the teachers are not able to reach to the expectations of the students?
- What specific qualities are required to reach such high standards of performance as that of Professor Raj?
- Pick the names of few teachers from your institution who ranks equal to the performance of Professor Raj and delineate their strengths.

5

Teacher Empowerment

You get the best out of others,
when you give the best of yourself.
When you discover your mission,
you will find its demand. It will fill
you with enthusiasm and a burning desire
to get to work on it.

—W. Clement Stone

Introduction

Professional development of a teacher ultimately culminates in teacher empowerment. It means to further one's own scholarship, research, and thereby maintain higher standards of performance. It also means focusing on students' learning objectives, developing students' intellectual skills and preparing them for careers. It also results in improving the standards of the institution and the quality of life through positive contributions for the growth and progress of the society at large. Moreover, it ensures proper development of the teacher in all phases of faculty development. "The professor must be first of all one who 'professes', who has a commitment." Professional development is looked upon as the teacher's total commitment to quality. According to Edwards Deming quality is pride in workmanship which comes from continuous improvement. In fulfilling his obligation to the profession, the teacher exerts every effort to raise professional standards on a continuous basis. The knowledge base is the core of professional development. It is this knowledge base which standardizes teaching profession and empowers the teachers.

The aim of education, according to John Dewey is development of individuals to the utmost of their potentialities. It is only a teacher with a professional outlook who will be able to help the student to tap his full potential for his development. Hence, professional development leads to empowerment of teachers. Macroff (1988) states that helping teachers become more knowledgeable about teaching and assisting them in developing a repertoire of strategies to teach is a requisite for empowering them. In the twenty-first century, when all the finest institutions in the world are assiduously bringing a more global perspective to the curriculum and raising the standard of education, empowerment of teachers by adhering to professionalism is the most practical method which can be chosen by teachers. Indeed, empowerment is considered a pre-requisite for not only improving the quality but also the status of a teacher.

The empowerment of teachers enables them to play a pivotal role in the decision making process, facilitates them to have control over their work environment, and helps them to take up more responsible positions of leadership. Bolin (1989) has defined empowerment as enabling teachers to participate in the determinations of institutional goals and policies, and to exercise professional judgement about what and how to teach. Lucas, Brown and Markus (1991) define teacher empowerment as readiness to make administration share their autonomy with teachers whose commitment is necessary to make the educational programme function at the highest degree of efficiency. Empowerment, which is a major characteristic of professional development, is the realization of one's potentials and shouldering the aspirations of the society when they entrust their children in the hands of teachers.

Empowerment also refers to developing self-esteem and confidence in one's own capabilities, which is another characteristic of professional development. Empowerment is the creation of an environment in which the teacher has the ability, confidence, prowess, motivation and commitment to take responsibility to continually improve the quality of teaching and initiate the required action to enhance the quality of students assigned to them in order to achieve the overall objectives of the institution. Glenn (1990) observes that the real power behind the concept of empowerment is authority derived from the command of the subject matter and essential teaching skills. It has been found that only an empowered teacher can create an empowered student who possesses outstanding qualities. An empowered teacher will voluntarily take the entire responsibility to accomplish the whole task within the time schedule. Empowerment focuses on continual development of the self and the core competence of the institution. It positively addresses issues pertaining to changes, both internal and external.

Effective professional development focuses on individual, collegial, and organizational improvement. It reflects the best available research practice in teaching, learning, and leadership and enables teachers to develop further expertise in the subject matter and teaching strategies, uses of technologies, or other essential elements in teaching to higher standards. It is driven by a coherent long-term plan (Fred C. Lunenburg, Beverly J. Irby, 2006). As teaching involves the intelligent use of a set of processes and procedures to produce effective learning, teachers are expected to internalize the core competence in this intellectually demanding profession from the very beginning of their career. Those teachers who have a professional mindset will naturally follow certain essential key strategies to improve their professional conduct, like, enrolling themselves in continuing professional development programmes, attending specialized training programmes, conferences, seminars and workshops—national and international—updating knowledge by private study, participating in workshops and courses, webinars, engaging in serious research and becoming a part of the networked learning communities and online discussion groups, forums and blogs. In addition, they would publish books and articles, use the services of peer-mentors, attend training programmes or faculty development programmes for upgrading skills on the job, make presentations at seminars, conferences and workshops, attend industry-academia conferences and become a part of a professional body of teachers—national and international. It would be one of the challenging propositions to be considered seriously by the distinguished colleagues of the fraternity, especially those who do not have the habit of publishing papers, to at least come out with 3 to 4 publications in the next two to five years in referred journals of national or international repute. Becoming a part of networked learning communities and online discussion groups on specific subjects, of both national and international groups have become a common feature, especially amongst accomplished academics. Such continuous interactions within the academic communities would invariably facilitate access to resources, promote faculty engagement, and excellence in teaching, and thereby, considerably strengthen the core competence of teachers. A teacher with a streak of professionalism would certainly engage himself energetically in most of the above-mentioned activities so as to transform himself as a teacher par excellence and thereby serve the society with pride and contentment.

A simple method to empower teachers to become more professional in their approach and in the practice of teaching is to maintain exclusive journals. Recording whatever is important about one's profession—whether it is about what has transpired in the classroom, or a matter of special interest or concern noticed in a new book, or a suggestion for self improvement, or about an observation made on one's own presentation or about the presentation made by another teacher—are of much help to improve one's quality of teaching. "Journals can promote a closer interaction between the personal and professional self and can assist the writer to determine and measure growth." This is one practical tool which has to be constantly used by teachers, whether a novice or senior, "to reflect on their practice, which gives momentum to the learning process. Habitual reflection needs to begin at the outset of professional development. In this way teachers can initiate practices that will provide them with frameworks for reflection over time throughout their careers." (*Methods and Technologies for Learning*, 2005). This practical tool will be of immense help for any teacher to do a self assessment of one's teaching and find appropriate development activities to be learnt and practiced as part of the professional development strategies.

Journal Writing

Journal-writing would serve several of the following purposes:

- To record experience;
- To facilitate learning from experience;
- To support understanding, and its representation;
- To develop critical thinking or a questioning attitude;
- To encourage metacognition;
- To increase active involvement in the ownership of learning;
- To increase ability to reflect and think;
- To enhance problem-solving skills;
- As a means of assessment in formal education;
- To enhance reflective practice;
- To lead to personal development and self-improvement;
- To enhance creativity;
- To improve writing skills;
- To support planning and progress in research or a project;
- To do a self-appraisal of one's current level of skills in communication.

In addition, lecture journals can be used to reflect on the content of the lecture, providing opportunities to deepen, and thereby, to improve the quality of learning. Other forms of journal-writing are: web logs or blogs. (Adopted from *Learning Journals*, Jennifer A. Moon, 2006).

Professional development is defined as those processes and activities designed to enhance the professional knowledge, skills, and attitude of educators so that they might, in turn, improve the learning of students. In some cases it also involves learning how to redesign educational structures and cultures (Thomas R. Guskey, 2000). From the observations given above, we can realize the unique position and responsibilities of a teacher in education. What is required of a teacher with a professional attitude is a quest for excellence that would constantly motivate him/her to engage the students with passion and understanding.

The term "empowerment" can be synonymous with 'professionalization'. Macroff, 1988). Lee (1991) defines empowerment as the environment in which the teachers act as professionals and are treated as professionals. Their findings explain how empowerment of a teacher is, to a great extent, interlinked with his/her professional development. Stephen Covey asserts that an empowered organization is one in which individuals have the knowledge, skill, desire, and opportunity to personally succeed in a way that leads to collective organizational success. Clearly, then, empowerment at the individual and institutional levels produce remarkable outcomes of success and contentment which leads to growth and development of both the individual and the organization.

The following twelve significant characteristics of an empowered teacher are the key indicators for success in this ennobling profession. Some of the characteristics mentioned here are inborn and others are acquired through practice which involves perseverance and commitment. But all the characteristics are equally important. If a teacher feels that he lacks any of the characteristics mentioned below, he will have to pay special attention to its development.

12 C's of an Empowered Teacher

1. Competence
2. Character
3. Caliber
4. Confidence
5. Creativity
6. Credibility
7. Command over language
8. Clarity of Expression
9. Clarity of instructional objectives
10. Cordiality
11. Calmness
12. Co-operation

The following factors have been found responsible for preventing a teacher from getting empowered. Usually, teachers who are not self-motivated and whose attitude to teaching is negative, have these traits. Subsequently they become a liability for the institution. They are responsible for spreading negative vibrations in the environment. Through effective training such teachers could be made positive-minded even though it would be an uphill task to instantly change their already existing negative mindset.

The Common Barriers to Empowerment

1. Inadequate expertise
2. Resistance to change
3. Lack of responsibility and authority
4. Lack of support from significant persons
5. Ego clashes and inferiority complex
6. Improper leadership style

7. Lackadaisical and lethargic attitude
8. Unwillingness to upgrade skills
9. Prone to academic dishonesty
10. Lack of enthusiasm
11. Highly critical of others
12. Wavering in their opinions

Administration is sometimes found lacking in its ability to build a harmonious and highly focused organization, and is often held responsible for the non-empowerment of teachers. First of all, administration has to realize that there is no conflict of interest between them and the teachers in the attainment of the overall objectives of the institution. Both are expected to act in unison, in the best interests of the institution, and are expected to feel that both are partners who steadfastly engage themselves in the pursuit of common goals of the organization. Administration's duty must be to foster and facilitate a collaborative approach by enlisting the co-operation of all the stakeholders of the institution, especially the teachers, to achieve the common goals of the institution. In this context, administration can improve matters in the organization by cultivating a culture of empowerment and cooperation by adhering to the following guidelines.

A Checklist for Administration to Facilitate Teacher Empowerment

a) Administration is expected to lead by respecting the abilities of the teachers.
b) It is expected to develop an atmosphere of free and open communication system embedded in mutual dialogue and respect.
c) It is expected to understand that the objective of teacher empowerment is to bring out the best out of teachers.
d) It always listens to teachers with respect.
e) It clarifies the expectations of administration from time to time.
f) It follows bottom up management style of functioning.
g) It celebrates together the achievements of teachers and the institution and their contributions made in the realm of academia by way of innovative and creative practices and strategies for development.

The following classification can throw light on the different types of teachers who perform far better than others by using their potentials:

a) The Master Teacher is the one who possesses the expertise to work with superior quality of performance. He is a model teacher who sets examples for others to emulate.
b) The Mentor Teacher is the one who assists other teachers in their professional development.

c) The Meritorious Teacher is the one who has excellent standards.
d) The Accomplished Teacher is the one who creates 100 per cent results for the institution.
e) The Committed Teacher is the one who is fully devoted to the profession.
f) The Enthusiastic Teacher is the one who carries students with him.
g) The Creative Teacher is the one who can experiment and break the pattern.

Teachers who are fortunate enough to possess a fine blend of the qualities mentioned above naturally become role models for others.

Personal Enablers

The following are the essential 'Personal Enablers' which essentially strengthen the qualities of a teacher:

a) Develop professional proficiency;
b) Be well-versed in the methodologies of teaching;
c) Cultivate a desire to go beyond a subject and learn for the sheer joy of discovery;
d) Set SMART (Specific, Measurable, Attainable, Realistic, Time-bound) goals;
e) Adhere to continuous self-evaluation;
f) Have control over the choice of technology to be used in the class;
g) Share the vision of the institution;
h) Build strong leadership qualities and be a team player;
i) Support initiatives to change;
j) Lead by example;
k) Be a source of inspiration;
l) Make noteworthy positive contributions to the institution;
m) Be trustworthy;
n) Continually demonstrate commitment to quality;
o) Be proactive.

The Five Big Dimensions of Personality and Effectiveness of a Teacher

The five big dimensions of personality have been used by theorists in different situations to analyze human behaviour. I am using the same dimensions to collate them with teacher effectiveness.

1. *Conscientiousness:* A teacher could perform well as a conscientious teacher, and be well organized, industrious and persistent or could be disorganized, lethargic and unreliable.

2. *Extroversion-introversion:* Extrovert teachers are outgoing, gregarious and sociable whereas the introvert teachers are reserved, timid and withdrawn.
3. *Agreeableness:* It shows the extent of co-operation, warmth and agreeable attitude on the one hand and an unfriendly, aggressive and disagreeable nature on the other.
4. *Emotional stability:* It shows the degree to which teachers are secure, happy and pleasant on the one hand and insecure, sad and anxious on the other.
5. *Openness to experience:* It shows the extent to which some teachers are creative and proactive whereas some are pessimistic and narrow-minded.

If we try to find these traits or characteristics in the behaviour of teachers, we may come across teachers who are goal-oriented, committed, well organized, sociable, industrious, open-minded, optimistic and possessing positive attitude. On the other side of the spectrum, we see teachers who are non-cooperative and keep themselves aloof from the team. They are lazy, disorganized, belligerent, depressed, pessimistic, demotivated and critical. In the former group, we come across teachers who are enthusiastic and motivated and in the latter group we have teachers who present a gloomy and bleak picture. The former group belongs to a community of path-finders and energizers whereas the latter group belongs to a community of negative-minded and unenthusiastic teachers. The second type of teachers are usually spoilsports and try to considerably dampen the spirits of the proactive teachers. It would be difficult to train these teachers as they resist new ideas due to their dogmatic and uncompromising nature.

The overall sense of well-being found in the first group of teachers is lacking in the second group as there is a marked difference in their attitude and value systems. The second group invariably holds negative views about themselves. They usually interpret ambiguous statements negatively to support their personal views.

Teachers must Rise to the Occasion

Some teachers feel that students are only comfortable with their lecturing method and uncomfortable with other methods of teaching. The reason for such ill-founded belief is that they are not at all comfortable with the other methods, mainly because they lack confidence and expertise in handling the class when they switch over to other methods of teaching. The point is, some teachers, unfortunately, lack skills and initiative to understand the implications of instructional objectives and effective use of a variety of appropriate tools and methodologies of teaching. Often they make excuses that since their lecture classes are well appreciated, they would stick on to the lecture method of teaching. This is a situation which is created by the teacher himself to avoid appropriate teaching methods in a challenging and changing environment. If the teacher does not change his mind-set and adapt to the changes in the pedagogical demands in a learning environment, if he does not familiarize himself with new effective methodologies of teaching, he will soon become a square peg in a round hole, and, may be asked to quit.

The teachers who have a positive disposition towards the course content will definitely be able to transfer their passion to receptive students with ease and efficiency. There is always a high correlation between a teacher's enthusiasm and a student's achievement. Enthusiasm will act as a motivational embellishment which enhances students' interest in the variety, novelty and creativity of the presentation. To deepen the understanding of the subject one teaches is a paramount duty of a teacher. Lewis B. Mayhew, *et al.*, 1990, suggest that academic and intellectual qualities are most likely to be enhanced when a number of intensively prepared professors continue over time, to deepen their understanding of the subject they teach and offer a series of interrelated courses that, according to an explicitly stated logic or rationale, are intended to develop student knowledge, and ability to apply that knowledge.

Benchmarking and accreditation of educational institutions have become a top priority goal. It is vital for most institutions of higher education, especially for those who aspire to be leaders in the profession. The two main concerns addressed in this context are quality and efficiency. The quality and efficiency of teachers are examined in depth by any accreditation-peer group. If they identify any problem related to them, they specifically mention them in their report, mainly to draw the attention of the administrators to the lapses of teachers, which create an unwholesome impression about the academic standards of the institution. Administration should identify such lapses in the beginning and take appropriate corrective measures to set right their weaknesses before the accreditation process starts. If the teachers are not aware of their crucial role in the accreditation process, they would bring about adverse consequences.

It is the paramount duty of an institution to obtain accreditation or ranking, and never compromise on the quality expectations of the stakeholders. Eventually, the administration will be able to assess the quality performance of teachers by obtaining feedback from students and from other internal sources. Any kind of non-conformity to the predetermined standards will end up in chaos and the results will be reflected soon in the performance of students. The teachers are always expected to be alert and conscious of their duties, especially in complying with the standards fixed by the administration and other bodies like the university to which the institution is affiliated.

Emphasizing the importance of teaching as a profession, A.P.J. Abdul Kalam states that as a teacher, one must not merely aim for the success of a few of their students. Instead, he should strive to ensure that students who are considered below average are provided the necessary assistance to improve their standards. Only then can the person become a great teacher.

The statement reminds us of the key responsibilities of teachers—not to simply concentrate on the development of the gifted students, but also provide the necessary help and guidance to the mediocre and poor students.

As significant developments are taking place in the field of knowledge, resulting in conceiving and designing newer courses, adopting large-scale technology, teachers must keep abreast of the advance in knowledge with respect to their subjects and constantly update their skills in the use of appropriate technology. In addition, they are to be proficient in the various methods of teaching. They can also play a key role in designing or improving the curriculum so as to meet the demands of modern education. They can contribute much in developing the appropriate pedagogical skills.

A teacher, who periodically attends the faculty development training seminars and workshops with simulated environments for teaching practices, will be able to familiarize himself with the new trends, techniques and methodologies of teaching and thereby conform to the standards of the profession. The overriding idea behind professional development of teachers is that knowledge enhancement and honing the skills in teaching make the teachers more efficient and facilitate improvements of students' achievements. Professional development is, by all means, an ongoing systematic process which requires constant attention by the teacher whether he is working in a school, college or university. Teachers, as professionals, are at the heart of educational development, and in many cases play a dual role, both as teachers and as administrators.

Environmental Challenges Affecting Teachers

Environmental challenges, by which I mean the forces external to the institution, naturally affect the performance of teachers. The first challenge is the drastic changes taking place in the system of education due to the impact of globalization. Higher education is undergoing rapid changes to meet the new demands of various sectors of the economy. One of the dramatic changes is the entry of foreign educational institutions. They bring along high standards of performance and highly successful courseware that are suitable for international environments. Since there is faster movement of workforce to countries where employment prospects are higher, students are attracted to the new foreign educational institutions to enhance their quality of education. To maintain higher standards, and compete with them, the institutions operating in the country are also forced to drastically improve their standards and quality. The universities and school boards of administration are changing their curriculum in a phased manner. They are incorporating newer subjects/content material brought about by changes in the external environment. But, competing with an already well-established global education institution is a gargantuan task for the *deshi* institution, which has already been beset by formidable challenges in its internal and external environment. Globalization is forcing more competition in the labour market which demands constant enhancement of knowledge and skills. Competition in a global scenario can produce disastrous results for the *deshi* institutions if they do not upgrade their standards, especially in higher education.

In this fast changing world, a teacher's knowledge of his subject becomes obsolete at a faster rate. The rapid change in the educational technology affects the methodology, strategy and tools used in teaching. In effect, these external forces are putting the teaching community under a great deal of stress. Several institutions face the threat of closure as students do not opt for out-dated courses or avoid inefficient institutions.

The second challenge is the explosion of knowledge due to the impact of internet. Some students are better informed about a subject as they have access to internet. The internet, has such a pervasive impact that the teacher finds it hard to cope with its demands. In fact, there is information overflow, which makes the teacher much concerned.

The third challenge comes from the imposition by the authorities to continuously follow the accreditation policies by ensuring quality enhancement as reflected in the national and/or global education environment. In a challenging environment, they are forced to gain a competitive advantage by tapping the right resources to maintain quality in all spheres of its functioning on a continual basis. Institutions either volunteer or are forced to obtain accreditation from national accreditation bodies in the respective countries and/or obtain ranking from international bodies. In addition, some obtain ISO certification to add one more feather to their cap.

After securing accreditation and/or ranking, the institution faces yet another challenge: to continuously show evidence that they have been implementing quality enhancement programmes continuously. The net result is that the teachers have to upgrade their skills and maintain quality in the teaching-learning environment, which are always documented by the inspection team at the time of accreditation. The new challenging situation expects the teachers to possess distinctive capabilities to create unsurpassed competence in selective areas of their performance. It is yet another daunting task for the teaching community.

Principles of Positive Change

The following ten principles, can bring about positive changes in a teacher. He/she may adhere to these principles and reap rich dividends.

1. Never think or speak negatively about yourself;
2. Learn about your strengths and encourage yourself;
3. Never compare yourself with anybody else. Everyone is unique;
4. Focus on your potential, not on your limitation;
5. Find out what you like to do and do it well. Strive for excellence;
6. Have the courage to be different;
7. Learn to handle criticism;
8. Determine your worth;
9. Do a self-assessment of your performance;
10. Focus daily on your greatest source of confidence.

How Successful are You as a Teacher?

The following self-assessment tools could be used by a teacher to carry out self-evaluation effectively, and thereby become a conscientious teacher and set things right.

1. I consistently work the hours I am paid for;
2. I take full responsibility for my actions, behaviours and attitudes;
3. I avoid passing the buck or blaming others for my problems and mistakes;
4. I know and follow all the rules established by the organization;
5. When given a task or assignment, I regularly try to complete it before the deadline;
6. I make a habit of volunteering for work;
7. I am a considerate co-worker;
8. I make special effort to co-operate with other members of my team;
9. I am committed to provide the best of my service;
10. I remember my promises and commitments;
11. I make special effort to keep the commitments and accept and support change rather than resent it;
12. One can count on me to bring about new things willingly;
13. I look for and seize opportunities to help my colleagues;
14. I treat everyone with the same sense of dignity and respect that I want for myself and the people I care about;
15. I value and appreciate people with ideas;
16. I make an effort to be patient with my students and colleagues;
17. I respect my organization and protect its interests;
18. I perform my duties with ethics and integrity;

19. I look for every opportunity to go the extra mile;
20. I always put myself on a path to success.

In the present education scenario, lots of radical changes are taking place, which may not be fully understood and appreciated by the teachers who are either ill-informed about or disinterested in them. The educational system is bound to change because of internal and external factors. The teachers who do not appreciate changes and resist it affect their performance adversely.

Major Reasons for Resistance to Change

The major reasons to resist change by teachers are the following:

1. The fear of potential personal losses;
2. An apprehension of the unknown;
3. Lack of knowledge, skills, etc., to implement the change;
4. Lack of communication from the authorities;
5. Lack of conviction about the purpose of the change;
6. Conflicts due to various groups' perception;
7. Ineffective leadership and resultant confusion;
8. Absence of courage to implement the change;
9. Poor motivation;
10. Incompetent to manage the complex organizational and employee transition to the desired end state;
11. New responsibilities due to changes;
12. Lack of initiative to do something different;
13. Misunderstanding;
14. Lack of trust;
15. Low tolerance for change;
16. Habit;
17. Lack of information;
18. Resentment towards the initiator.

It is noticed that teachers, like any other employee, do resist changes, depending on one's level of apprehension. Resistance takes place on an individual or a group basis. It could be in the form of a mild or an aggressive reaction.

When the administration introduces a change in the system, some teachers turn a deaf ear to the new suggestions and behave indifferently. They try to avoid the new responsibilities either ignoring the new changes or by attending to the new tasks indifferently. This is a subtle form of resistance to change, but the hidden agenda is to scuttle its objectives. For instance, if the newly introduced programme envisages the learning of new skills, the teachers would become slow learners and evince the least interest in the programme.

Another method by which they resort to sabotage the efforts of the administration to introduce change is by launching a collective action. When resistance takes the form of organized resistance, it leads to a head-on collision with the administration's policies. When a group is in conflict with the institutional goals, tempers run high and the atmosphere is vitiated by conflicting views and perception. It leads to ego clashes between the administration and the hostile group. In some situations the collective action is taken up by trade unions. In all such situations, it is advisable to discuss the matter with the trade unions or groups in advance and take them into confidence by convincing them about the need for change in a particular area of work. A consensus approach is ideal to tackle such problems. The main problem associated with resistance to change is that it breeds hatred and frustration among the affected parties which can have a disruptive effect on the institution. To avoid such unpleasant situation, it should be the priority of administration to plan and implement changes in a phased manner through a process of mutual discussion and acceptance. On matters affecting the future prospects of teachers due to the introduction of changes, it is advisable to have an open discussion with the teachers' organizations and arrive at decisions which are acceptable to the teaching community, administration and other stakeholders.

I would like to add some very useful tips, especially for the new teachers so as to improve their quality of teaching. A masterly teacher is warm, accessible, enthusiastic, caring, sets high expectations for all students and maintains professionalism in all areas. The following tips, if used properly, can bring out the best in a teacher.

Tips for Better Results in Teaching

- Be aware of the responsibilities of a teacher;
- Be thorough with the topics;
- Be familiar with the students of the class;
- Keep abreast of the changes in syllabus, curriculum and pattern of question papers;
- Be natural in presentation;
- Be informative;
- Teach with enthusiasm;
- Use audio-visual aids;
- Be punctual;
- Be honest;
- Be supportive;
- Appreciate the needs and understand the problems of students;
- Conduct periodic assessment;
- Give feedback;
- Always do self-assessment and take steps to consistently improve the quality;

- Always teach by following this principle: From simple to the complex;
- Introduce the level of difficulty gradually;
- Put to use different methods of teaching;
- Make teaching interesting and effective;
- Respect diverse talents and ways of learning;
- Build positive rapport with students;
- Be approachable;
- Possess exemplary communication skills;
- Have sense of humor;
- Be a centre of influence by leading by example.

CASE STUDY

THE NEW PROCEDURE

In the Great Easter College, the major problem the administration faced was, whenever a new procedure was adopted, or work was allotted to the teachers, they desisted from doing that task en masse. They argued that it was not a part of their duty as they have not done it earlier. The opposition came first from the informal leader of the group, who was an elderly and lethargic teacher. The administration noted that whenever a new task was given, the teachers unanimously took a decision to sabotage it. It was found that such informal leaders held a secretive meeting and decided to remain silent over the matter or inform administration that it was totally impossible to do the job. This became a regular feature and the teachers were determined not to take up any new task. If at all they took it up, they deliberately did it half heartedly or delayed the completion of the work. Some informal leaders demotivated those who did the work properly.

When a new principal was appointed, as part of official procedure, he wanted to take stock of the library books. He entrusted some teachers, after the annual examinations when they were totally free, to verify the stock with the assistance of the office staff. No sooner than this notice was circulated a senior teacher who was their informal leader convened a secret meeting, and the teachers announced in unequivocal terms that they would not assist in the verification of library books as it seemed to be a menial job. The teachers considered it an arbitrary decision and refused to work. They were both arrogant and adamant in their attitude, and they passed sarcastic remarks about the new principal.

☞

- What should be recommended to overcome this type of resistance to change?
- If one comes across such irresponsible and impolite behaviour on the part of the teachers how should one react? Does one think that teachers generally shirk their responsibilities when persuaded by their leaders? Is lack of professional attitude and ethics factors which make the teachers behave this way?

6

Learning, Performance Appraisal and Feedback

Thought is the blossom; language the bud; action the fruit behind it. —R.W. Emerson

He who has a why can endure anyhow. —Friedrich Nietzsche

The proper aim of education is to promote significant learning. Significant learning entails development. Development means successively asking broader and deeper questions of the relationship between oneself and the world (Laurent A. Daloz, 2012).

Findings related to Research on Learning

To begin with, we should have a brief idea of the findings pertaining to research on learning as summarized by Bransford, Brown and Cocking (2000). It throws light on certain fundamental principles of learning. Among these findings are:

- Students have preconceptions about how things work and these preconceptions (often misconceptions) need to be taken into account while indulging in learning activities.
- The development of competence requires fundamental knowledge, a conceptual framework, and the ability to organize and retrieve knowledge.
- Metacognitive approaches facilitates learning and improve performance.

These findings are consistent with and reinforced by model-facilitated learning (Milrad, Spector, and Davidsen, 2003), cognitive apprentice (Collins, Brown and Newman, 1989), model-centered (Seel, 2003), and such other instructional design approaches.

Lowyek and colleagues (Lowyek, Elen, 2004; Lowyek, Poysa and Van Merrienboer, 2003) also provide a compact and meaningful summary of the findings of learning research that have implications for instructional design and effective use of technology. Their findings pertaining to goal-oriented learning include the following:

- Learning is an active process that typically involves mental effort;
- Learners interpret their experiences and construct internal representations;
- Learning is cumulative, new knowledge is most useful when it is integrated with prior knowledge;
- Effective learning is self-regulated;
- Learning occurs in contexts that include both physical and socio-cultural aspects.

  (*Learning and Instructional Technologies for the Twenty-first Century*, Edited by Leslie Moller, Jason Bond Huett and Dourglas M. Harvey, 2009).

One would like to include in the definition at least some of the following elements: (1) learning as a process, (2) the acquisition of knowledge and skills, (3) a change of behaviour, and (4) self-activity (Richard M. Gorman, 1974).

Teachers' Duties to Improve Learning

Teachers can take a lot of positive actions to improve learning in the classroom. According to Donald C. Orlich, Robert J. Harder, *et al.* (2010), planning is at the heart of teaching. One hallmark of teaching as an organized activity is the process of planning. If one wishes to instruct in a systematic manner, one will have to devote a substantial proportion of one's time and activity to planning–deciding what and how one wants one's students to learn. Master teachers exhibit three common traits: They are well organized in their planning, they communicate their instructional objectives effectively to their students, and they have high expectations from their students.

The teacher, through effective planning, will be able to address the needs of students, importance of student-centered teaching and its effectiveness in enhancing their learning skills. As the responsibility to bring about positive changes in students rests on teachers, they are always expected to create productive educational experiences in the classroom. According to Bruce Joyce, Marsha Weil, and Emily Calhoun, (2011), people come to teaching with different degrees of warmth, sociability, academic learning, and conceptual development, and we can see all these in their stylistic variations.

Whatever be the stylistic differences, the following are some of the clear-cut practices, which, if implemented diligently by teachers, would result in improving the learning habits and skills of students.

Practices Leading to Effective Learning

1. Teachers must be thoroughly prepared to handle the classes and each class must turn out to be a unique experience for students.

2. They must constantly update their knowledge; improve upon their skills and methodologies of teaching.
3. They must collect and return the assignments and homework in the class.
4. They must give credit for prompt submission of assignments and homework.
5. Periodic tests are to be conducted and the valued papers to be distributed in the class.
6. If web-casts are provided by the teacher, it should be used by students as an additional resource material, and it must not be considered as substitute for attending classes.
7. Monthly attendance percentage and scores of all internal examinations are to be put on the notice board, and parents to be informed about the progress achieved by their wards.
8. The regular feedback regarding the performance of students must be given by teachers and, if special attention is required to improve learning skills, it should be done methodically and recorded.
9. Students must be provided with details of source materials for reference.
10. It is the first and foremost duty of teachers to take attendance in the beginning of a class. The students must understand that attendance is mandatory and that skipping classes is an indicator of indifference on their part. The teacher must make the students aware of the need to attend all the classes and make them understand that those students who regularly attend classes fare well in their examinations.

In "*The Teaching Portfolio—Capturing the Scholarship of Teaching*", R. Edgerton P. Hutchings, while delineating on "Products of Good Teaching," narrates the significant results of good teaching practices:

Results of Good Teaching

- Students' scores on teacher-made or standardized tests, possibly before and after a course, are taken as evidence of learning;
- Students work on laboratory workbooks and other kinds of workbooks and logs is taken into account.
- Student's essays, creative work, projects or field work reports are duly assessed;
- Publication by students on course related work is encouraged;
- Records of students who select and succeed in an advanced courses of study in the field is properly maintained.

These are products of good teaching and are pointers to the effectiveness of teaching, and teachers are expected to pay special attention to them.

Richard M Reis, in, "*Tomorrow's Professor*," explains the connectivity between teaching and learning as follows:

"I believe that learning can and should be fun, and that students who are active participants learn much more than whose participation is largely passive. Teaching and learning involve an inherent contract. Students must agree to take responsibility for their learning in order to engage, and teachers must be willing to be engaged, as well." This statement reveals candidly the importance of active participation by students in the process of learning, and about the active role of a teacher to be fully engaged in the process of teaching. These two factors can be considered as the two pillars of classroom teaching and learning, which would determine the success or failure of education.

Roger Saljo (1979) interviewed students about what they thought learning was and he found five qualitatively different ways of making sense of learning in an academic sense:

- Learning as a quantitative increase in knowledge; that is, learning as 'knowing a lot.'
- Learning as memorizing; that is, learning as storing information that can be reproduced.
- Learning as applying, skills or information.
- Learning as understanding, making sense or abstracting meaning.
- Learning as interpreting and understanding something in a different way.
- Learning as comprehending the world by reinterpreting knowledge.

In 1993, a study by Marton *et al.* identified an additional conception of learning:

- Learning as changing a person.

Here learning involves not just seeing the world differently but seeing one's own position in the world differently (Elaine Martin, 1999).

A teacher is supposed to know the learning styles of students he teaches. Neil Fleming's VAK model which consists of the following three learning styles throws some light on this concept:

- Visual style,
- Auditory style, and
- Kinesthetic style

Teachers should be able to understand the preference of a student in his/her learning style, and teach accordingly to get the best results. Visual learners do have a preference for seeing while learning; the auditory learners are more comfortable in learning by listening and the Kinesthetic learners learn effectively through experiences. Teachers are supposed to get a feel of the class; know the qualities of their students, particularly, their learning styles, and make teaching suited to the needs of students. Hence the need for a combination of teaching tools, aids and methodologies are always recommended to produce better learning outcomes. The quality of the teacher, the quality of learning and of the outcomes of learning are all indispensably interlinked. Indeed, one leads to the other.

There are further well-researched principles about how people learn. In "*Teaching at its Best*" Linda B. Nilson elucidates these principles: People are born learners, beginning from infancy with an insatiable curiosity and an increasing awareness of their learning. They absorb and remember untold billions of details about objects, other people, their languages, and things they know how to do (Bransford, Brown and Cocking 1999, Spence, 2001). People learn through elaborative rehearsal, which means connecting new knowledge to what they already know and believe (Bransford *et al.*, 1999). They learn what they regard as relevant to their lives (Svinicki, 2004). They learn socially by constructing knowledge in a group, (Kinzie, Stage, Muller, and Simmons, 1999), otherwise they learn one-on-one on their own (Spence, 2001). People learn when they are motivated by the inspiration and enthusiasm of other people in their lives (Feldman, 1998). They don't learn well when their major learning context is teacher-centered, that is, when they passively listen to a teacher talk in a monologue. Rather, they learn when they are actively engaged in an activity, a life experience. The human brain cannot focus for long when it is in a passive state (Bligh, 2000; Bonwell and Eison, 1991; Spence, 2001; and Svinicki, 2004). They learn best when they receive the new material multiple times but in different ways – that is, through multiple senses and modes that use different parts of their brain (Kress, Jewitt, Ogborn, Charalampos, 2006; Tulwing, 1985, Vekiri, 2002). They learn when they actively monitor their learning and reflect on their performance—a mental operation called metacognition or self-regulated learning (Bransford, *et al.*, 1999). People learn better when the material evokes emotional and not just intellectual and physical involvement (Leamnson, 1999; Mangurian, 2005).

The key learning principles mentioned above have some complimentary principles, which are as follows as suggested by Lois. J. Zachary.

Complimentary Principles of Learning for Teachers

- Hold your students to high expectations;
- Start where the students are;
- Make the material relevant to the student's lives;
- Demonstrate enthusiasm and passion for your subject and for teaching it, as they are contagious emotion;
- Assign creative, inventive, and challenging tasks to small groups

and more routine tasks, such as standard problem sets as individual homework;

- Use active learning technique, and when you lecture, do so interactively;
- When possible, use experiential methods, those that place students in real life problem-solving situations, simulated or genuine;
- Teach in multiple modalities—Give students the opportunities to read, hear, talk, write, see, draw, think, act, and feel new material into their system;
- Teach your students how to learn your material and build in assignments that make them observe, analyze, and assess how well they are learning;
- Build into your course plenty of assessment opportunities, including practice tests, in-class exercises, and homework assignments;
- Motivate and reinforce learning with emotions;
- Make learning experience dramatic, humorous, surprising, joyous, maddening, exciting, or heart-wrenching;
- Integrate engaging case and problems to solve, simulations, and games, role plays, service-learning and other experiential learning opportunities into your courses;
- Let students reflect debate and consider multiple points of view, write down their reactions to the material, and work cooperatively in groups. Any emotion will aid learning by inducing more enduring changes—that is, the generation of new, lasting synapses—in the brain.

Pedagogy is articulated either directly or in the generalized statements in theories of learning, or indirectly as instantiated in the curriculum materials, textbooks, videos and software (Diana Laurillard, 2008). Epistemology, which deals with the theory of knowledge, androgogy, which are teaching strategies developed for adult learners, and pedagogy are important in higher education as well. Pedagogical strategies are of immense help in enhancing the quality of learning. It is Piaget who made it clear that through a process of accommodation and assimilation, individuals construct new knowledge from their own personal experience. Constructivism is a theory propounded by Piaget which conveys the concept of the student as the creator of knowledge and meaning through their interaction with one another, their environment and with their teachers. In a constructivist classroom, teachers and students share responsibility and decision-making as well as demonstrate mutual respect.

While blending learning methods, both traditional and technological supported, the teacher not only lectures but also uses ICT-enabled learning method to enhance the quality of learning and teaching.

In the collaborative learning method, a variety of educational approaches are put to use by the teacher to make teaching effective. For example, a guided design as a structured approach to group problem-solving is followed to assist students to find solutions to problems by carrying out sequential tasks.

In the active learning method the student is effectively engaged in the learning process. It provides an opportunity to him to think about what he is doing rather than passively listening to the teacher. This method helps him to develop independent learning skills and the ability to apply knowledge in real life. John C Maxwell summarizes the impact of learning as follows: "Change is always the goal of learning. You cannot have growth without change." From this point of view, we can understand that growth and change are interconnected, one leading to the other. Every learning experience brings about visible and invisible changes in the individual which primarily affects his way of thinking and behaviour, and evidently has lasting impressions on the human psyche.

Experience and learning are intimately interconnected. David A. Kolb, (1984) in *Experiential Learning*, defines learning as "the process whereby knowledge is created through the transformation of experience." Learning through experiences has been considered one of the most practical ways to learn effectively. Those who learn better by using the kinesthetic style of learning would always prefer learning through experience as they would be more comfortable and productive when they follow this method.

According to Jenny Rogers, effective learning takes place when the learner really needs and wants to have knowledge; when he knows how to apply it drawing on his own experience, when he knows he will be rewarded one way or another for having it; when he knows he can learn at his own pace and style and is encouraged to learn about where to find and how to judge information; when he is challenged; when he is supported; and, when he is treated as an individual with unique needs by whosoever is helping him to learn.

What is found pertinent in the whole process of learning is that the will to learn plays a dominant role in deciding the effectiveness of learning. It stems from an inner desire to learn and achieve success. If a student is on the will to learn mode of motivation, he need not be coerced or coaxed to learn. He becomes an ardent and strong believer in the principle of self-efficacy on his own. Such students are regular, systematic and methodical in their learning activities. They are the self-starters who are self-motivated to achieve success. Learning becomes a pleasure, a play for them.

A wide spectrum of factors contributes to the effectiveness of learning, apart from the IQ and memory retention capabilities. It is a long list, indeed—Factors, like the culture and influence of one's home and institution, curriculum and inputs, quality of teaching, peer culture and influence, self-image, readiness to explore and enquire, observation and analytical skills, attitude, interest, focus, creativity, language skills, competitive spirit, willingness to take risks, evaluation systems, level of motivation, health, study routine, distraction-free environment, ambience of the study room, avoiding time wastage, using speed-reading skills and memory techniques, goal, and task-orientation— all these determine the effectiveness of learning.

Johann Wolfgang von Goethe's advice can be used by every teacher to enrich the qualities of a student: "If you treat an individual as he is, he will remain how he is. But if you treat him as if he were what he ought to be and could be, he will become what he ought to be and could be." Every student has immense potentiality which has to be nurtured and nourished by an intellectually astute and insightful teacher. Every student can demonstrate confidence in learning if the teacher is capable of creating hope and confidence in him.

James M. Banner, Jr. and Harold C. Cannon (1999), state that study is the opposite of indulgence and indolence. It calls for repeated application, concentration, focused thought, and often solitude—all challenging demands. Although study can bring one great pleasure and reward, actual study is always tedious. Satisfaction comes from its results, rarely from the activity of studying itself. Its benefits are often found in the indiscernible future. Studying and learning are therefore the opposite of all the material trophies that our commercial culture extols.

The following story will ignite the minds of teachers who want to make teaching an exciting experience for students:

A story told about Louis Agassiz, a natural history professor at Harvard University, and his students over a century ago (Corey, 1980) underscores the importance of reflecting on experience to reach deeper levels of understanding.

Agassiz assigned his student the task of observing a fish and left him alone. The student, bored with the assigned work, concluded after a short while that he had "seen all there is to see". To spend his time while waiting for Professor Agassiz to return, he took a pencil and paper and draw the fish— and as he drew, he discovered features he had not previously observed. When the Professor returned, the student eagerly reported what he had found from observing and drawing the fish.

Agassiz praised his student at first and remarked, "A pencil is one of the best of eyes," later be challenged him, saying, "You have not looked carefully! Why is it that you haven't even seen one of the most conspicuous features of the animal, which is as plainly before your eyes as the fish itself. Look again, look again."

This scene between Agassiz and his student was repeated over and over again. And for every new observation by the student, Agassiz offered a compliment, followed by a challenge to "look, look again."

There are many lessons to be learned from this classic story, For example, rather than telling the student the answer, Agassiz provided an opportunity for him for self-discovery and reflection. In addition, he paced the learning to be sensitive to the student's need and continuously encouraged him to examine the fish from different perspectives and look more deeply (*The Mentor's Guide*, Lois. J. Zachary, 2000).

Relevance of Feedback and SWOT (Strengths, Weaknesses, Opportunities, Threats): An Analysis of the Self-Evaluation Process

Obtaining feedback on one's quality of teaching is a pre-requisite to ascertain its effectiveness. Of course, the management of any institution is interested in conducting the evaluation of teachers to decide about his suitability for further employment. But I would strongly recommend that the teachers themselves carry out frequent evaluation and just do not wait till the end-of-the-semester or term questionnaire circulated by the management amongst the students. The purpose of evaluation in such contexts is clearly delineated in the questionnaire. The teacher must be aware of not only the purpose of such mechanisms, but also, understand the nuances and implications of each statement and response made by each student. It is advisable for the teacher to peruse the end-of-the-semester questionnaire for evaluation in the beginning of the semester and prepare well to handle the class, keeping always in mind the instructional objectives to be achieved. Unless and until he is ready to function with an open mind to adapt to the specific requirements of this profession, he will not be graded as a proficient teacher. If he is true to the profession, he himself would encourage students to give feedback about his classes from time to time. This healthy practice would become the basis for his better preparation for the class. It is prudent on his part to obtain both positive and negative feedback so that he could maximize his strengths and minimize his weaknesses. The teacher can also undergo a SWOT analysis to carry out self-assessment about his performance. Such an analysis, if carried out in all earnestness, would reveal all the inherent strengths possessed by him, the weaknesses faced, and several opportunities available for taking corrective measures to improve the quality of teaching. He can visualize the kind of threats faced by him to prevent him from attaining the goals set for improvement. A fledgling teacher can make use of this effective self-assessment tool to enhance the quality of teaching, and thereby gain confidence to become a proficient teacher. A brief idea is given here to assist the teacher to pick the related factors for self-analysis under the SWOT Analysis method of self-evaluation.

The teacher may consider factors like one's own inherent strength—qualification, capabilities like thorough knowledge of the subject, good communication, analytical skills, mastery of pedagogical practices, creditable experience, positive attitude, outstanding performance, etc. As weaknesses, factors like lack of proper qualification, inadequate knowledge of the subject, poor communication skills, lack of mastery of pedagogical practices and experience, negative attitude, gap in performance, etc., may be considered for analysis. As regards opportunities, factors like, new qualification, library facilities, training, research and publications, attending seminars and workshops, etc., may be considered. Finally, regarding the threats factors, like newer education technologies, competition from similar institutions—from national and international players, accreditation or ranking requirements, new educational policies, etc. may be considered. It is up to the teacher concerned to find the different factors in the four areas of analysis as most of them are personal factors. Usually, while analyzing the strengths and weaknesses, factors which are mostly internal, as far as the institution and the person are concerned, are taken into account. While analyzing the opportunities and threats, factors which are external to the institution are considered separately. But, to make the SWOT analysis effective and useful, the teacher has to pick up the factors by being true to himself. If he cheats himself by concealing facts to avoid unpleasant results, he stands to lose from this beneficial exercise. In the end, after a thorough analysis, what he is expected to do is to maximize his strengths, minimize his weaknesses, and seek new opportunities to grow and excel.

Peer Observation and Other Practices in Evaluation

Peer observation has an important part to play in facilitating effective teaching. It is the observation of teachers by teachers, usually, though not always, on a reciprocal basis. Pairings may be mentor/ novice or experienced teachers. In the first situation the focus is more clearly on assisting the novice to develop his teaching skills. In the second situation, the purpose is to provide opportunities for the experienced teacher to reflect on his teaching practices.

In "*Effective Teaching*", Daniel Muijs and David Reynolds (2001), give us a very effective practice carried out in Japan to improve the quality of teaching—a particularly interesting form of classroom observation is the use of 'research lessons' in Japan. There, teachers regularly present research lessons to colleagues, in which they demonstrate some innovative strategies and practices they follow while teaching their subjects. Such an innovative presentation necessarily enhances the confidence of the teacher. I would recommend that this unique, useful and challenging method be tried out in all the institutions of higher education in all countries.

Peer observation and evaluation can be effectively used to ensure professional development of teachers by giving them an opportunity to learn from one another in a non-threatening environment. It is hoped that teachers will share ideas and suggestions openly and constructively to their mutual professional benefit. It is a powerful and most useful tool to disseminate good practice of teaching and thereby help the less experienced or fledgling teachers to improve their teaching skills and also to absorb the shared values of the institution. In most cases the institution provides the framework for the observation and evaluation but remains uninvolved and uninformed about the outcome of the observation. They leave it to teachers to reap the benefits of such voluntary efforts for self-improvement.

Peer observation and evaluation can also be used by an institution as part of its quality assurance procedures. In this mode, the head of the department is asked to constitute a committee of teachers who assess and report formally on the performance of their colleagues according to certain criteria set out by the institution. Such healthy practices can bring about qualitative and positive changes in the presentation skills of teachers to a great extent.

From the point of view of sound administration, the effectiveness of teaching and learning must be determined by all the stakeholders of an educational institution, starting from the teachers themselves, then by the administration, and parents and students. It is imperative to find out the source of weakness in the delivery—whether the teacher himself is responsible for the poor quality of teaching or whether there are organizational failures which have led to the weakness in teaching or whether there are any failures in the systems in the organization which have acted as stumbling blocks to effective teaching and learning—all these have to be analyzed to identify the root cause of deficiencies in teaching and learning. The possible causes for poor quality of teaching have to be thoroughly examined by the end of each term and corrective measures are to be taken to stem the rot at the appropriate time.

In some institutions, a 'suggestion box' or a 'grievance redressal box' is placed at the entrance of the main hall so that every student gets an opportunity to write down any suggestion or complaint and drop in it matter related to the activities of the institution, including performance of the teachers and other members of staff. Students are permitted to drop their remarks with or without their names on them. This is a good system provided to obtain first hand information about the quality of teaching, facilities provided, standards maintained and also about the expectations of students.

Reflective Teaching

Reflective teaching is a very useful and effective method of self-evaluation which reveals the strengths and weaknesses of one's own teaching. It is followed by conscientious teachers to improve their teaching skills. Reflective teaching means looking at what teachers do in the classrooms, thinking about why they do it, and a process of self-evaluation. This important exercise initiated by the teacher himself, helps to identify and explore one's own teaching practices and underlying beliefs, the benefit of which is the consequential improvements in teaching. Reflective teaching is, therefore, an effective means of professional development which begins in the classroom itself.

Reflective teaching is a cyclical or spiraling process, in which teachers monitor, evaluate and revise their own practice continuously. It provides a dynamic basis for teacher action. Lawrence Stenhouse (1975) argues that teachers should act as 'researchers' of their own practice and should develop the curriculum through practical enquiry. Teachers are principally expected to plan, make provision and act. Reflecting teachers also need to monitor, observe, and collect data on their own and on the intentions, actions and feelings of their students. It needs to be analyzed critically and evaluated so that it is shared, judgements are made and decisions taken. Finally, this may lead the teacher to revise his or her classroom policies, plans and provision before beginning the process again. It is a dynamic process which is intended to lead through successive cycles, or through a spiraling process, towards higher-quality standards of teaching. This model is simple, comprehensive and could certainly be an extremely powerful influence on practice (Andrew Pollard, 2006).

To make reflective teaching a meaningful means to improve the quality of teaching, one has to maintain a teacher's diary or a journal. After each lesson the teacher can write in the diary or journal about what happened in the class. He may also describe his own feelings and reactions and those observed on the part of the students. Peer observation is another method to collect information about teaching and the different patterns of interaction. Video or audio recordings of lessons can also provide very useful information for reflection. Yet another method which can be put to use by the teacher is the student feedback which can be obtained by circulating questionnaires.

The reflective teaching method has to be followed from the very beginning of the career so that the teacher can become aware of his strengths and weaknesses at an early stage. The teacher will be prompted to teach effectively by initiating changes in the method of teaching in the beginning of his career, and thereby become more quality-conscious. And that is what professional development is all about.

If this important method has to be made useful, the teacher must be willing to maintain a record of the changes initiated. He can use reference books and other publications which throw light on improving the quality of teaching, and attempt to implement new ideas. Reviewing new teaching materials, adopting new methodologies of teaching and attempting instructional innovations and evaluating their effectiveness, and participating in professional seminars and workshops intended to improve the quality of teaching will be of great help. Another, practical method for a new teacher is to observe the experienced teachers' classes, and make a note of the good practices that could be emulated. In addition, he could have informal discussions with experienced teachers so as to understand the classroom situation and what really works for learners.

As learning environments and instructional methodologies are diversified, teachers become self-reflective about their performance, thereby striving to achieve better learning outcomes.

As a research tool, self-study allows teachers and teacher educators to implement and extend the principles of reflective-teaching—questioning one's practice, gathering evidence related to these questions, and reflecting on the evidence in order to understand the processes of effective teaching better (Jere Brophy, 2005).

Performance Appraisal

The Gnanam Committee in the report submitted to the University Grants Commission (UGC) clearly stated that the university must see that the faculty divisions and colleges have accomplished the purpose of imparting higher education by evaluating the effectiveness of teaching.

The purpose of performance appraisal is to inform the teachers how they are performing their duties. Performance must be based on standards that are developed by the academic bodies and made known to teachers. The standard or criteria must be useful in identifying the achieved level of teachers' performance. The performance standards are made known to the teachers in the beginning of the term as they provide a mandatory guideline on performance appraisal. It is also required of teachers to maintain documents to substantiate their claims related to their level of performance. Performance appraisal, in general, provides a basis for promotion, increase in salary, counseling, training, incentives and special recognition. It also provides data about the strengths and weaknesses of teachers in critical areas.

While using performance appraisals, the appropriate rating scales are to be chosen by the administration. The team which carries out the appraisal is to be well trained for making the system of appraisal foolproof. If promotion decisions are made on the basis of performance appraisals, it is better to entrust an independent body to decide on such important matters. The performance appraisals conducted by the administration must be supported by peer and student feedback. The final decision for promotion, increase in salary, etc. could be made after analyzing the findings of performance appraisal, peer feedback and student feedback.

Criteria for Performance Appraisal

In the performance appraisal forms, the following criteria are rated in the following order—'Outstanding, Exceeds job requirements, Meets job requirements, Needs improvement, Unsatisfactory.'

1. Knowledge of subjects and understanding of assigned duties and responsibilities.
2. Technical skills in terms of setting instructional objectives and their realization.
3. Quality of performance in terms of teaching-learning outcomes.
4. Quantity of work in terms of successful completion of work according to schedule.
5. Leadership skills in terms of planning and execution of programmes.
6. Judgment in terms of effectively responding to problems.
7. Attendance and punctuality.
8. Flexibility in terms of positive response to changing work requirements.
9. Interpersonal relations.
10. Cooperation.

Performance as a Teacher

The teachers are to be evaluated at the end of each term so as to find out whether they have performed according to the standards of performance stipulated by the administration.

Regarding the first criterion, it must be ascertained whether the teacher concerned possesses sufficient knowledge in the subject he has taught, and has been aware of all the duties and responsibilities assigned to him as per the Teachers Manual of the institution.

Under the second criterion, the competence of the teacher in developing the instructional objectives of each topic and their fulfillment are to be examined in detail.

Under the third criterion, it has to be ascertained to what extent the instructional objectives have been met in relation to teaching-learning outcomes.

Under the fourth criterion, the performance of the teacher has to be quantified in terms of the topics taught, assessment of students, by way of tests and examinations, and success and failure of students.

Under the fifth criterion, teacher's leadership skills in the planning and execution of all academic, co-curricular and extra-curricular activities are to be evaluated.

Under the sixth criterion, the teacher's skills and quality in judging the matters related to barriers in learning and discipline are to be evaluated.

Under the seventh criterion, punctuality of the teacher in the conduct of classes and the overall percentage of attendance secured by the teacher has to be looked into.

Under the eighth criterion, what has to be examined is how the teacher adjusts positively to the specific changes introduced by the administration from time to time.

Under the ninth criterion, the human relations skills of the teacher are evaluated.

Finally, whether the teacher possesses a willingness to extend cooperation and how far he has extended his cooperation for the smooth functioning of the class and institution has to be evaluated.

Parents' Feedback and Perception of the Standard of the Institution

Nowadays parents are more concerned about the quality and standards of education of the institution. They demand better performance of teachers if they find them lacking in competence. More parents are now concerned about the standards of the institution as their expectations have become higher and education has become costlier. The parents do not hesitate to take up the issue of haphazard performance of teachers and/or staff and unwholesome and unethical institutional practices directly with the administration and strongly demand change of such personnel and practices. If they are dissatisfied with the performance of the teachers and staff and institutional practices and, if the administration is not taking corrective measures, they may withdraw their wards from such inefficient institutions.

Areas of Interest and Concerns

The major areas of interest and concern for the parents are the following:

a) The progress and achievement of the student;
b) Quality of service provided by the administration;
c) The institution's environment;
d) Reputation of the institution;
e) Accreditation policies and achievements;
f) Periodicity of dispatching report cards;
g) Respect for parents;
h) Action on complaint;
i) Strive for continuous improvement;
j) Working conditions in the institution;
k) Quality of performance of teachers and staff.

Parents always keep track of the education of their wards. They may or may not attend the parent-teacher meetings, but are very much concerned about the general standards maintained by the institution. Most of them interact with the teachers through an open system of communication facilitated by the respective institutions. The parents give a lot of publicity to good institutions, which in turn attracts a large number of students to such institutions. Indeed, the parents play a significant role in publicizing the reputation of the institution.

The administration of an institution is duty-bound to pay heed to the suggestions given by the parents and try to implement them for its better development. If one scans through the history of successful institutions, it is noticed that most of them have incorporated the valuable suggestions given by the parents regarding their functioning. Parents and alumni always support the institution financially when it needs funds for specific projects. The administration can use the parent-teacher meetings as a platform to ensure mutual support and co-operation but it must listen to the suggestions given by parents. During the parent-teacher meetings, teachers must be responsible and alert. Some parents might even write down questions related to their wards' progress and hand them over to the principal or the chairperson of the meeting. Some parents may be tempted to blame the teachers for their wards' failure or difficulties in the learning of subjects. Some of them make use of such occasions to appreciate the good job done by the teachers or congratulate the administration for introducing healthy practices or providing better facilities to students. We should note that the best outcome would be achieved when teachers, students and parents work together to improve the quality of students.

The administration can make use of the parent-teacher meetings to articulate their ideas for improving the atmosphere in the institution and to seek the co-operation of parents for its future development. The parent-teacher meetings must be well-planned, the notice containing the agenda circulated well in advance, and the meeting effectively conducted to bring out better results. It can be considered one of the important PR exercises, which, if organized effectively, would generate a lot of goodwill, esprit de corps, camaraderie and satisfaction on the part of parents.

It is always advisable to get acquainted with the parents by giving the name and contact number of the teacher in charge of tutorial activities to them in the beginning of the academic year. The teacher can, in turn, inform the parents the best time to call them.

Importance of Feedback

While going through a bunch of feedback forms in an institution, the administration came across suggestions written by students at the bottom of the form about the attire worn by some teachers which, according to them, was unacceptable. Some made comments on offensive and objectionable language used by the teachers. Most students try to avoid giving a dispassionate and true assessment of their teachers as they do not want to see them penalized. Even if there are few negative responses, they are to be taken up seriously by the administration as well as the teachers. In general, students are afraid of their teachers, which prevents them from providing their correct assessment to higher authorities.

The classroom assessment of students on a continual basis is an essential process carried out by teachers to collect data on student learning. It is usually carried out by asking questions, listening carefully to the questions or comments made by students and by observing and monitoring their body language. It can also be carried out by giving them home work, assignments and small projects. Classroom assessment helps in bringing about attitudinal changes in students and thereby making them actively interested in the process of learning. It is through such evaluation that the progress of students can be measured. When the student obtains satisfaction from the learning environment after such assessments, he is further motivated to complete his course successfully. Constant assessment of students brings about positive changes in them. They are motivated to do whatever is possible to improve their studies. Teachers are also able to know how helpful they are in improving their learning capabilities. The classroom assessments are followed by monthly tests and terminal examinations in which the data generated through classroom assessments are not used for grading purposes.

It is the paramount duty of a teacher to reflect on teaching continuously. It's a sort of a process of self-observation and self-evaluation. It means, looking at what the teacher does in the classroom, thinking about why he does it, and whether it works. When he collects relevant information about what goes on in the classroom, and analyzes and evaluates it, he can identify and explore his own methods, practices and beliefs. This self-analysis may then lead to improvement in his teaching method. It can create enthusiasm in the teacher to aspire for professional development, which in turn, would bring about positive changes in his outlook and performance.

What is the most ideal way to carry out a process of reflecting on one's own teaching? First, the teacher has to maintain a diary wherein he records all details of the class, including his own reactions and feelings. Secondly, he goes in for a peer observation by inviting his colleagues to the class and collecting peer feedback about the class. Thirdly, he can record his lesson by using an audio recorder or video recorder and find for himself what went on in the classroom. Fourthly, he can obtain students' feedback and then analyze their opinion and perception. From such self-observation and self-analysis, he is likely to find out his strengths and weaknesses as a teacher and plan to attend an in-service training programme or obtain guidance from experts and other sources to rectify the mistakes.

Let us have the "One Minute Feedback," which may be used by a conscientious teacher to obtain instant feedback about his performance.

ONE MINUTE FEEDBACK

So far I find this class to be (circle your response)

Interesting	1 2 3 4 5	Uninteresting
Too fast	1 2 3 4 5	Too slow
Too easy	1 2 3 4 5	Too difficult
Relevant	1 2 3 4 5	Irrelevant
Organized	1 2 3 4 5	Disorganized
Relaxed	1 2 3 4 5	Tense

Source: Adopted from: *The Ultimate Training Workshop Handbook*, Bruce Klatt, 1999.

Evaluation of Teachers

The importance of evaluation of teachers by students has to be reiterated here. The purpose of periodic evaluation is to help the teacher to be aware of the strengths and weaknesses of his teaching method. It is certain that students are the most reliable judges to evaluate the performance of teachers as they are the only persons with whom the teachers constantly interact in the classrooms or laboratories.

Now a days, standardized evaluation forms are readily available which are put to use by the managements to keep a close watch on the performance of teachers. These reports are referred to when the management decides finally to re-employ the person for another term. In good institutions, teachers themselves circulate the feedback forms at the end of a term to elicit response from their students about their quality of teaching. Some teachers circulate these forms after completing a topic so that they are able to make necessary adjustments in their methods of teaching. The anonymity of the student is protected in all such feedback forms by asking the students to drop them in a box separately maintained for this purpose.

One simple method used to evaluate teaching is the 3P's Method. The form for evaluation addresses three important educational indicators i.e., 3P's—Proficiency, Perception and Professionalism. The three key performance indicators are:

Proficiency: Are you being taught with effective teaching and communication skills with properly organized lesson plans and contents?

Perception: Are you able to perceive and swiftly produce the content taught in the class? Does the teaching standard make you think beyond what you have learnt?

Professionalism: Are you being taught with the fair, impartial and professional attitude in the class?

The three indicators are to be mentioned on the form along with the specified places to fill the numerical data. The form structure addresses two different columns for each parameter. One contains the current numerical data about a certain indicator assessed by the students out of 100. The other column is filled again by the student with numerical target data, again estimated out of 100. The expediency and dynamism of this model is apparent from the fact the targets are set by students and they are not dynamic. Throughout the course, the students' conceptual and perceptive grooming changes to higher and higher levels. It will be reflected in the target data as given by students. This method also measures the differential efforts that teachers use in a class with students of different calibers.

Evaluation of teachers by the administration serves a number of purposes in an educational institution. It provides important inputs for the administration to take decisions on crucial matters like, promotions, transfers, and terminations. The evaluation reports will, amongst other matters, pinpoint teaching skills and competence. Based on the evaluation reports the administration can conduct specific training programmes to upgrade the skills of teachers. These reports can be used as a base for providing feedback to teachers on how the administration views their performance. Furthermore, teacher evaluation becomes the basis for reward allocations by the administration.

Medley and Shannon (1994) identified three facets of teacher quality: teacher competence, teacher performance, and teacher's effectiveness. These three characteristics will decide how a teacher becomes a conscientious and committed professional. They impact a teacher's zeal and passion for teaching. Therefore, it is appropriate for the teacher to constantly undergo self-evaluation and be self-critical.

One best way of evaluating the qualities of a teacher is to look at the test scores of one's own students. "Research on the quality of teachers and teaching has shifted in focus over the years, from traits to behaviour to student outcomes. While researchers have not lost sight of classrooms, the place of classroom events in teacher evaluations has diminished as student test performance has taken centre stage" (*Assessing Teacher Quality*, Edited by Sean Kelly, 2012).

7

Challenges in the Classroom

If you work upon marble, it will perish
If on brass, time will efface it,
but if we work upon immortal minds
and imbue them with principles
we engrave on those tablets
that will brighten to all eternity. —Daniel Webster

Handling the Heterogeneous Group

One of the major problems faced by the teacher in the classroom is his difficulty in addressing the needs of a heterogeneous group of students, viz., some gifted, some good, mediocre and yet others, poor. The gifted students respond faster, the mediocre take some time and the poor do not respond at all. The gifted students get bored once they have learnt; the mediocre ones get bored once they too have learnt. In between the poor students get lost, and they too are bored. It would be better if the teacher avoids normative comparisons of the sub-groups based on their IQ level. He must be able to understand, over a period of time, the speed at which students in the above-mentioned sub-groups grasp, and devise methods by which the mediocre and the poor students can be guided effectively. Teaching demands active listening and observation at close quarters. Teachers would then be able to identify those students who require special care and assistance. In all such situations, he must have ample patience to provide all support to enhance their level of achievement and also continuously monitor the progress made by them. Attending to individual differences is a major task of a teacher.

Another area of interest for the teaching fraternity is the application of the theory of Multiple Intelligence as propounded by Howard Gardner in 1983. Gardner's theory argues that intelligence, traditionally defined, does not sufficiently encompass the wide variety of abilities of human beings. He advocated the recognition of the unique set of talents of individuals and the need to foster them for their personal and collective good. The eight 'multiple intelligences' introduced by Gardner are as follows:

1. Linguistic intelligence: sensitivity to the meaning and order of words.
2. Logical-Mathematical intelligence: ability in mathematics and other complex logical systems.
3. Musical intelligence: the ability to understand and create music. Musicians, composers and dancers show a heightened musical intelligence.
4. Spatial intelligence: the ability to "think in pictures," to perceive the visual world accurately and recreate or alter it. Spatial intelligence is highly developed in artists, architects, designers and sculptors.
5. Bodily-kinesthetic intelligence: the ability to use one's body in a skilled way for self- expression or toward a goal. Players, dancers and actors are among those who display bodily-kinesthetic intelligence.
6. Interpersonal intelligence: an ability to perceive and understand other individuals relating to their moods, desires and motivation.
7. Intrapersonal intelligence: an understanding of one's own emotions. Counselors use their own experience to guide others.
8. The Naturalistic intelligence: the ability to recognize and classify plants, minerals and animals. It also includes ability to recognize cultural artifacts.

As Ian Gilbert (2011) has stated: "when it comes to democratizing learning, the effective understanding and use of Multiple Intelligence Theory has no equal." Credit goes to him to have simplified the eight intelligences as follows:

1. Linguistic intelligence	words
2. Logical-Mathematical	numbers
3. Musical intelligence	sounds
4. Spatial intelligence	sight
5. Bodily-kinesthetic intelligence	action
6. Interpersonal intelligence	people
7. Intrapersonal intelligence	feelings
8. Naturalistic intelligence	nature

The Multiple Intelligence approach encourages teachers to delve deep into diverse intellectual capabilities of students. If the teacher appreciates its immense impact, classes can be made more interesting. Most students are stronger in more than one type of intelligence. However, all teachers could not be equally competent to assess strengths of their students in relation to their proficiency in a particular type of intelligence.

Traditionally, educational institutions have emphasized the development of logical intelligence and linguistic intelligence. Gardner's theory gives importance to the use of different methodologies, exercises and activities to reach the students who excel in other varieties of intelligence.

In "*The Element*", Ken Robinson provides ample insights into the vast powers of imagination, intelligence, feeling, intuition, spirituality, physical and sensory awareness inbuilt in every one of us. Teachers have to make use of the diversity of intelligence, the power of imagination and creativity to transform education to meet the challenges of living.

In the modern day curriculum, emphasis is given to the study of interdisciplinary subjects and a choice is given to the students to select subjects of their interest in some semesters. These changes in the curriculum pinpoint the strengths of multiple intelligence in learning.

Attending to the Basic Needs of Students

There are instances in which good students, hailing from respectable families, all of a sudden, turn into students with a callous and indifferent attitude. Such students end up even spoiling their entire career, and may live a reckless life. As an educationist, I am of the opinion that both parents and teachers are in a way jointly responsible for causing such deviant behaviour on the part of students. To set things right, the teachers who are considered surrogate parents of the students at school or college are to be smart enough to attend to the basic needs of students in the campuses. Those teachers who closely observe the behaviour and activities of their students and maintain good rapport with them could easily detect their deviant or irresponsible behaviour. This is not one kind of added responsibility to be shouldered by the teachers with skepticism or reluctance.

A road map to fulfill the basic needs of students could be worked out by the teachers after considering the peculiar needs of the students. In general, the following proposition would be highly beneficial to introduce a viable plan of action which would attend to their basic needs.

The objective should be to formulate a plan of action which would develop an inner desire for learning in the minds of students. "Within a positive learning environment we stand a chance of fostering motivation. For that motivation to be intrinsic and not just for end-goals or pleasing others, the learning experience taking place within that environment need to be meaningful and connect with learners' lives and aspirations." (Janet Collins, Joe Harkin and Melanie Nind, 2002). Many good teachers try to establish from the beginning that they expect students to be active participants in the classroom—that the purpose of the course is not teaching, but learning. That usually means requiring students to take some responsibility for the conduct of the course and to take some risks in the process of learning (*The Chicago Handbook for Teachers*, 2011). Teachers can prepare an academic plan of action suited to cater to the academic interests of students on a weekly, monthly and yearly basis. Some good institutions expect the teachers to maintain such academic plan of action for the entire year, split up as a weekly, monthly or term-wise scheme, which is made by each teacher after incorporating the institutional annual academic plan. In this academic plan, teachers are expected to mention clearly the topic-wise academic skills to be achieved by students. The lists of resource and reference materials which are useful to the students to master the academic skills are to be included in the academic plan. The details of assignments, homework and field study, if required, are to be included in a chronological order. Details regarding tests, term examinations and semester/annual examinations are to be shown date-wise. The students are to be made aware of their responsibilities and duties as per the requirements of the academic plan. When a well planned academic plan of action or academic calendar is in vogue, a counsellor must be appointed to support the academic initiatives. He can supplement the academic needs of students if teachers do not find adequate time to attend to the problem-students. Other issues which crop up in an educational environment could be better tackled by an expert counsellor rather than by the teacher. Counsellors can also advise the students regarding particular courses of study they could take up when they pursue higher studies.

As a practical step to solve most of the behavioural problems related to adulthood in the educational institutions, the service of an educational counsellor must be made available. Either one or two teachers can be trained for this purpose or a professional counsellor can be appointed or a cluster group of institutions can make use of the service of a counsellor by turn. The students who face problems while learning or who reveal characteristics of deviant behaviour will have to undergo counselling periodically until they become perfectly alright.

As a special case, the newly admitted students as well as their parents must be made aware of the institutional policies, rules and regulations and the academic plan of action in the beginning of the year. They have to be familiarized with the new environment and culture of the institution. It is advisable to make an easy access to teachers as an essential requirement as it enables students to establish good rapport with their respective teachers. One effective way of controlling a class is by knowing the names of each student. When students know that the teachers not only know their names but also some essential information about their families, they change their attitudes considerably. They become more responsible, docile and attentive in the class. Another method which helps the teacher to make students more responsible and attentive in the class is by monitoring their progress on a daily basis. If they notice unsatisfactory performance in studies, irregularity in attendance or deviant behaviour, the matter must be taken up by the relevant academic committee in consultation with the class tutor. It is the bounden duty of the committee to inform the parent about such lapses of the student without any delay.

For the smooth implementation of the academic plans, the teachers can maintain a checklist to keep an eye on the activities to be completed every day by him/her and the student. This system of preparing checklists enables teachers to streamline their academic activities efficiently. If students shirk their responsibilities, it is the duty of the teacher to see that they complete the task assigned properly within the time limit. Again, it is the duty of the teacher to enforce discipline in the class and monitor the progress of each and every student and report it to higher authorities to take appropriate action against those who violate the rules and regulations of the institution.

Significance of Discipline and the Teacher's Duty to Enforce Discipline

In broader terms, the purpose of education is to discipline the mind and body of the student. It should take place as a natural result of a sound learning process initiated and controlled by able teachers. The student who is well-initiated into a healthy, proactive and productive educational environment, will never lose sight of his goals and move astray from his charted course. Generally, teachers are good at spotting the students with any trace of deviant behaviour and tame the wayward ones within no time.

Indiscipline cannot be tolerated as it corrupts the minds of students at a younger age and later leads to disastrous consequences. Problems such as ill behaviour in the classrooms or on the premises of the institution must be tackled by the teacher concerned. They are authorized to take appropriate action as recommended by the rules and regulations of the organization. Counseling may be required in specific situations to correct the deviant behaviour of students. In such situations the institution must readily make available the service of a counsellor. Punishments, if necessary, are to be meted out immediately after the occurrence of the undesirable behaviour.

It has to be noted well that everyone must be punished equally for the same misbehaviour. One common practice followed in educational institutions is meting out punishment progressively. In the beginning, mild punishments are given and if repeated, the severity of punishment is increased with each successive violation. Those students who intentionally misbehave may have behavioural problems, which have to be addressed by a counsellor. Passive disruption in the classroom could be stopped by the teacher by giving a stern warning. It is appropriate to institute a commission of enquiry in cases where the nature of deviant or misbehaviour is grave and demands serious consideration to decide the severity of punishment. In most institutions, a disciplinary committee is appointed to maintain discipline, keep control on situations where disciplinary problems creep up and conduct enquiry in matters of gross indiscipline.

It has been noticed that most disciplinary problems develop in a class where the teacher is either too lenient or careless. An effective warning regarding the expectations and standards of behaviour and disciplinary practices followed in the institution, is clearly given in the rules and regulations of the institution, in the beginning of the course. The teacher has to enforce discipline for the whole academic term. A practical advice on how best to manage such problems is to apply rules consistently. However, it is expected of a teacher to influence the behaviour of students from day one in such a way that he is not forced to award punishments. Good teachers often minimize the need to use disciplinary measures as they instill in young minds the cardinal values of life which promote self-discipline among them. According to William Goodwin and Herbert J. Klausmeier (1975), the basic message is that good discipline is a function of good teaching. This observation holds good as it is known that only very few disciplinary problems arise in classes where teachers are accomplished and resourceful.

James M. Banner, Jr. and Harold C. Cannon, discuss the importance of self-discipline as follows:

> "What do we mean by self-discipline? It's the order you impose on yourself out of full understanding of what is best for you. Self-discipline is structured industry, some kind of plan or method by which you direct your efforts and schedule your time. Its study and activity tied to your aspirations and pursued with perseverance and method. For everyone, the plan will differ; but for everyone the plan will be essential."

If students can understand and appreciate the value of self-discipline, the classrooms and campuses would become better places to learn. Good teachers, in particular, and the campus culture, in general play a decisive role in inculcating the value of self-discipline.

Teacher, the Constant Motivator

Some teachers take their own time to give feedback to students after the conduct of tests. This practice has to be discouraged. The teacher concerned must return the evaluated answer sheets promptly as soon as the tests are over and inform each student personally about his performance. Efficient teachers constantly challenge their students in their academic pursuits. Proper advice is given to each student to ensure proper learning and also to instill in their minds effective learning habits.

The teacher must appreciate the performance of good students and simultaneously, encourage the poor performers to do better. In the beginning of the course, the teacher must set his expectations and goals, and make students accountable to complete the study of the portions on a time bound basis. It is the teachers who can certainly raise the achievements of students to a higher level by constantly motivating them. Here again, only stimulating, interactive and engaging classes can result in effective learning. The teachers can either make or mar the future of their students. Outstanding teachers create a bright future for their students.

Enhancing Professional Competence of Teachers in Classroom Management

Classroom management is a key area, which both the teacher and the administration have to closely monitor. As this most critical area decides the future of the teacher, he is expected to undergo specialized training in classroom management. Teachers are supposed to undergo frequent training programmes to enhance their competence to meet the specific challenges in a classroom environment. It is the duty of the institution to organize in-house training programmes on a regular basis for teachers and also enlist them for effective training programmes conducted by the Staff Training Institutes or other professional organizations. In some reputed institutions, the administration itself encourages teachers to join professional bodies which focus on enhancement of their qualities.

According to Donald C. Orlich, Robert J. Harder, Richard C. Callahan, Michael S. Trevisan and Abbie H. Brown (2010), effective teachers monitor student behaviour in the classroom. They make each student responsible for some work during the learning activity and then see that it is actually accomplished. Such teachers are strong student motivators (Wood, 2001).

The administration must be able to identify teachers with exceptional skills who can develop better methods in classroom management or methodologies in teaching or develop better aids and tools for teaching. It should facilitate such creative teachers to present innovative practices in staff training institutions and at seminars and workshops for teachers. The details of such contributions from the part of competent teachers are to be published in professional journals. A lot of research and studies have been carried out in the field of enhancement of the quality of teachers, especially on classroom management at the school and college level by national and state educational bodies and universities. But, institutions neglect this crucial area of teacher development as the system is clogged by routine preoccupations. Teachers are generally not motivated by the administrators in this regard for want of time and financial resources. Teachers themselves shy away from such responsibilities to get trained or to present their innovative skills or practices in seminars or training programmes. In any large institution, there are many self-motivated teachers who are ready to offer their services for the enhancement of the quality of their colleagues, especially the novice teachers of the same institution. But, due to the bureaucratic set up of the administration, which is often lethargic, no one takes the initiative to make use of such potential qualities of teachers for the purpose of enhancement of the qualities of their own colleagues. Team teaching, cluster group interaction, seminars and workshops are some of the platforms where exceptionally talented and efficient teachers can share their knowledge and skills to empower new teachers.

8
Methods of Teaching

I hear and I forget;
I see and I remember;
I do and I understand. —Ancient Chinese proverb

If you cannot do great things, do small things in a great way.
—Napoleon Hill

The tragedy in the teaching profession is that once a teacher becomes comfortable with a particular method of teaching, he sticks to it till the end of his career. Teachers are expected to try out new methods of teaching, and find time to review different methodologies. Or else, they end up labelled as antiquated species. The level of achievement of a teacher depends on the right choice of methodology of teaching. Students learn better and more quickly if the teaching method matches the students' preferred learning styles. Ellis, (1985) describes a learning style as a more or less consistent way in which a person perceives, conceptualizes, organizes and recalls information. The teacher must not only be thorough with different methods of teaching but also know the efficacy of a particular methodology in a specific situation while handling a class. Some of the important methods of teaching are narrated below.

The Lecture Method

The origin of the lecture method is traced back to the mediaeval university-teaching practices. In those times, lectures were of two kinds,—"ordinary" and extraordinary or "cursory". The former were given in the morning by professors; the latter in the afternoon, either by professors or students about to take a bachelor's degree. The purpose of lecture was to read and explain the text of the book or books of the course. The character of the lecture was largely determined by the fact that all text-books, till 1500, were in the form of manuscripts, and many students were unable or unwilling to purchase or hire their copies. A large part of the lecturer's time was thus consumed in the purely mechanical process of reading aloud the standard text and commenting on them. To them he could add his own explanations; but the simple ability to "read the book" intelligently was sufficient to qualify a properly licensed Master or a Bachelor preparing to take the Master's degree, to lecture on a given subject (Arthur O. Norton, 1909).

The invention of printed books made a discernible change in the practice of teaching. Book printing had far-reaching consequences for university teaching. When the ordinary student began to buy books, the written words became dominant in university teaching. Not only were the sources made more immediately and comprehensively accessible, but commentaries, textbooks, and polemics ceased to be monopolized by teachers and could be purchased from the market. Thus, diverse views and new insights became objects of intensive discussions and of individual debates within the larger scientific community (Walter Ruegg, 1992).

The Chicago Handbook for Teachers (2011) suggests that giving lecture provides one with many opportunities for creative expression, for imaginative presentation, and for projecting personal charisma. It also cautions thus: A lecture depends heavily on the style of its presentation, to be sure. But it is, at its heart, a way of conveying ideas and information to students. Even the most stylishly and engagingly presented lecture will be of little value if it does not contain real substance, and if it does not challenge students to think. The most important part of a lecture, therefore, is done before one even enters the classroom: preparing and organizing one's own ideas about the subject.

Studies conducted to understand the suitability of this method in various teaching- learning contexts reveal that this is a preferred method depending upon instructional objectives. The proper use of the lecture method is to be understood by a teacher, which helps him to select this method in different situations. N.L. Gage and David C. Berliner (1991), help us gain insights into the proper uses of lecture as stated below:

Use of Lecture Method

Many writers (Bligh, 1972; McKeachie, 1967; and McLeish, 1976; Verner and Dickinson, 1967) have concluded from their reviews of studies that the lecture method is suitable when:

- the basic purpose is to disseminate information.
- the material is not available elsewhere.
- the material must be organized and presented in a particular way to a specific group.
- it is necessary to arouse one's interest in the subject.
- students need to remember the material for only a short time.
- it is necessary to provide an introduction to an area or directions for a learning task that is going to be taught through some other teaching method.

These authors believe that the lecture method is inappropriate when:

- objectives other than acquisition of information are sought.
- long-term retention is necessary.
- the material is complex, detailed, or abstract.
- the learner's participation is essential for the achievement of objectives.
- higher-level cognitive objectives (analysis, synthesis, evaluation) are the purpose of instruction.

The lecture method has been the target of much criticism for many centuries (Paul Klapper, 1920). Even when a teacher knows that his lecture does not receive the purposeful attention of the majority of students in a class, he continues with it to complete his course whether students learn effectively or not. Here is a practical suggestion with regard to lecturing: 'Rarely present a matter or an argument for more than 15 minutes at a stretch' (Erickson, B.L. and Stommer, D.W., 1991). There is more scholarly advice on this age-old method of teaching.

Teaching for more than twenty minutes usually mean that a good portion of audience has ceased to listen, that their minds have wandered off, away from the speaker toward all that really matters in their life. When we as a culture begin to be serious about teaching and learning, the large lecture will no longer occupy the prominent space that it has held for years. For, in many ways, the lecture is the teaching moment that most promotes passivity and discourage participation from learners (bell hooks, 2010).

The first few seconds of the lecture are critical to the ultimate success of a teacher. They affect the kind of response a teacher will get from his students. If a teacher cannot deliver the first few sentences effectively and create a good impression on students, it would be difficult for him to maintain their attention. "The beginning is the end", though a philosophical idea, matters much in teaching, especially in the lecture method. The teacher is expected to make use of different methodologies of teaching to make learning interesting and interactive. Some teachers, in this hi-tech era, do not make even an attempt to change the one and only method they know, i.e., the most conventional method of teaching, the lecture method. I am not downplaying the importance of the lecture method as we all know how a well-delivered lecture can not only assist to impart knowledge but also motivate the student to have better insights into the subject. But, it has been proved that it does not meet a student's pedagogical needs if the teacher follows only this method. According to Annette L. Breaux, "Lecturing is one of the least effective means of teaching. It does not encourage unfettered thinking even though an interactive lecture can open up a meaningful response." That is why Robert Boice, asks us to "abandon the non-stop 50-minute lecture; it reinforces passive listening, verbatim note-taking, and superficial info-processing strategies." Many students attend a boring lecture for the simple reason that attendance is mandatory in most of the institutions.

As a methodology of teaching, the lecture method has been commonly used for a long time in schools and colleges. It has survived all criticisms as it is found suitable in most situations in the classroom teaching. The efficient teacher, who is also good at lecturing, can hold the attention of students at a stretch for twenty to twenty five minutes by relating the facts to the topic of study or assignments prepared and read by students. A deep knowledge of the subject and a comfortable command over the language enables the teacher to lecture with confidence for a certain period of time. A lecture becomes a waste of time and effort if it is neither thoughtful nor interactive.

There are other viewpoints regarding plus and minus points about the effects of the Lecture method. Samuel Johnson, the great English author, was quoted by Boswell, his biographer, as saying: Lectures were once useful; but now when all can read, and books are so numerous, lectures are unnecessary. If your attention fails, and you miss a part of a lecture, it is lost; you cannot go back as you can upon a book. The point has often been made over the centuries (McLeish, 1976). What Johnson surmised has been confirmed time and again by research. After reviewing 208 studies made between 1890 and 1980, Welwert (1984) concluded that visual presentation is more effective than auditory presentation in improving retention and comprehension of hard or medium-hard text, especially for students over age 13, whose reading ability has developed fully. Lectures have been called an anachronism. They have been criticized for fostering a passive role for students in the learning process. Although criticism has been loud and severe, there are those who defend lectures, who find it valuable for surveying a whole field of knowledge through the medium of a living personality, and for arousing active interest that leads students to understanding. Lectures can repeat material in different words, something books rarely do. They can give students a framework, an overview, a critique, unlike anything in any available printed material. Lecturers can bring to their material their own aesthetic pleasure and enthusiasm to a far greater degree than can the printed page. The lecture method gives some teachers and students a kind of reinforcement that is not available in other educational methods. A professor of art wrote: I enjoy the lecture method. It is the most dramatic way of presenting to the largest number of students a critical distillation of ideas and information on a subject in the shortest possible time. The bigger the classes the better I perform intellectually....How are students reinforced? By the lecturer's warmth, humor, drama, intensity, logic, enthusiasm, and attention—to say nothing of the knowledge and comprehension they acquire (N.L. Gage and David C. Berliner, 1991).

A variation of the lecture method is the '*lecturette*', which is a brief oral presentation lasting less than five minutes, followed by a brief discussion by involving students. This method can be best interspersed in a workshop to make it both interactive and interesting.

As a training method, the purpose of lecture is, in fact, specific and quite limited. In the continuum of knowledge, understanding, and skill or behaviour, the lecture can focus on understanding. When, through reading assignments and experience, participants have become fairly familiar with information about a subject, the lecturer can relate the facts to one another and fit them into a memorable scheme, an understandable whole, a thesis, a theme. This may be more memorable than, say, reading a book, because of the living voice and manner, and "the ambience" associated with the lecture. The lecturer can make facts "come alive," imbue them with vitality and significance. The tested results of lectures, therefore, encourage only their rare and deliberate use. A lecture is effective at that stage of the learning process which seeks to increase intellectual understanding. For passing knowledge on, the lecture is inefficient. People remember only about half of the lecture's content immediately after delivery, no matter how carefully they think they have listened. Two months later they remember about twenty- five per cent or less. Incidentally, those who remember the most are not necessarily the most intelligent. An underlying fact is that people think several times as fast as anyone speaks. Their attention to a lecture, therefore, depends markedly on what they do with that spare time (Rolf P. Lynton, Udai Pareek, 1990).

It has been noticed that the lecture method does not foster to a great extent much of the critical thinking required of a student when compared to the effectiveness of certain other modern methods of teaching in stimulating critical thinking. If the teacher is able to clear the doubts of his students in the same class, this method holds some promise as students gain confidence in the teaching and learning process. However, a problem erupts when the teacher is not able to respond effectively to the questions raised by students. In such a situation, he is looked upon with contempt. As a teacher is expected to refer to the topic in detail, he should come thoroughly prepared to clear doubts raised by students.

As an established method of teaching, this conventional method will continue, provided the teacher takes real pains to prepare the topic well and present it methodically. However, a combination of different methods of teaching which would produce better results and engage students effectively and productively is preferred by those teachers who have realized their significance and use. It is imperative on the part of the teacher to make a zealous effort to learn and use different methods of teaching, viz., individualized teaching, buzz group, brain storming, case study, seminar and symposium, discussion group, demonstration, in-basket exercise, simulation, role playing, assignments, projects, business games, field trips (real, simulated or virtual), programmed instruction, etc. It will bring about a cogent and purposeful learning outcome. Some of these teaching methods are given below.

Individualized Teaching Method

This method is highly essential to give special coaching to students who wish to learn a new skill for personal reasons or to the weak students. From the perspective of achievement, research indicates that new and lower-achieving students often need more planning and structuring by the teacher to facilitate individualized teaching. The teacher, in this context, identifies students with special needs and devises individualized coaching to help them acquire the necessary knowledge and skills. It may be a time-consuming task. The teacher will have to adequately space out the routine work to find time to complete the additional task. In the teaching of mathematics, accounting, computer application, production management and similar subjects, individualized teaching will yield better results. In the individualized teaching method, the teacher focuses attention on the particular area in which the student is deficient by imparting knowledge and the necessary acquisition of skills. This one-on-one method of instruction is the ideal way to learn for the weak students or for those students who need special attention due to other personal reasons. The teacher, in this case, meticulously prepares to help the student to understand the topic covered and encourage him to ask questions to clear whatever doubts he has. Since the feedback is readily available in this method of teaching, it helps the teacher to prioritize the key areas to be taught by a step by step method. In the classroom, the slow learner finds it hard to follow the class and also faces humiliation for being a slow learner, a fact he wants to keep suppressed. Later it may turn out to be a psychiatric case. But the same student, while learning under the individualized teaching method, finds great relief and learns the subject far better than in the regular class. In this method, the student response is continuously evaluated and the teacher observes at close quarters whether the student has grasped the subject. He encourages him to make correct responses.

Buzz Group Method

Under this creative method of teaching, the teacher forms smaller groups of students and assigns tasks to them to find solutions to problems. The advantages are, mainly, the understanding of group dynamics and developing certain important skills required to analyze and make a group presentation by involving the members of the group. In this system, the participants get a golden opportunity to apply what they have learnt, thereby, getting exposed to practical knowledge. This group exercise can be titled as the Buzz group activity. The

Buzz group activity is a problem-solving process where the teacher must have a comprehensive idea of the problem under discussion and be proficient to handle the discussion in order to find solutions. The teacher must have a vivid idea of the topics or problems selected for exploration. It is advisable to monitor the developments that take place in this group-exercise by way of involvement of all members and their contribution to find solutions to a problem. The teacher has to act as a guide and provide broad guidelines to the group. He acts as the discussion leader and explains its format and procedures. The group has to elect its own leader or chairperson and a spokesperson. It is advisable to divide the class into small clusters of five to seven members. If several small groups are formed, all of them must have similar pattern of leadership. The chairperson of each group is responsible to provide leadership to the group in matters like, deciding a plan of action, assigning specific roles to various members of the group, arriving at decision, etc. The spokesperson of each group is responsible to air the views of the group as and when the discussion leader asks the group to present its ideas. One of the members can write on the board the recommendations presented by each spokesperson. The final presentation of each group must be evaluated by the teacher and the performance of each group graded. While the group analyzes a problem, the teacher should ensure participation by all the members. The inactive members must be encouraged to contribute constructive ideas to find solutions.

Buzz groups set a very conducive environment to group communication which ultimately enhances the confidence of individuals to present ideas before a group convincingly. The audience also gets an opportunity to listen to divergent views and see for themselves how groups function independently to formulate decisions on common problems. In Buzz groups, in the beginning, a teacher is assigned the role of the discussion leader and later experienced students are asked to take over his/her role.

Brainstorming Method

A commonly used method of teaching is the 'Brainstorming' session by which the teacher is able to elicit different ideas about possible action to be taken to solve a problem or to take a decision on any matter of concern. The participants are given the freedom to suggest any number of solutions they think fit. This is a creative, freewheeling, no-holds-barred approach used to find solutions to problems in both small and large groups. Brainstorming can be freewheeling as it promotes wild ideas, wishful thinking, hitchhiking or building upon other student's ideas. The teacher narrates the problem in the beginning and asks students to think for a while and suggest as many solutions as possible. One of the students can volunteer to write on the board all the suggestions made in the class. The participant's ideas are not criticized at any point of time. The purpose of this exercise is to generate as many ideas as possible and even facilitate further hitch hiking on the idea. The purpose of a brainstorming session is to make one idea spark off other ideas, almost spontaneously. It has been noticed that the scope for evolving newer ideas by hitch hiking the ideas already contributed by others from the group replenishes the stock of ideas already generated. As time passes by, the quality of ideas substantially enhances thereby producing incredible and unimaginable results. In fact, brainstorming makes the participants both active and keeps them involved throughout the session.

Alex F. Osborn, an advertising executive and the founder of the Creative Education Foundation, has been given the credit for introducing this creative method which has been copiously used by generations of people to generate new ideas. The concept was developed by Alex to stimulate thinking, and thereby, generate new ideas without any inhibition.

Brainstorming is one of the effective methods of teaching which necessarily provokes students to come up with fresh ideas within a flick of a finger. It spontaneously produces divergence in thinking. This method is highly useful to generate creative ideas within a short period of time. This method of teaching, no doubt, improves the students' quality of thinking. When the teacher finds that the group has almost run out of their ideas, he screens them and writes the selected ideas on the board for the purpose of evaluation and to finally choose the best ideas as solutions. This method also enhances creative thinking at a faster pace.

Case Study Method

An interesting method used, especially in the masters' degree and undergraduate programmes, is the case study. This, as far I know, was used as a method of teaching at Harvard Law School way back in 1870, and was later adopted by the Harvard Business School in 1908. A case presents a realistic situation which is analyzed and solutions worked out individually or collectively. Cases are, for all practical purposes, narratives designed to serve as the topics for classroom discussion. As it represents a real life situation, the student is able to come to grip with practical problems and is able to apply theoretical knowledge to find solutions. In management studies, case study method is commonly used to obtain better insights into the subject. The analysis of a case sharpens the analytical skills of a student. It also enhances his problem-solving skills as the situation necessitates marshalling of ideas so as to weigh the pros and cons of solutions. Case studies can be given individually or group-wise. In the beginning simple cases are preferred. As students progress in their studies, more complex cases can be given for analysis. In modern texts, one can notice a good number of cases on different subjects. The teacher must be judicious to select the ideal case from among a large number of cases or must be resourceful to develop his own cases suitable for the situation. This method can be focused on specific learning objectives. According to Selma Wassermann (1994), a good case is the vehicle by which a chunk of reality is brought into the classroom to be worked out by the class and the instructor. A good case keeps the class discussion grounded upon some of the stubborn facts that must be faced in a real life situation. It is the anchor on academic flights of speculation. It is the record of complex situations that must be literally pulled apart and put together again for the expression of attitudes or ways of thinking brought into the classroom (Lawrence, 1953).

A case is a written description of an enterprise, an event, an incident and information about its many facts. It generally contains the history of its internal and external environment. A case is the narration of events or episodes of an organization covering some or all aspects during a particular point or period of time. The case method triggers a high degree of mental stimulation on the part of students and is essentially a discussion method. Confronted with cases as a medium of learning, the student experiences a gradual growth in the maturity of his point of view, but the path is not smooth. The Case method has several advantages. This can be used for research as it may uncover some very meaningful insights and hypotheses for further testing. It can be most useful when experimented in actual situation as a means of gaining and sharing experiences. It can develop an individual objectively and imaginatively. It generally gives confidence to a student to deal with the real life situations (Upinder Dhar, Santosh Dhar, 2007).

Primarily, a case must be exciting and challenging. It should generate adequate interest in the problem and suggest at least a few alternative solutions from which the discerning student is able to select the best alternative. Cases are followed by analytical questions, which in turn create the excitement to an enquiring mind to probe deep into its different aspects. Once all the students present different solutions to the problems, a group discussion is initiated to carry out a thread-bare discussion on the central and incidental problems of the case. This complex educational instrument is an excellent method for the exploration of solutions to complex issues. Cases as such do not offer their own analysis. Instead they offer opportunities to the student to test his ability to apply the theory that he has learnt in a 'real world situation'.

Case study is one form of narrative research that is particularly valuable for understanding a decision or set of decisions that are made within a bounded context (Yin, 1984). Using narrative case studies enables the group—singly and collectively—to explore professional and personal experience as a text for learning (Jere Brophy, 2005).

Role Play Method

In role play, which is considered as an active teaching method or strategy, the student faces hypothetical situations by reenacting assigned roles and improvising his behaviour. Students are provided advance information regarding the context, the situation and an outline of their roles. Role plays are particularly useful for developing demonstration, managerial, communication and decision making skills. This method is suitable, especially for adults, to learn effectively, as they are naturally attracted to the element of realism and practicality involved in a role play.

In role-playing, the student assumes the character, feelings, and ideas of another person as they experience a hypothetical situation drawn from real life. The purpose of the activity is to analyze the human problem. A few students serve as the role players, while the rest of the class observes the action in order to identify what the characters feel, what their underlying motives are, and what other possible solutions to the problem are.

In structured role play, students are provided elaborate details about the situation, the character outlines and the purpose of the role play so as to develop their interpersonal skills.

In a single role play, roles are allocated to a chosen group of students. The non-performing group analyses the interactions and learns from the interactions of the performers. In the multiple role play, all the students are divided into groups which take turn in acting out the roles assigned to them. Each group analyses the interactions and shares the analysis with other groups.

The most important aspect of role playing is the analytical discussion, known as debriefing, which takes place after the enactment. During debriefing sessions, the participants recall their feelings, attitudes and responses while they enacted. It helps the student to understand and appreciate his experience and enables him to discuss his insights with the whole group. This method provides ample opportunities to students to practice skills. The participants can be videotaped while role playing and given feedback on their skills. The participants are active and challenged.

According to Rolf P. Lynton, Udai Pareek, 1990, role playing is mainly useful for training in behavioural dimensions.

In-Basket Exercises Method

The students, in this quite practical method of teaching, deal with specific situations of a nature they come across in life. They are asked to really work in a formal situation with full in-baskets. The participants are provided with letters, memos, reports, forecasts, and other details as if they are operating in a real life situation. The prepared items are given to the participants as if they have arrived in their baskets. They pose a series of problems to handle, which they sort out one by one. They prioritize, make decisions, handle the difficulties, respond to deadlines, and in the process, they make use of all the channels of communication to find solutions to the problems they face.

The development of in-basket exercises by the teacher requires familiarity with the kind of roles participants play. The advantage is that the students can learn from actual experience selected from real life situations.

Seminars Method

Seminars and symposiums, like the group discussion method, provide ample opportunities to students to exchange ideas, information and views on the subject. In a seminar, a small group of students and a teacher discuss a particular topic, which is open for discussion by others at the end of the session whereas in a symposium, each participant covers only one specific phase of the topic. In these discussions, the moderator introduces the participants and the subject and controls their presentations. He informs the audience about the procedure to be followed, including that of a forum discussion at the end of the presentation. He keeps control of time so that each participant gets equal opportunity.

This method stimulates fast thinking on the part of the participants. It helps them to broaden their outlook and develop an attitude of give and take. In such seminars, interested students from other classes could be invited. If students of different background and disciplines are brought in, the discussion becomes more interesting and fruitful. Since these types of teaching methodology create a broad spectrum and scope for exchanging ideas, the participants find such opportunities more challenging than the usual lecture method of teaching. They come well prepared to attend such seminars or symposiums. They take responsibility to prepare the material for presentation and discussion and play a leading role in making the seminar or symposium a success. They are ready to answer questions for which they burn the midnight oil to scan through source materials. It would be both fun and challenge if all the participants are active in such meaningful intellectual exercises. Usually, the teacher plays a secondary role, he organizes the sessions and leaves it to the students to run the programme. He forms the group, gives topics for the seminar and guides them as to how to organize it effectively. The other teachers are also invited to see the performance of the group. It is noticed that the participants become so enthused in these sessions that they improve their communication skills by leaps and bounds.

The purpose of seminars, symposiums, and other general discussion methods is to provide participants with opportunities to exchange information, views, ideas and recollections of experience. Through exchange, they stimulate one another's thinking, broaden their outlook, and also gain experience in the kinds of give and take that commonly occurs in such meetings. This process develops tolerance for the views of others. The methods are most promising if the group consists of people who come from different backgrounds. Symposiums and seminars aim generally at widening the participants' horizons and providing opportunities for exercising the mind: reading, preparing material for discussion, and participating in and leading discussions (Rolf P. Lynton, Udai Pareek, 1990).

Group Discussion Method

Group Discussion is one of the finest teaching methods which could be preferably introduced in the end of a semester/term as by that time students will be well aware of the scope, contents and the importance of the subject. The students are also aware of the practical application of the subjects and thereby are in a better position to analyze the problems in a much more critical way. They are able to gather different viewpoints and present convincing ideas which are substantiated with proof. In a group discussion, the teacher has to exert caution in selecting the topics for discussion. He can give assignments on different topics with questions which help them to go deep into the topic. They can be prompted to do some research to obtain the relevant information on the topic. Group discussion would encourage them to search various sources of information and update their knowledge. As an important method of teaching, group discussion considerably improves the learning skills, and enables students to gain a degree of self-direction.

In most of the excellent centers of higher education, teachers make it a practice to form 'Discussion Groups' of those interested students who meet regularly to discuss matters of importance. This method attracts students who assiduously participate in all the proceedings of the discussion with enthusiasm. At the end of the year, some institutions find this programme so interesting that they conduct inter-collegiate competitions in group discussion. It enables the students to gain confidence to exchange ideas freely in a group so that they get rid of their inhibitions. The participants learn through the hard way how to present their ideas in a group. As they gain more experience, they garner more strength to present their ideas with courage of conviction. In the process of articulating them, they become skilful communicators.

Functions of the Discussion Leader: Donald C. Orlich, Robert J. Harder, *et al.* (2010), elucidate the functions of the Discussion Leader as follows:

- *Initiating*: Getting the group going and keeping it moving when it is bogged down or goes off on a dead-end tangent (for example, by clarifying certain statements or asking questions that call for more than a *yes* or *no* answer).

- *Regulating*: Influencing the pace of the discussion (by summarizing or pointing out the time limits).
- *Informing*: Bringing new information to the group (but not by lecturing).
- *Supporting*: Making it easier for members to contribute (by harmonizing opposing viewpoints, voicing group feelings, varying member's places in the group, and helping group members to get acquainted).
- *Evaluating*: Helping the group evaluate process goals (by testing for consensus or noting the group's progress in some area).

Difference between the Lecture and Discussion Methods of Teaching

Generally people think that lecturing is just about as effective as the other methods. Dubin and Taveggia (1968) reviewed the data (not just the conclusions) of nearly a hundred studies performed over a forty-year period. They tallied the results of eighty-eight independent comparisons of scores of final examinations of students taught by the lecture and discussion method, as reported in thirty-six experimental studies. Of these 51 per cent favoured the lecture method and 49 per cent favoured the discussion method (N.L. Gage, David C. Berliner, 1991). This study makes it clear that the discussion method is favoured by a large section of students.

There is more evidence to prove that the discussion method is much more effective than the lecture method: McKeachie and Kulik (1975) found that in comparison to the lecture method on measures of retention, higher-level thinking, attitudes, and motivation, the discussion method tended to be favoured. As discussion allows students more activity and feedback, it is, according to them, more effective than lectures in promoting the understanding of concepts and development of problem-solving skills (N.L. Gage, David C. Berliner, 1991).

As in the case of case study, in a group discussion too, students are to be taught the proper skills required to solve a problem. They must possess adequate knowledge and the methods and techniques to solve the problem. Only then they will be successful in choosing the appropriate solution. The teachers must make it a point to provide as many opportunities as possible to help students improve their metacognitive skills which can be put to use while solving a problem.

Programmed Instruction Method

In this method the participants are presented specific steps to perform a task with the aid of a computer or printed text. They, in turn, respond to the directions and proceed through the exercise until they know how to perform the specific skill. The peculiarity of this method is that the participant learns through a self-paced method. The teacher can provide immediate feedback to the student.

Apart from the methods cited above, teachers can also follow the project method, simulation, sensitivity training, skit, tele-conferencing, storytelling, etc to enhance the efficacy of teaching and learning.

A careful analysis of the methodology of teaching will definitely lead us to the conclusion that without their use, teaching would lose its charm and variety. The different methods of teaching definitely create a lasting and valuable impression in the minds of students and enhance the quality of teaching by making the learning environment both interactive and productive.

The following study conducted by Professor Carol Kauffman of Harvard Medical School is of great help to guide the teachers in the selection of various methods of teaching. He summarized the research on how people retain from various methods of instruction as follow:

Method	*Percentage Retained*
Lecture	5
Reading	10
Audio-Visual	20
Demonstration	30
Discussion	50
Practice	75
Teaching others	90

Source: *Adults Learning*, Jenny Rogers, 2007.

The following is an at-a-glance table which will give a teacher a probable match between objectives and methods.

Objectives	*Possible Methods to Consider*
Acquiring information	Reading, delivered through reading list or via, website and other media. Quizzes, tests, questionnaires. Problem-based learning. Facilitated discussion
Acquiring a skill	Demonstration—live or recorded Observation Skill practice solo or in small groups with feedback Role play Coaching
Discrimination, Diagnosis and Problem solving	Reading Guided observation

	Problem-based learning Case studies Simulation Role play Facilitated discussion Project work Coaching Action learning
Changing attitudes	Facilitated discussion Case studies Role play Coaching Project work Simulation and game.

Source: *Adults Learning*, Jenny Rogers, 2007.

ABC COLLEGE OF TECHNOLOGY AND MANAGEMENT

ABC College of Management and Technology has been one of the oldest colleges in the region, having a sizeable number of students. Of late, it has been facing several problems. The worst one is teacher turnover, which has affected its reputation. The administration was able to identify this problem, but could not recommend workable solutions. The disturbing factor was that the turnover rate had been increasing every year. The administration conducted a study of the salary pattern in the region to find whether there was any disparity in the amount of salary paid as compared to other teachers. The variance was low. Even then, they took actions to rectify the anomalies. Still, the turnover rate was a matter of great concern for administration. They tried to figure out the problem, but neither succeeded in identifying any major issue nor recommend a viable solution.

Appointment of a Task Force

To do an in-depth study of the problem they appointed a Task Force consisting of five members drawn from administration and teaching. This group of senior personnel conducted a detailed study of administrative policies, working conditions, scope for advancement, salary structure, etc., and submitted their findings. The administration introduced certain modifications in the general policies and changes in salary structure, as recommended by the Task Force. Even though the teachers were satisfied with the changes introduced, at the end of the year, some of them resigned. Before leaving, the teachers were asked what prompted them to quit. The answers given by them were not convincing for the administration. It was apparent that they left due to some dissatisfaction. The real cause could not be identified.

At a meeting of the Management Council, the matter was discussed at length. It was found that some efficient teachers were also leaving the institution. The administration tried to find out where these teachers took up new assignments and what was the service condition provided there which had attracted them. They found the service conditions were almost the same. The chairman of the Management Council made this final remark. "I don't know where the problem lies. We are even losing good teachers. I have a fear that this is a fishy and mysterious problem. Let us bring an educational consultant who could find a permanent solution to this nagging problem."

The Council approved the suggestion of the chairman to appoint an educational consultant. In the middle of the ensuing academic year, the consultant was appointed who made an in-depth study of the situation, but, he too failed to identify the cause. However, this setback did not dampen his spirits. He started visiting classes and made very critical observations about the classes, especially, the practice of teaching and the feedback he received from the students. This phase of his study provided a revealing insight into the root cause of dissatisfaction among the teachers. He called them one by one and sought information about the method of teaching and the problems confronted by them in the class. He conducted a detailed analysis of the information collected from the teachers, and was able to pinpoint the real cause of the resignation of teachers. The major problem emanated from the class was revealed by the feedback received from both the students and the teachers.

The educational institution was imparting education at the undergraduate and post-graduate levels. The students came from various institutions. Some of the institutions from where they came were top notch in the region, where the quality of teaching was very high. Such students who were used to high standards of teaching based on different methodologies of teaching were dissatisfied with the quality of teaching at this new institution. Within a short period of study in this institution they became a disgruntled lot and who complained to the principal about the poor quality of teaching. The teachers had no other choice, but to leave the institution as they felt they were gradually losing control of the class. As one group of students were always disgusted at the poor quality of teaching and were complaining to the administration, the teachers were demoralized and were not able to improve the quality of teaching; they had never undergone any training in the newer and more effective methods of teaching.

The administration congratulated the consultant for cutting the Gordian knot, and decided to allocate a separate budget for teacher training. They conducted specialized training programmes in the new methods and techniques of teaching.

☞

- Do you consider money as the single most deciding factor in motivating a teacher?
- Do you recommend any changes in the training process in the light of your observations of this case?
- What is the importance of feedback given by students? How often feedback has to be collected to ascertain the quality of teaching?

9

Effective Communication

The overriding cause of most communication problems is perception, which can be defined as a person's view of reality.

—Richard M. Hodgetts

Without dialogue there is no communication,
And without communication there can be no true education.

—Paulo Freire

The teacher's major task revolves around constant transfer of ideas and an understanding of their meaning. It is basically the art of communication. The quality of communication and its effective transmission determine the success of a teacher. Effective communication fosters rapt attention, effective listening and motivation to learn well. As verbal communication involves both emotional expressions and other non-verbal messages, there is an immense impact of communication on students. As a two-way communication takes place in a classroom situation, the immediate feedback helps the teacher to gauge the effect of his teaching. If the teacher cannot communicate effectively, neither his scholarship nor his love for the profession is of any help to him. Gilbert Highet (1989) makes this point clear by stating as follows:

"After the teacher has prepared his subject, he has to communicate his knowledge to his pupils. If he fails in this, he has failed as a teacher. He may still be an inspiration for a few youngsters because of his selfless devotion to scholarship or the charm of his character; yet that will scarcely make up for his central failure." He further states that: "Communication is an essential function of civilization. Teaching is only one of the many occupations that depend upon it, absolutely."

The process of communication which occurs in a classroom is almost the same as that of any communication system, but the methods and purpose are different. The key parts of this process are given below.

Main Components of the Communication Process

1. The sender
2. Encoding
3. The message
4. The channel

5. Decoding
6. The receiver
7. The physical environment
8. Clarity
9. Acceptance
10. Feedback
11. Follow up
12. Conclusion

The sender of the message, in this context, is the teacher who initiates a message by encoding a thought. The message is the physical product which is encoded. When the teacher speaks, the speech is the message. When he writes, the written words are the message and when he gestures, the movements of his arms and expressions on his face are the message. The channel in this situation is the formal channel i.e. the classroom presentation. Decoding is done by the receiver, the student in this context, by translating the symbols into meaningful ideas or message. It is the process of converting the message back into the teacher's original ideas. The physical environment in this case means the classroom with its physical settings which may or may not be conducive to handle the class well as external disturbances can result in distractions to the students' listening capabilities. Clarity denotes clarity of ideas and its expression. In this situation, if the communicated message is not free from perceptional problems, semantic difficulties, cultural differences or information overload, the meaning is distorted; the intended meaning is not the same as the one understood by the student. Acceptance denotes the comprehension of the ideas expressed by the teacher as understood by the student. It is through feedback information collected by the teacher that he finds out whether the received message is the same as the intended message that was communicated. It enables the teacher to modify his method, contents and language. Receiving feedback allows the teacher to determine whether his messages have been understood properly. A follow up is essential to findout whether the student has followed the instructions. Conclusion is the final stage when the teacher shifts to another topic after being fully convinced that effective learning has taken place.

Major Barriers in Communication in the Classrooms

Language: It is expected of a teacher to possess a sound vocabulary and a perfect knowledge of grammar so that he is able to articulate the ideas with confidence. He has to choose apt words and use them in the right context to convey the message without any ambiguity. Language plays a pivotal role in expressing ideas effectively. The quality of language enables the teacher to communicate with a free flow of relevant ideas which, in the end, justifies the purpose of communication. It basically fulfills the instructional objectives. The teacher who does not have a command over the language cuts a sorry figure in front of his students. The teacher who is well-versed in the knowledge of the subject, but lacks language skills, faces severe communication problems while explaining the topic. Improper use of language creates unnecessary confusion in the minds of students.

Emotions: The emotional balance, facial expressions and gesticulations of the teacher do influence, to a great extent, the acceptance and interpretation of the message by students. Extreme emotions can create indelible impressions on their minds. We remember the teacher who taught us a Shakespearean drama by enacting the scenes with full emotions. Those scenes are ever etched in our minds. If the teacher fails to use emotions in appropriate contexts, his discourse may become dull and drab. The teacher must know how to use emotions to drive home a point clearly. Emotional imbalances can disrupt the smooth functioning of a class.

Filtering: The filtering of the ideas can severely affect the purpose of communication as it tends to distort the message. In the classroom the scope of filtering is more as there is a knowledge gap between the teacher and the student. Another key factor which encourages filtering is the fear of students for the teacher, especially the strict ones. Hence, in most cases, when the teacher seeks to know whether the students have understood the topic that has been taught, they answer in the affirmative to please him. Filtering also takes place when the teacher is not able to explain the topic with clarity, confidence, brevity, comprehensiveness and to the point.

Information Overload: Students have a finite capacity to assimilate the ideas expressed by a teacher. If the teacher in his anxiety to complete the course indulges fast in overloading the students with too much information at a given point of time, it results in defeating the objectives. The student either picks up ideas according to his whims and fancies or ignore many of them, including the main points. In the end, it cripples his level of comprehension. Teachers who do not take pains to prepare well and are not adept in time management usually end up in overloading students with too much information at a time.

Selective Perception: Perception involves how a person organizes and interprets his sensory impressions in order to give meaning to his environment. What a person perceives can be substantially different from the objective reality. Perception denotes one's view of reality. Factors like attitude, interest, motive, exposure, expectations and experience decide the nature of a person's perception. A student's perception about the teacher may differ from that of another student. There are numerous chances of eruption of perceptional problems which, in turn, affects the acceptance of the ideas expressed by a teacher.

Making Learning Possible

The most important steps involved in learning are—Revise, Retain, and

Retrieve or Recall. The student who frequently revises his lessons is able to retain the contents of the topics in his memory and is thereby able to retrieve from his memory what he has learnt. Efficiency reflected in revision and the concomitant efficiency reflected in retrieval are inter-dependent. Here comes the role played by a teacher to constantly repeat the important points in the class so that the student remembers what is important. Different methods are followed by students to retain the points in their memory. Some retain what they have revised far better than others due to their well-organized and productive learning habits. Learning is, to a great extent, an individual process, both retention and retrieval depend on his competence. Learning is influenced by the students' genetic makeup, previous learning experiences, culture and his societal exposure. According to Sue Davidoff and Owen van den Borg (1990), a teacher may follow four steps: plan, teach/act, observe and reflect. He has to observe the learning habits of students and take follow up actions to see that they learn their task properly. Some students may prefer a visual, auditory, kinesthetic, or tactile way of learning. According to McCarthy (1980) they can be grouped as innovative learners, analytic learners, common sense learners or dynamic learners.

The teacher has to evaluate the student on a continual basis to ascertain the effectiveness of both teaching and learning. It is a part of the duty of all teachers to consistently guide the slow learners. Without putting the blame on the weak students in the class, the teacher has to attend to them individually either in the teacher's room or at a convenient place. The teacher is partially responsible if the student fails. He has to put in extra efforts to enthuse his students to take studies seriously. He has to guide them effectively so that in the end they perform well and he gets credit for their performance.

A very helpful strategy to learn the subjects is to divide the material into small parts. Reading five to seven pages of a text each day is better than reading the whole chapter in a hurry a day. The student has to summarize the key points by connecting them to examples and by generating questions to find answers about the topics studied. Repetition is the key to success.

Need for Constant Assessment of Reactions of the Learner

The teacher must use effective methods to assess student's reactions to his instructional innovations. Whenever he introduces a new teaching method and instructional innovations to improve the quality of learning, he ought to obtain timely feedback so that he could make necessary changes in his method of teaching and instructional innovations. In this context, Classroom Assessment Technique, which is a specific procedure or activity designed to assist a teacher to obtain immediate and useful answers to focused questions about student learning, is the ideal method to be used in schools and colleges. If the teacher finds that the new teaching method and instructional innovations has not improved student learning, he has to immediately bring about the necessary changes so that the student improves his learning capabilities. In a classroom situation, the teachers who ensure regular feedback on student learning and reactions are able to ensure their professional success.

It is through a continuous feedback system that the teacher is able to assess the students' level of confidence in the application of knowledge and skills. The high achievers will naturally have a high level of self-confidence. The students would appreciate the introduction of modern teaching methods, instructional innovations and classroom assessments which play a significant role in their overall academic performance.

Efficacy of Communication and Planning in Teaching

Teaching requires certain fascinating skills to attract students. For instance, the introduction of a new topic must be captivating and result in assuring full attention of students. The very first part of the introduction of the topic should be appealing and stimulating to create some excitement in the minds of the learner. If the teacher could relate the subject to a real life situation, the student would be all ears to his presentation.

Efficient teachers state the main points of the lessons both in the beginning and at the end of the class. They do not cover more than four to five main points, at a time. They describe the points one by one in a sequential order and explain them by using appropriate illustrations. The teacher reinforces the idea by not only repeating or restating it, but also by using a combination of well-crafted teaching method. It is through a well thought out lesson-planning that the teacher is able to fulfill the instructional objectives in a methodical manner. The teacher, who takes pains to plan the lesson well, ultimately becomes the apple of eye of students. Senior teachers who are masters in the field revise the topics before they go to teach, even though they are proficient in handling the subjects with years of rich experience. They incorporate the changes and add new illustrations to make the topic interesting. Without lesson planning, teaching is a total failure. Poor classroom management results from poor lesson planning also.

Though a variety of assessment tools are available, most teachers do not assess the current knowledge of the student on a subject. This is a serious flaw and causes serious concern for the students who are not able to digest the topics for lack of rudimentary knowledge of the subject. To develop confidence in the minds of students in a newly taught subject, in some institutions teachers follow the practice of conducting a short term Bridge course or a Foundation course in which the fundamentals of the subject are explained so that the students get an idea of the basics of their subjects. This is an excellent method to be adopted in every institution.

Simple to the Complex Principle Makes Communication in Teaching Effective

One of the cardinal principles in communication/teaching is to proceed from the simple to the complex. This method is relevant at all levels of teaching, irrespective of the nature of the subjects taught. When the teacher bypasses this principle, his students find learning too strenuous and burdensome. Some teachers are in a hurry to complete the lessons and overlook this fundamental principle; they neglect the teaching of the basics of subjects, especially at certain rudimentary and crucial levels of learning. The teachers have to invariably follow the age old principle of proceeding from the familiar to the unfamiliar. This method results in a better understanding of the subject. It ensures the connectivity between the major concepts in a subject. It also guarantees a smooth transition from one topic to another. It is indicative of a sense of continuity from the old to the new or from the known to the unknown. This process of planning a lesson lays a solid foundation for effective sequencing of major concepts. One best method of planning the teaching of a lesson is, to plan a clear and brief outline of topics taught with the sub-headings and major points. The outlines must plainly delineate how the sub-topics are connected to the main topic.

Eye Contact and Communication

It has been mentioned that the teacher must have eye contact with all students. As successful speakers maintain a steady intense look on a large audience, teachers have to maintain continuous eye contact with students whether it is a small or large class. This is essential because without eye contact a teacher would fail to perceive the efficacy of teaching. The facial expressions and the body language of students can convey vital and spontaneous feedback about their attentiveness in the classroom. The teachers must be able to extend the attention span of students by resorting to a long pause, putting questions or by shifting from one method to another. Proper eye contact reveals whether students are attentive. The teacher is continuously able to obtain visual feedback through eye contact.

If the teacher fails to maintain eye contact, over a short period of time he loses control over the class, leading to even disciplinary problems. Indeed, lack of proper eye contact results in poor classroom management.

Tips for Effective Use of the White/Black Board

- It is the duty of every teacher to erase the white or black board when he/she leaves the class.

- For whiteboards, use different, but suitable, coloured markers and for blackboards, use suitable but different, coloured pieces of chalk.
- Be mentally prepared about the scheme of things to be carried out effectively on the board.
- Always use bold capital letters.
- Never speak while writing on the board. The moment it is written, look at the students, and read it aloud. It is a good practice to be followed.
- Write the headings first, and then, the points, in a sequential order.
- There should not be any overlapping of points as it may confuse the student.
- Circle or underline the major points as and when required.
- Always use the left side of the board for writing the major points or steps and the right side for working out calculations or pointing out connected matter or questions that need further clarification.
- At intervals, move to the rear side of the class to ascertain whether the writing is legible to all.
- Check at random whether students are taking down notes properly.
- If solving a problem, write down the steps in a methodical way.
- Do not miss the steps while giving a solution as it hampers the learning process.
- Always use a different colour or dotted lines while making changes to an already drawn diagram or while comparing that particular topic with another topic which was discussed previously.
- Invite students to work out a problem or to give illustrations on the board.
- Invite them at random so that everyone would remain alert, expecting an invitation from the teacher.
- Appreciate the students who perform well.
- In the end, repeat the main points and give necessary assignment or home work to reinforce learning.

10
Qualities of a Good Teacher and His Role in the Academia

The more I learn about myself
The more I become different self. —Ashleigh Brilliant

Quality can mean many things, they include:

Quality teaching and administration;
Quality development;
Quality control;
Quality assessment;
Quality assurance.

Much has been discussed about the teaching profession, so far. We will now examine the characteristics of a good teacher, ethics of teaching, and other significant aspects, which decide his future.

Lord Ashby, a few years ago, wrote a paper on "A Hippocratic Oath for the Academic Profession". It was a courageous start on a momentous undertaking. The academic ethos is hard to grasp and resistant to systematic formulation. But we all have some traces of it in our consciences which have been formed and nurtured by our own training in universities, our long experience in them, and the academic traditions which we inherit. It is that element which we must affirm and strengthen (Edward Shils, 1997).

To the question, 'What is good teaching?', Stuart Palmer (1998) states:

> "It consists of guiding and helping others to understand and contribute to knowledge. Required is an intellectual grasp in depth of the given field of knowledge. Also required is enthusiasm for the field and for learning and discovery, not necessarily loud enthusiasm but a sense of importance of the field. Necessary as well is effective communication about the field of knowledge and the learning process. Added to that a good teacher must have the capacity for hard work because preparing for and teaching classes is just that—time-consuming, hard work. To organize material well, look up points unclear to oneself, create lectures and discussions that are informative

and interesting, connect with and motivate students —these are difficult."

Most of us are quite concerned about the pre-requisites of effectiveness of teaching displayed by effective teachers, which according to Baker, Boggs, and Putnam (1983) are the following:

- a student-centered orientation
- a value for the learning process
- a need to influence individual behaviour, and
- a belief that the teacher possesses the power to produce a desired effect in the learner.

A teacher's knowledge, skills, and abilities are a critical resource for instructional reforms. Such reforms envision changes in pedagogy, thereby, creating an expectation that teachers enact new instructional practices (*Educational Leadership and Reform*, edited Wayne K Hoy and Cecil G Miskel, 2005).

Teachers' thinking is directly influenced by their knowledge. Their thinking, in turn, determines their action in the classroom. Therefore, to help teachers change their practice, they have to expand and elaborate their knowledge systems (Burko and Putnam, 1995).

Characteristics of a Good Teacher

1. Sound knowledge of the subject;
2. Effective preparation;
3. Clarity of expression;
4. Enthusiasm;
5. Stimulating interest and intellectual curiosity;
6. Encouraging discussion;
7. Selecting appropriate tools and methodologies of teaching;
8. Fostering creativity;
9. Attending to individual differences;
10. Punctuality;
11. Concern about student's learning;
12. Building rapport with the students and their parents;
13. Assessing instructional effectiveness;
14. Desire to improve one's quality;
15. Professional credibility;
16. Integrity;
17. Instilling confidence;
18. Inspiring fascination for learning;

19. Reliability;
20. Making use of collaborative efforts.

In fact, these characteristics can also be used as pointers while doing a self-analysis by a teacher to assess his efficiency.

Ethics of Teaching

The teaching profession demands ethical standards of a high order. The ethical standards adhered to by the teacher have a ripple effect as it percolates in the society. They are considered bright spots of the academic ethos of an institution as they foster positive academic growth and development. "Teachers are ethically committed to make decisions that best serve their students' needs and interests. Teachers are accountable and responsible for their students' learning" (John S. Lofty, 2006). Moreover, teachers are always expected to encourage students in their quest for knowledge, giving them all possible assistance in the free exploration of ideas. They must understand, appreciate and strictly follow the ethical practices which are given below:

Ethical Standards of a Teacher

1. Must be fully aware of the pedagogical requisites;
2. Must fully understand the instructional objectives pertaining to each topic;
3. Must possess the expertise and professional competence as required of a teacher in the relevant subject;
4. Must be fully aware of the specific needs of the learners in relation to instructional objectives;
5. Must be fully prepared to handle the class with essentially needed tools and methodologies;
6. Must carry out diligently effective methods of evaluation in a systematic order;
7. Must clear the doubts of students on a priority basis;
8. Must support the needs of weak students;
9. Must possess an upright character;
10. Must be trustworthy;
11. Must be punctual;
12. Must never discriminate any student on the basis of gender, colour, religion, caste, or ethnicity;
13. Must respect all students and be fair in judgement;
14. Must imbibe the spirit of the vision and mission of the institution;
15. Must believe that the quality of the teacher's service directly influences the society.

The Real Teacher Mesmerizes

While I was a student of a reputed school in a historic town, I always noticed that the teachers used to come well-dressed. At a young age, we were able to understand the value of appropriate dress. In fact, in whatever position we are, the dress we wear communicates our status in life and the degree of confidence we possess. Our appearance in a class, which is closely observed by each and every student, determines our attitude to life and displays our confidence. I salute those teachers as my role models who dressed immaculately and taught us passionately. They took care of their health admirably well, which was reflected in their grooming and deportment. They were so punctual that the local people used to set their watches when these teachers passed by. They were all held in high esteem, and were highly acceptable in the society. Pin drop silence was maintained in the class from the moment they entered till they left. They taught us so well. Their communication skills were excellent. Their command over language was superb. The beauty of their class was that they had no occasion to scold us. They were role models for generations of students.

What attracted us to those illustrious teachers were their impeccable manners and dedication to the profession. The high quality of teaching maintained by them throughout their career put them on a pedestal, quite apart from the ordinary teachers. They were a class by themselves. They were not only teachers, but also educators and pedagogues. As educators, they were the best leaders of the institution and society. As pedagogues, they were responsible for developing the personality of students by fostering human values in them. It is when we come across such teachers that we proudly announce—teaching is the noblest of all professions.

Interpersonal Skills of a Teacher

Teachers of the modern times are exposed directly to the needs of a multi-ethnic community with socio-economic, linguistic and cultural differences. They must possess interpersonal skills apart from the pedagogical and other skills. Given below are some of the major interpersonal skills a teacher must possess which would lead to a supportive, creative and relationship-oriented approach to teaching.

Interpersonal Skills of a Teacher

1. Empathy;
2. Supportive nature;
3. Patience;
4. Tolerance;
5. Sympathy;

6. Sense of humor;
7. Fairness;
8. Flexibility;
9. Affection;
10. Active Listening;
11. Leadership (Student-focused);
12. Communication with understanding.

Even though teaching is the very cornerstone of this profession, sadly enough, it has been found that some teachers fail in their duties. The shortcomings of such teachers have become a matter of great concern for both administrators and parents. Evidently, now educational administrators pay considerable attention to this nagging problem.

A major reason for the poor standard of teaching can be attributed to the failure of teachers.

Major Reasons for the Failure of Teachers

- The teacher goes to the class without preparation or with haphazard preparation;
- He has an indifferent attitude to teaching;
- He presents himself in a casual dress and his demeanor is unbecoming of a teacher;
- He shows scant respect for the needs and feelings of students;
- He metes out unfair treatment to students;
- He displays a bad tempered or ill-mannered behaviour;
- He follows unethical and unprofessional practices;
- He speaks ill of students;
- He reports to the class without being punctual or leaves the class early;
- He gives inappropriate explanations or uses wrong illustrations;
- He ignores the needs of gifted as well as weak students;
- He has inefficient training;
- He receives incompatible compensation and rewards;
- He lacks administrative support;
- He lacks access to modern technology;
- He has poor library facilities;
- He resists changes.

The root cause of these problems is lack of awareness, motivation and training on the part of teachers. Such teachers are also found uninterested in continuous teacher improvement programmes. Researchers have emphatically brought out the close relationship between poor teaching and poor academic performance of students. Any achievement gap in the student's performance has been mainly attributed to performance gap in the teacher's instructional practices. If students are taught by poor teachers, it is necessarily reflected in the poor quality of the students who may face severe disadvantages in their career. When the teacher fails to do his duty, the student fails in his subjects, and thereby the institution fails in imparting education effectively. Indeed, the resultant ripple effect has disastrous consequences.

Here is a perceptive analysis of the behaviour of the teachers with poor quality as noted by Therese Huston (2009).

Research shows that instructors tend to lose credibility with their students when they:

- show up late to class;
- lack familiarity with the text;
- cannot explain difficult concepts;
- rarely ask whether students understand their explanations;
- do not make any attempt to answer students' questions;
- provide unclear and vague answers to students' questions about course policies, tests, quizzes or other graded assignments;
- fail to follow the course policies outlined in the syllabus (particularly when they change grading policies); and
- fail to remind students of upcoming deadlines and due dates.

Seven Steps to Enhance the Quality of Teaching

The teachers may consider the following suggestions to improve their quality of teaching and avoid failure and unnecessary setbacks in their profession.

1. Be Fully Prepared for Handling the Class: Academic competence comes first from how efficiently the teacher handles the class, which depends on his attitude and orientation regarding the preparation for engaging a class. Before entering the class, the teacher must be fully organized with the *what*, *why*, *when*, *whom*, *where* and *how* of teaching. To understand how well a teacher has to prepare on a daily basis and deliver it effectively by upholding quality standards, the teacher has to follow the guidelines narrated below.

2. Develop Instructional Objectives and Explore: It is advisable to begin teaching by doing an objective and purposeful soul-searching—a frank and honest self-assessment. The strategies and techniques to be followed must be identified, preceded by a proper understanding of the instructional objectives to be attained during the class. The teacher must be familiar with the syllabus and curriculum as both are interconnected. The former delineates on what has to be taught and the knowledge, skills and abilities which have to be deliberately fostered and the latter deals with the content-teaching procedure and about the connected learning experiences—all necessary to achieve the educational purpose of the programme. A thorough understanding of the syllabus and curriculum helps the teacher to figure out his instructional objectives.

3. Be Ready with the Appropriate Inputs: Inputs to teaching add to the objectives and value of teaching. They mainly consist of the essential materials which throw light on the contents. They have to be first digested by the teacher before entering the classroom. Research for the inputs requires certain amount of patience and focus. Some teachers seek the assistance of experienced teachers to refer to the best materials. Selecting the right instructional materials is of immense importance as it nourishes and satisfies the quest for excellence of a teacher and makes the presentation worthy and effective. A teacher with passion goes to any extent to keep all materials ready for reference to prepare for an exciting class.

4. Make the Right Choices regarding the Methodology and Educational Technology: One of the key purposes of teaching is to provide a variety of opportunities to students to learn. Here comes the need to choose the right blend of teaching strategies. The right mix of methodologies of teaching which suits the needs of students brings about positive changes in the teaching and learning environment. Selecting the appropriate technology or using multiple teaching methodologies makes teaching not only effective and interesting but also stimulating and interactive. Inputs, methodology and technology chosen would speak volumes about the professionalism the teacher has.

5. Be Conscious about the Needs of Learners: Adult learners have greater expectations for the quality of teaching. They are more experienced about life and look forward to task/problem-centered learning. They are to be self-directed and made conscious of a perceived need. A more student-oriented, experience-based, problem-oriented and collaborative method of teaching is ideally suitable for adult learners. The quality of teaching is always closely linked to improved learning outcomes, and the adult learners expect a high level of student-interactive, co-operative and stimulating teaching-learning environment. At this level, the teacher must be able to cultivate critical thinking skills, stimulate real interest in the topic, and encourage self-initiated learning.

6. Take Care of Students: As teaching progresses, an emotional bond is established between the teacher and the student. A closer understanding develops between them which fosters mutual trust and respect. The more efficient is the teacher, the stronger is the bond. It is expected of all teachers to develop a positive rapport with their students to especially understand and appreciate their individual needs and problems. Some of them need special care by way of special assistance to improve their learning skills. A committed teacher is never reluctant to provide this extra care.

7. Always be a Professional in Outlook, Delivery, and Qualities: In this knowledge-era, education has a massive potential in transforming economies into social engines of growth. In this context, teachers play a crucial role in ensuring the transformation of educational institutions into centers of excellence with a national perspective. The evidence of professionalism is linked with the qualities a teacher possesses, like, academic and subject expertise, educational leadership, continuous development, positive outlook, integrity, inspiration, and vision. Teaching has become a complex process which demands a high degree of professional standards at all levels. It has become both an intellectually demanding and socially challenging profession.

Good Preparation is the Key to Success

Even though, the preparation of the teaching materials requires hours of earnest and meaningful contemplation and reflection on the topic concerned, some teachers have the dubious habit of using the same notes over and over again. The art of preparing lessons cannot be taken up lightly for the simple reason that, if the notes smack of lethargy and ineptitude, the results are disastrous. Some teachers consider teaching notes as a mere addendum, used just to remember some points while delivering a lecture. It is not so. Preparing notes is one of the most important tools used in the proper delivery of lecture in a step-by-step manner. It is the workable framework which steers the course of the curriculum to its culmination. It is the end result of thoughtful meditation over a particular subject for a long time. If a teacher neglects this crucial tool, his future is doomed.

Some teachers underestimate students' potentials and drag on with a monotonous lecture. In today's world not a soul would listen to an hour's lecture without showing periodic signs of fatigue. Students need interactive, stimulating and intellectually focused classes which would make them think to find solutions to critical problems. They look forward to undergoing a process and an activity which stimulates their process of thinking. If teaching boils down to a one way communication mode, they will be quite exhausted, and dash to the nearest food court to cool down and relax. Teaching has to invigorate the learner to explore further into the unlimited boundaries of knowledge. It has to be intellectually challenging to motivate students to set higher standards; it has to encourage self–initiated learning. Teaching, in the end, reveals the indomitable spirit of a master mind.

New Roles of Teachers

In most institutions there are student councils which provide students opportunities to learn about the art of leadership, effective communication, creativity, negotiation, human psychology, stress-and-time management, group dynamics, assertiveness, decision making, human relations, parliamentary procedures, etc., so that they develop an integrated, harmonious and holistic personality. A very important outcome of these healthy practices is that the student community gets ingrained in the fundamental principles and practices of democratic functioning of public bodies. In some institutions a teacher is put in charge of this significant co-curricular programme or a person designated as a student co-coordinator is assigned the task of supervising the functioning of the students' council. In this situation, the teacher must be thorough with the procedures of organizing and conducting a meeting. At times a teacher is assigned the task of conducting the open house or parent teacher association meeting or a meeting in connection with a community extension programme organized by the institution, often conducted outside the campus. As modern institutions are becoming more and more integral part of the society and collaborate with other social organizations to serve their community, they must be prepared to meet such eventualities or exigencies that the community is committed to.

In these circumstances, a sound knowledge about the management of meetings is a requisite competency for the job of a teacher. There are certain basic rules to be followed while conducting a meeting. In all formal meetings there will be a chairperson or a presiding officer who will officially run the meeting by strictly adhering to certain parliamentary procedures. The chairperson of a meeting is the controlling officer as regards the conduct of the meeting is concerned and has the authority to commence the meeting, conduct and conclude it at an appropriate or predetermined time. The chairperson has to religiously follow the agenda of the meeting which is set prior to the meeting by discussing with the principal and the secretary of the meeting. The secretary of a meeting, in the case of a student council, its secretary, shall prepare the minutes of the meeting and read it before the meeting to be adopted by the body. The chairperson of the meeting, in this case, the chairperson of the student's council will take up the business of the house one by one, discuss the propositions or proposals and decide the future course to be taken in respect of the proposition as and when the proposition becomes a resolution passed by the house. This proposition or proposal which comes before the house is known as a motion which is the subject matter for discussion and finally when a decision is arrived at that motion becomes the resolution passed by the body either unanimously or through a voting procedure. The students who address the house must address the chairperson first and present his or her views, suggestions, etc., on the subject matter. It is the chairperson's duty to give opportunities to all those who would like to speak in favor or against the motion or move amendments to the motion as suggested and passed by the meeting. The body can appoint committees to study further the implications of a proposal and suggest better methods or actions.

The chairperson must see that the meeting commences and concludes on time. If a participant uses foul, discourteous or unparliamentary language, the chairperson should disallow it. He must ensure that all the speakers, including himself/herself, use clear, unambiguous and concise language whenever addressing the house. The chairperson must also ensure that when a speaker has occupied the floor, he should not be interrupted by others. He must be sensitive to the feelings of the members and should not tolerate any personal affront or attack. He should be diplomatic and tactful while dealing with members. He should be able to gauge the sense of the house and should not prolong unnecessary discussion. He should not act in a partisan or prejudiced manner.

Now-a-days, there is much emphasis on student support services, academic and social skill developments, soft skill development, personal growth and career planning. Orientation programmes for the freshers, leadership development programmes, public speaking training programmes and a host of other programmes are organized by the institution with the help of faculty members who can volunteer themselves to organize them with competence, authority and efficiency.

Educational institutions make it a point to conduct outreach programmes and serve the community in a big way. The purpose is to enhance the standards of students so that they demonstrate a positive attitude and keenness to learn well. For instance, the high school students can now experience college life through student summer outreach programmes. Such institutions introduce programmes to reach out to the community and enable as many students as possible to prepare them for the future. Some institutions conduct bridge programmes in English and other languages, and in subjects like, Mathematics, Accounting, and IT. Some even conduct programmes in TOEFL, IELTS and the like to assist students to move to international institutions. New facilities like 'Soft skills Enhancement' programmes, 'Finishing schools', 'Achievement Academies' and 'Learning Foreign Languages' are provided in campuses, mainly to facilitate employability. Teachers can make these facilities available easily by running them with a professional touch.

In the current scenario, educational institutions have a duty to provide career education to all. They must ensure that all students receive timely and appropriate career advice and guidance. The government or local bodies can share a part of the expense involved as it helps the citizens to obtain employment.

The importance of various clubs in educational institutions has increased as they facilitate the holistic development of personality. They not only unite students of diverse backgrounds but also enable them to expose themselves beyond the classroom. Teachers may volunteer to provide such opportunities to students to develop their latent potentials, without any compulsion. The institution may form small committees to oversee the functioning of arts, sports and other clubs and encourage teachers to develop programmes that provide students a robust campus life.

Institutions can promote Drama club, Quizzing club, Entrepreneurship Development club, Adventure club, Creativity club, Writers club, Debate club, Discussion Group club, Nature club, Students Forestry club, Literacy club, Book club, Performing Arts club, Management Skills Development club, IT club, Energy Conservation club, Sitcom club, Leadership Development club, Consulting club, Heritage club, Film club, Photography club, Department-based clubs, etc., to provide effective platforms for the self-development of students.

Building Trust

Obviously, building trust is one of the major goals of a teacher. When the students know that the teacher would strive hard to assist them in their acquisition of knowledge, they trust him. Some teachers are considered more trustworthy than others. The reason is they carry out their obligations sincerely and perfectly, on a time-bound basis and reach out to every single student. They are appreciated for their competence and admirable performance.

Benefits of Teacher Involvement

In the institutions where teachers are involved at different levels of decision making process, the organization benefits which, in turn enhances the confidence of teachers. This approach not only provides opportunities for continuous improvement, but also ensures unstinted co-operation of the teaching fraternity in realization of the overall objectives of the organization. The untapped ideas, innovations, and creative thoughts of teachers can make a big difference in the performance of the institution. In a competitive environment, it is prudent on the part of administration to make use of the resources of proficient teachers to enhance the quality of the institution. When the institution treats teachers as partners in its development and progress, teachers' involvement increases and it enhances their prestige. Naturally, such teachers take pride in contributing to the general welfare of the organization. When the leadership shares information about the institution's priorities, challenges and future plans with the teachers, they feel that they are also taken into confidence. It is prudent on the part of the administration to solicit teachers' views on important academic and other related matters.

Need for Effective Teacher Involvement

1. Teachers are competent to make better decisions using their knowledge and skills to improve the quality of the institution, especially in academic matters.
2. They are able to keep track of the areas requiring improvement and take corrective action in academic matters.

3. They are most suited to pinpoint trouble spots and find immediate solutions on academic matter and matters of general interest.
4. Their involvement ensures better rapport between the administration and the teaching fraternity.
5. Their involvement increases morale by creating a sense of belongingness to the institution.
6. They are better focused on changes, and accept changes when they become part of a team that decides on crucial matters related to the impact of change on the institution.
7. They can voluntarily lend their support to make the teaching process effective, efficient, and adaptable.
8. They can assist the administration in setting newer benchmarking policies in the academic pursuits as a core parameter of growth and development.
9. They can assist in establishing regular feedback from students and take steps to enhance the quality of teaching.
10. They can be more competent in solving problems and thereby enhance the quality of the institution.
11. Their commitment to fulfill the institutional goals is much higher.
12. They can be proactive in their approach when it comes to the overall development of the institution.

Let us conclude by narrating a very small but interesting story. Jan Carlzon ends his book, '*Moments of Truth*', with a story about two stone cutters who were chipping square blocks out of granite. A visitor to the quarry asked what they were doing. The first stone cutter, looking rather sour, grumbled, "I'm cutting the damned stone into a block."

The second, who appeared to be pleased with his work, replied proudly, I'm on the team that's building a cathedral."

When the teacher feels that they are the 'builders of cathedrals' in the field of education, they become the true social engineers who will carve out the future of a great nation with vigour, optimism and strong determination.

Importance of Meetings in Educational Institutions

Meetings of administrators and teachers take place periodically to plan, organize, communicate and control the conduct of the curricular, co-curricular and extra-curricular activities of the institution. In the commencement of the academic year/semester, they decide all the events that have to be included in the academic calendar for the year. The allocation of classes, assigning of all duties to teachers, maintenance of specific documents, university/college regulations, quality assurance programmes, the conduct of tests and examinations, students progress, scheme for month-wise completion of portions, submission of assignments/projects, guidance for project/dissertation/research, classroom management and resource allocation and utilization are the main matters that are decided in the first meeting of the year/semester. Similarly, all matters related to co-curricular and extra-curricular activities to be taken up during the academic year/semester are decided in this meeting, and duties are assigned to various teachers. All meetings are guided by specific agenda prepared in consultation with the staff concerned. They facilitate dialogue and promote good interpersonal relations between administration and teachers. In some institutions, they conduct monthly meetings, especially to evaluate the performance of departments or classes at different levels. For all the meetings, the agenda is circulated before the meeting so that every participant knows its purpose. In addition, special meetings are convened to address specific issues. The administration makes it a point to ensure that the atmosphere of the meeting is congenial. The differing views are treated with respect, and domination by a few is not encouraged. Democratic procedures are adopted so that those who want to speak are heard. If gender and cultural differences crop up in the meeting, they are discouraged. The organizers see to it that every participant feels free to air his/her views. It is the bounden duty of the chairman of the meeting to skillfully manage it and strive hard to meet its purpose.

Meetings are also convened for the purpose of giving specific instructions related to the decisions taken by the administration from time to time. For instance, when new organizational procedures are introduced, a meeting of the teachers and staff is convened to disseminate information regarding the change in procedures. When the administration decides to address other specific issues related to academic matters, meetings are convened. Such meetings are chaired by the head of the institution.

When the administration wishes to solicit views of teachers about changes to be introduced, meetings are convened. The intention of such meetings is to enable teachers to be aware of the impending changes and also to enable them to contribute their suggestions on matters of common concern. It facilitates a dialogue between the administration and teachers on organizational issues.

Departmental meetings are convened regularly to discuss how the departments are performing and contributing to the fulfillment of the overall objectives of the institution. They also address the specific issues faced by them, find solutions and initiate corrective measures. Sometimes, inter-departmental meetings are convened mainly to share information and seek cooperation in the matter of collaborative programmes.

11

Use of Technology in Higher Education

Nothing is impossible,
the word itself says,
I'm possible. —Audrey Hepburn

All technical progress has three kinds of effects:
The desired, the foreseen, and the unforeseen. —Jacques Ellul

Introduction

Times have changed. Technology has been integrated into the personal lives of billions of individuals all over the world. It has simultaneously opened up unimaginable opportunities to both teachers and students globally. The impact of information technology explosion on modern classrooms is truly amazing. Technology is now playing a pivotal role in improving the methods of teaching and learning. Universities are grappling with new realities: including more conscious and tech-savvy generation of students. In the classrooms, technology has revolutionized both teaching and learning processes. Teachers have started laying emphasis on video and media-rich technologies, such as holographic projections to create new learning environment. Some renowned universities in the world which experimented with the virtual education community environments have introduced systems like Second Life. Likewise using 3D immersive technologies as well as cloud-based tools have tremendous potential in schools and colleges. College Portals with Public Domain Information, Student Hub, Teacher Hub, Knowledge Portal and many more facilities have become a part of the common usage of ICT applications in colleges and universities. As technology is going to influence all spheres of life, its impact on education is no exception. According to Alberto Leon-Garcia and Indra Widjaja, "technology always plays a role in determining what can be built. The capabilities of various technologies have improved dramatically over the past two centuries. These improvements in capabilities have been accompanied by reduction in cost. As a result, many systems that were simply impossible two decades ago have become not only feasible but also cost-effective." That is good news for educators too. In the words of Warren Bennis, (1989), technology has done what ideology could not, it created a worldwide community of the wired who are well-versed in computer and information technology. We should feel lucky to live in a virtual world of all kinds of possibilities and opportunities. The proliferation of the ICT has covered vast areas of human population. James J. Duderstadt, in "*Challenges Facing Higher Education at the Millennium*", asserts that the emerging information technology has removed the constraints of space and time. We can now use powerful computers and their networks to deliver educational services to anyone, at anyplace and anytime; it is no longer confined to the campus or the academic schedule. Technology has created an open learning environment in which the student has evolved into an active learner and consumer of educational services, stimulating the growth of powerful market forces that could dramatically reshape the higher education enterprise.

In *Digital Youth*, Jonathan Alexander (2006) reminds us that "literacy is changing. Or, more specifically, what it means to be literate in our society is undergoing a transformation. Since the advent of the World Wide Web (www) in the mid-1990's, and the increasing use of Internet technologies throughout the west, digitally enabled mass communication has enabled millions to communicate with one another, have access to greater amount of information, and share their own thoughts, desires and dreams through web pages, e-mail, instant messaging, and other electronics venues." The East has also been impacted by this universal change taking place in the virtual world of communications using the Internet. According to Michio Kaku, the author of *Physics of the Future*, the internet is the beginning of a Type 1 Planetary telephone system. This process will accelerate as nations lay even more fiber-optic cables and launch more communication satellites. This process is unstoppable.

Multimedia PowerPoint, Pod casting, Spreadsheets, SMART Board skills, etc are used in modern classrooms to make the teaching-learning environment effective. Thanks to human ingenuity and creativity, more and more innovations are taking place in this crucial area of human development. Indeed, teaching and technology go hand in hand. In this millennium, a large number of institutions provide a technology-enabled learning environment to facilitate an effective learning process. The integration of iPads, interactive boards, e-Books, online resources, etc has become common tools and aids to teaching.

In the new pedagogical paradigm aided by IT-enabled teaching, "IT has the power to transform education by supporting shared creation, collaboration, and mastery of knowledge" (Dede, 2000). IT creates an appropriate environment for teachers and students to easily engage in active learning/problem-solving in a collaborative approach. In this Information Age, ICT cannot be confined to just the software or hardware used, but it is applied in all courses, programmes, services and administrative practices at all levels. Moreover, developing life-long learners is the ambitious goal of higher education. Thus information literacy has assumed more significance in the modern world than ever before.

In *Teaching with the Internet*, Beverley E Crane stresses the importance of internet activities which would heighten motivation by engaging students using a variety of media and allowing them to feel as if they were a part of the subject matter. In turn, it would make them more interested in the topic under discussion, and enable them to invest more mental energy in the process of learning. When students articulate and share their thoughts, they grasp the meaning of a subject and understand it better.

Another rare feature of the Internet Technology is that students have opportunities to converse with experts, research on almost any subject, and work in classrooms worldwide on similar projects, in the process of learning how to locate, organize, interpret, and present information (Beverley, 2000). This remarkable facility has enabled hundreds of students all over the world to interact with one another and exchange ideas in their relevant field of study. However, studies have revealed that students get an easier opportunity to evaluate their teachers based on their social media profiles. It has been found that teachers with a professionally oriented profile are more respected by the students and parents than others.

Advantages of Internet-Enabled Teaching

1. It is a technology-enhanced instruction.
2. It is student-centered.
3. It fosters critical thinking.
4. It ensures a multipath progression.
5. It is a multisensory aid.
6. It enhances cooperation.
7. It facilitates the teachers.
8. It creates an active learner.
9. It is exploratory.
10. It adheres to preferred learning steps.
11. It deals with the real-world situation.
12. It is the best practice to enhance quality.
13. It enables a flexible schedule.
14. It facilitates the use of a variety of teaching methods.

The opening lines of Castell's, *The Rise of the Networked Society* (2000), are revealing: "Towards the end of the second millennium of the Christian era several events of historical importance transformed the social landscape of human life. A technological revolution, centered around information technologies, began to reshape, at accelerated pace, the material basis of society". Educational systems are experiencing a paradigm shift, basically driven by IT. Teachers are now expected to not only possess educational expertise in the subject but also in technological expertise that is needed in different situations. If teachers are not fast enough to respond to this big change and uphold the quality of standards in all spheres of teaching, it would make them ill-equipped and they would be incompetent to handle classes productively.

Words of caution regarding the risks and promises of the Internet have been tacitly given by Nicholas C Barbules and Thomas A Callister, Jr., (2000):

> "The Internet is a vast, complex, and flexible information and communication medium. But it is not entirely neutral in structure. Certain features, such as the hyper-textual character of the Web and other elements in cyberspace, promote or encourage certain ways of organizing and accessing information, or communicating, and discouraging others. Still, on the whole, the Internet has remarkably broad and open set of capabilities, only some of which are being taken fully advantage of at present. Educationally, it is the most promising innovation since the invention of the book, and perhaps even longer back than that."

With the advent and development of cyberspace, the education sector has also undergone rapid change. Progress has been made in recent years to enhance global connectivity. which makes education accessible to millions of new learners at the higher education level. The more the global connectivity, the more would be the scope for imparting education to people throughout the world. Many people are denied educational opportunities due to the excessive cost of higher education. As an increasing number of countries now rely on the internet for providing services to their people, it is high time to take advantage of its immense potential in education. All universities of repute are now catering to students from different parts of the world to provide excellent quality of education. It has become possible as Information and Communication Technology (ICT) has already merged with educational pedagogy in many areas, and more and more course contents are digitized to facilitate faster dissemination of information. Given these circumstances, the need for traditional teaching to converge with the twenty-first century teaching and learning has become a high priority requirement. All prominent universities in the world are adapting to the new educational technology. As teachers, we have to welcome it.

In *The New Digital Age*, Eric Schmidt and Jared Cohen (2013), describe the impact of digital connectivity on a massive scale. They predict that soon everyone on the earth will be connected. With five billion more people set to join the virtual world, the boom in digital connectivity will gain in productivity, health, education, quality of life and myriad other avenues in the physical world from the most elite users to those at the base of the economic pyramid. Connectivity will not solve income inequality, though it will alleviate some of its more intractable causes, like lack of availability of education and economic opportunity.

Innovation and technology have significant impact on education. It is because it is a rapidly changing-wired world which is becoming closer, adapting swiftly, and evolving. Universities and colleges have a key role to play in proactively capitalizing on innovative practices in collaboration with successful national and international institutions. Much of the knowledge-based and innovation-driven economy depends primarily on advances made in science and technology. The rapid breakthrough in ICT and the phenomenal growth in technology-oriented courses have considerably influenced the academic world. The new generation wants to be well-equipped with the new century knowledge and skills. Universities and colleges have to play a dominant role to educate students; they must align themselves with the needs of the society, government and industry by embracing innovation. Universities and colleges must be committed to excellence, and contribute their mite to align technology with the academic objectives and pursuits. While universities are engrossed in research, they have to prioritize the needs of the society so that they meet the aspirations of the community. Otherwise they will be viewed as mere ivory towers.

Technology is pervasive, it cannot be regulated, and it will go anywhere (Bruce Pulling, 1985). This statement shows its enormous impact which affects the lives of almost every human being. According to James W. Hall (1991), the new interactive capacity of telecommunications technology possesses a transforming character which has the potential to alter dramatically the structure of the university, providing flexibility, convenience, and individual feedback and evaluation of both residential and off-campus students. As technology makes the locus of study less confined, more extended, the possibility of learning in a global campus becomes increasingly more feasible. However, the costs of technological infrastructure will exceed the fiscal capabilities of a single university, regional consortia and partnerships with state governments will be required.

As the Internet grows, educators have made increasing use of the web in both face-to-face classroom situations and distance education courses. The web is often touted as making education more accessible, promoting improved learning, and reducing the cost of education (Owston, 1997). Others suggest that the capabilities of the web can enhance the delivery of instruction (Starr, 1997, Renee E. Weiss, *et al.*, 2000). Our prediction is that universities will maintain ubiquitous web environments that are personalized, cohesive, and critical to the campus community as a renewed focus on social networks in the education process (Matthew Serbin Pittinsky, 2003). Teachers at all levels are expected to be sufficiently comfortable with navigation in an increasingly digital world. Of course, these twenty-first century skills are being incorporated in curricula the world over.

Technology brings positive learning outcomes. What this means is that in this high-tech era, students of a certain higher level of aptitude who are technologically oriented are able to progress faster than others. In such a challenging situation, teachers are expected to become the catalysts for change. They have to be open-minded to adapt to technological evolution, and thereby facilitate ICT-enabled teaching. Some teachers may be hesitant or even resistant in the beginning to try out the new methodologies and technologies of teaching. They will realize the full potentials of the new educational technologies once they become professionally competent to use them in the classroom. It is in this context that the relevance of professional development strategies in ICT-enabled teaching must be appreciated and practised by the teacher.

We may think for a while about the influence of technology on children in our homes. It has made their life quite hectic and exciting. It has changed their expectations. They are not happy to play in the garden or gathering shells on the beaches, make sand castles or read books. They are mostly engaged in frenetic activities on the computer. They are busy bees working with utmost concentration on computer games. They pester the parents to provide them with the latest-technology computers, the latest apps, TV videos, iBox or Nintendo to play games. In the process, they become fast thinkers, decision makers, goal setters and achievers, which, in a sense enable them to adapt changing technologies. When they come to school, they expect teaching and learning process to provide them the same thrill and excitement which they enjoyed when they were on computer games for hours together at home. The same challenge is applicable in the colleges and universities, but of a different dimension.

In today's educational environment, dramatic changes are taking place in our school/college libraries because of huge increase in the use of e-books. Students can access them from anywhere without being physically present in the library. What they need is a user name and password. Most books are available in electronic format. Modern libraries do not contain many books or journals in print. The layout of the library has changed a lot. It is easy now to source the books. Students request titles from the librarian who finds them and have them delivered. A student need not waste his time searching for books. Other library services available include online databases and even counseling services. The traditional libraries are undergoing a sea of change by converting themselves into fully digitalized bookless libraries.

There is yet another challenge in this highly volatile environment. The future of technology in the classrooms depends on the demands of the labour market as learning environments is increasingly tailored to suit the demands of industries. Everyone will benefit from the upgradation in technology provided educational institutions buckle up and make teaching and learning technologically-oriented. In essence, the institutions will have to prepare students for the relevant requirements and exposure at the workplace. The mismatch between actual teaching and nature of work at the workplace must narrow down. This is yet another challenge which the universities and colleges must be aware of while framing the syllabus and designing the curriculum.

In a technology-supported learning environment, teaching can be made effective with the use of technology. Such digital technology systems of imparting education has to be made capable of serving the content of courses to the learner. Such an innovative system backed up by technology has to invariably recognize the learning preferences of individual students. Also, the teaching methodologies and instructional objectives must focus on one's learning capabilities. A teacher has to understand the different methods by which students learn a subject and adopt suitable media, tools, methodologies and technologies that are compatible with and supportive of the learning process. The usual methods chosen by a student to assimilate an idea are: aural, visual, reading, writing and kinesthetic. Teachers must be aware of the nuances of these methods for effectively imparting knowledge. Ranjana Bhatia (2011) observd: "According to a study conducted by K. Gulati, S. Dang (2011) on teachers' perspective, their awareness level of specific technology and the roles this technology plays, it was found that many teachers lacked a functional computer literacy foundation upon which to build new technology and skills. The study revealed that the teachers had low level of technological knowledge and computers and related technologies have not been a part of their own educational environment. Data suggests that teachers in India need to be increasingly encouraged to explore the emerging technologies for teaching."

In some prominent centers of learning, students are able to obtain a truly global education with the introduction of Tele Presence technology in their classrooms. This is primarily a video conferencing technology, which can host up in many countries simultaneously. Those students will have access to teachers of erudition and exceptional qualities from around the world. Under this system the education center can offer the best courses in their classrooms. In some campuses, students are trained on the effective use of iPad to address the academic elements of learning by integrating textbooks, case studies, and other course materials, onto this device. In terms of using the iPad, some universities and colleges have adopted even mobile applications, like sending alerts to students.

It is a truism that new skills—technical, intellectual, and social—are becoming essential for participating actively in a knowledge society. While their scope extends well beyond "digital literacy," they are the basis on which the society depends. (European Commission, 2001) The ability to use ICT is essential in many sectors. *A European Reference Framework* (European

Commission, 2005) sets out the eight key competencies, which would be interesting to note, especially for the academics. They are: Communication in the mother tongue, Communication in the foreign languages, Mathematical competence and basic competencies in science and technology, Digital competence, Learning to learn, Interpersonal, intercultural and social competencies and civic competencies, Entrepreneurship; and Cultural expression. These competencies have been handpicked by this important body after contemplating over the future prospects of the citizens of European countries. They could be chosen as a model by all the countries in the world to stimulate growth of educational institutions and foster economic growth by providing the right opportunities to survive and prosper in a competitive global environment.

In a country like the UK, where they take pride in the fact that they have had several top ranking universities in the world for centuries, many middle-ranking universities face bankruptcy and are being forced to close or merge unless they embrace radical new teaching models using online learning. In the US, which has been maintaining iconic institutions for pretty long time, moves by leading colleges to publish their courses free online will rapidly make traditional campus universities out of date unless they reinvent how they operate. Sir Michael Barber has predicted that the traditional university lecture would be overtaken by new technology within a decade.

In *The Uses of the University*, MClark Kerr firmly states that higher education has become a preparatory ground for mid-career advancement which is bound to become more important as occupational skill levels continue to rise and the high skill occupations multiply. In the process, higher education will become less of an isolated institution and will be integrated into all individual and social life.

Authors like Gardner have come out with newer theories stating that students can use eight types of intelligence while learning, viz., verbal-linguistic, mathematical-logical, musical, visual-spatial, bodily-kinesthetic, inter-personal, intra-personal and naturalistic. Only an efficient teacher will be able to easily judge the different capabilities of a student in relation to the particular multiple intelligence skill in which he is proficient. Off late, proper pedagogy supported by technology has developed to meet the needs of different areas of multiple intelligence of the student, and teachers feel comfortable with the use of relevant educational technology and modern methodologies of teaching.

It has become imperative on the part of universities to integrate computer technology into curricula. They take the initiative via the Staff Training Institutes/Colleges to introduce professional development programmes in educational technology to ensure that ICT-enabled teaching is put to better use in universities and colleges with a view to enhancing the quality and standards of education. It has been proven that the closer the relationships between the syllabus, curriculum, course and well-designed classroom activities is with the new breed of learning technologies, the more effective is the learning environment for students.

It would be appropriate to assess the strengths and weaknesses of curriculum, especially to find out whether students are able to build their basic general competence and discipline-specific competence. It is in this context that the blending of technology-supported systems with the traditional system becomes relevant to get the best results in a classroom environment. But, in all such situations, priority has to be given to acquiring new knowledge, new skills and competence, without which students will not be fully equipped for employment in diverse work environments. Hence, teachers are expected to gain confidence in handling classes by using modern educational technologies and using technology collaboratively to develop the contents.

Getting technology tools into the hands of every student has become a standard practice at all reputed institutions all over the world. Most of the leading centers in higher education are helping their students to gain from the benefits of technology on the campus. Today, students bring laptops to the classroom and use technology to complete assignments. Institutions or teachers post the syllabi online and students take notes using laptops; most of them do not use pens and papers in the classrooms. Some smart teachers do conduct internet research from the classroom while engaging classes, if needed. The use of technology in the classrooms by the students has to be decided by the respective teacher. Modern colleges and universities are also implementing programmes that use technology to take standard practices to a new level. They extend their guidance to industries to adapt to newer technological advancements. If a country lags in the quality of teaching made available in the classrooms and in using appropriate educational technology, its young people will lose a variety of opportunities to grow and excel in a competitive world. The students are to be simultaneously exposed to excellent teaching and to the use of modern gadgets of educational technology. There is strong evidence that the more effective the academic instructions are and the better the use of technology, the better will be the performance of students. The moot point is that the student community should not be denied the enormous benefits of modern technology due to the sluggish and negative attitude of the administrators or policy makers in education. The more integrated and aligned pedagogy and technology are the more productive the educational environment becomes. Moreover, "rapid changes in information and communication technology require regular redefinition of literacy" (Karen Bromley, 2006). In this ever-changing educational scenario, where the speed of change of these new educational technologies has become mind-blogging, it is the teacher, with the support of administration, who can take initiative to set the new trend and bring about a world of difference on the campuses by making the best use of technology. Donald Kennedy (1997) reminds us of the need for adapting to the technological changes: Institutions and individuals will also have to adapt to the revolution brought about by computer technology, which has radically revised the way in which data and information are stored, retrieved, and communicated. Scientific communication, including publication, has been transformed by the Internet. Educational software is proliferating, and plays a significant role in instruction now.

The Enterprise Resource Planning (ERP) Solutions which were first used in manufacturing industries are now used in human resource management, and in the administration of higher educational institutions to not only monitor their functions but also the progress of teachers as well as students.

The purpose of Enterprise Resource Planning Solutions is to replace the existing administration-computer system by one that is more responsive to the needs of an ever-changing educational system. It is a software solution that integrates information and processes to enable information to enter into the system so that it may be shared throughout the institution. One of the main advantages of ERP in educational institutions is to improve access to information so as to provide a strong foundation to generate a data warehouse which can be used for improving both academic and administrative practices. It can assist in improving workflow and efficiency, thereby to improve the work environment. Teachers can keep track of the conduct of their classes, especially the completion of lessons and other duties assigned to them and report to their superiors about the targets attained during an academic session. Before incorporating ERP Solutions into an educational system, a detailed need-assessment and definition of requirements are to be conducted. A phased implementation plan has to be considered. If this new system is introduced in the educational institution all of a sudden, it shoots up costs to a considerable extent.

In the twenty-first century, teachers are necessitated by the forces of development in educational environment to make critical choices in their products and techniques. Educational technology is considered a timely and wise response to these needs. "Educational Technology is a systematic process of developing solutions to problems of teaching and learning. It entails analysis of educational aims followed by the design, production, field testing, evaluation and revision of programmes to achieve these aims." The teachers have to become the trail blazers to take advantage of these technological innovations.

PART II

12

Reforms in Institutions of Higher Education and their Ranking

We live in a moment of history
where change is so speeded up
that we begin to see the present
only when it is already disappearing.

—R.D. Laing

Need for Timely Reforms in Education

Global attention to various quality issues in the realm of higher education has reached an unprecedented level as nations prepare themselves to achieve higher economic growth. Advancing educational quality and productivity has become the priorities of developed and developing countries. Policy makers in different countries are aware of the correlation between educational quality and economic growth. They try to allocate sufficient funds to the higher education institutions to bring out the necessary positive changes for growth and development, especially to meet the increasing demands of the new generation which is prone to economic vicissitudes and imperfections of the educational system. Education reforms are a part and parcel of development in the modern systems of higher education in all nations irrespective of their political and economic outlook. People have a very critical view of the survival of higher education institutions. They are committed to a set of values and to a system of education that provides them the opportunities to develop their minds to full capacity. Such people have as a basic idea that education is important not only because of what it contributes to one's career goals but also because of the value it adds to the quality of one's life. Education can rebuild any economy in a balanced, sustainable and responsible way, and bring hope and contentment to the younger generation. To put in a nutshell, education can make things happen.

The need and dynamics of global teaching reforms have been captured by Maria Teresa Tatto and David N. Plank (2007) in the following observations:

> "Around the world, governments have increasingly come to regard education as the key to economic success. National boundaries and

> regulations are less and less significant in an increasingly integrated global economy characterized by high capital mobility, where workers find themselves in competition not only with their fellow citizens but also with their counterparts in other countries. The impact of globalization is further reinforced by the steady move toward an economy based on the control and exchange of information rather than the local production of goods and services. Under these economic circumstances, the race to occupy the high ground in the international division of labour is intensely competitive, and the ability to keep up is presumed to depend to an ever-growing extent on the quality of the national labour force. The importance that policy-makers assign to education has been further intensified by the advent of internationally comparable assessments of student performance, including TIMSS and its predecessors, and now PISA. Results from these assessments allow governments to compare the performance of their students with the performance of students in other countries."

The administration of institutions of higher education has become a formidable task as expectations are getting higher and more complex. Donald Kennedy (1997) explains this point thus: "Managing a university is harder and more consuming work than it once was. Institutions of higher education are complicated places, with more constituencies, more government involvement, and more stress." On educational reforms, Kennedy states that reform in undergraduate education has a deep and more philosophical side. Particularly in the most selective and rigorous undergraduate programmes, the academic "atmosphere" is intensely competitive." Teachers, non-teaching staff, students, managements, parents, government, regulatory bodies, funding agencies, accreditation agencies and collaborating agencies or institutions are the usual stakeholders in a broad sense. Each of these stakeholders has different expectations, interests and views about the function of the universities and colleges.

The UNESCO Report on Education clearly delineates the major functions of universities thus:

1. To prepare students for research and teaching,
2. To provide highly specialized training courses adapted to the needs of economic and social life,
3. To be open to all, so as to cater for the many aspects of lifelong education in the widest sense,
4. International co-operation.

It would be desirable for nations to follow these broad guidelines as the ultimate objectives of educational reforms in higher education. The recommendations of the UNESCO Report on Education, insists on the need to take cognizance of the key role played by teachers in the building of an educational institution. The Report states that in any event, no reform can succeed without the co-operation and active participation of teachers. This is one reason why the Commission recommends that the social, cultural and material status of educators should be considered a matter of priority.

Internationalization of Higher Education

The influence of internationalization of higher education, being a reality, has made its impact global in the knowledge-based societies. As Roger Goodman and David Phillips observe:

> "Globalization permeates higher education. As societies become globalized, higher education is also exposed to global standards. Great attention has been recently given to the quality of education and research, as well as competitiveness in the market. Globalization has been accelerated in knowledge-based societies with highly advanced information and communication technologies. Internationalization has been seen as a process which is responsive to globalization. de Wit (2000) and Vander Wende (2001) point out two paradigms in internationalization: competition and cooperation. Interestingly, both international cooperation and international competition occur in the context of globalization; they are two competing but co-existing dynamics."

Jane Green, (2011), reminds us of the impact of changes on higher education in the UK: The 1980's can be pinpointed as the high point also for managerialism to establish itself within higher education policy: from the first Thatcher cuts to the Jarrett Report on efficiency. "By the 1990's the metamorphosis of one concept of educational accountability into another was nearly complete…Then, soon after, with the publication of performance–('league') tables of examination results, there finally emerged a concept of educational accountability, attuned to the new 'quasi' market culture. In line with neo-liberal thinking, parents were to select schools, based on 'informed choice'. As the 'marketization'of education gained ground, parents were conceived as proxy clients acting on behalf of their children–the new 'consumers'.

From there onwards explicit standards for educational institutions were set along with the criteria for performance evaluation, the need for continuing professional development and such other control mechanisms in the UK.

Globalization, in general, is the flow of technology, knowledge, people, values, ideas, capital, goods, and services across national borders. It affects each country in a different way due to the nation's individual history, traditions, culture, and priorities (Knight, 2004). Contrary to widespread perception, internationalization of higher education did not, in reality, require standardization or homogenization of curriculum and the dilution of indigenous knowledge. Instead the system involved incorporating the unique strengths of various institutions for holistic development. The collaboration among universities was required for scientific growth, for developing social responsibility, and for producing students who were well-prepared to live in a more interconnected world (Knight, 2012). In Kemal Guruz's words, "the interdependent effects of globalization, technology, competition and forms of social and economic organizations are reshaping all aspects of international relations. A global higher education market has emerged that provides a much wider array of choices to today's e-literate youth, the children of parents educated in the past century's massified national education systems." He adds that, technology now makes it possible to tap into labour resources anywhere in the world without displacing people from one cultural environment to another. In the last decade, China and India have made use of the opportunities provided by trends toward outsourcing and offshoring to develop their people's skills and improve their standard of living. The most significant obstacle they face for further growth is the quality of their higher education systems. This is a common problem for many countries while integrating into the global knowledge economy and sharing its benefits.

The priorities of a nation for growth and development are typically and forcefully reflected in its education systems and reforms. When a country is subject to major societal shift—political, demographic, or economic—it focuses attention on its education system and seeks to 'reform' it so that it becomes more consistent with the changing societal context. Similarly, when drastic changes take place in the international arena which create repercussions all over the world in the field of education and employment, nation states are forced to face the new economic and social realities so as to benefit from the emerging newer technologies and innovative practices.

All countries have to take decisions on resource allocation, the quality of educational opportunities across diverse populations, access to higher education, students' testing and tracking, teacher accountability, school choice and innovation. These decisions, in turn, have a significant impact on students' educational experiences and on the distribution of educational opportunities across different population groups in the society. What a country does also affects educators' working conditions, and therefore, makes a difference in its ability to attract and retain qualified educators needed to maintain academic standards (Roger Goodman and David Phillips, 2003).

Educational leadership is taken seriously across the globe. There are now a considerable number of initiatives for its development in places as diverse as Canada, the UK, Sweden, the USA, Singapore, Hong Kong, and Australasia

(Bush and Jackson, 2002; Brundrett, 2002). It need not be mentioned here that these are some of the countries which produce top-notch institutions in the world now. In Canada, education policy, including that of higher education, is constitutionally the responsibility of each respective provincial government. Higher education is dominated mostly by public sector universities and colleges. Even though there are some private colleges, the involvement of government in providing equal opportunities to citizens is unique and unparalleled.

One has to appreciate the efforts of the UAE to bring laudable and drastic changes in its educational scenario. Within a short span of time, they have been successful in providing world-class education to its citizens due to their exceptional discernment and judgement in perceiving and implementing the right solutions. They have constituted several important authorities to oversee the development of education at all levels. The Ministry of Higher Education and Scientific Research of the UAE, the Abu Dhabi Education Council, the Knowledge and Human Development Authority in Dubai are some of the important authorities in the UAE which have been playing a key role in shaping the destiny of education. In their pursuit of excellence, they have been fulfilling the daunting task of maintaining international standards. In many of their educational institutions, they not only cater to the educational requirements of the local populace but also of a global community of expatriates. The relentless efforts put in by the Dubai Schools Inspection Bureau to ensure benchmarks of excellence in a large number of schools merit attention. Dubai is implementing an internationally acclaimed accreditation policy in the higher education institutions.

Here is yet another convincing explanation with regard to nations to prepare themselves to meet the challenges of competitive environments. William K. Cummings, (2003) states that the increase in global competition places pressures on localities and individuals to keep abreast of new developments and to prepare them for learning. Of particular importance in the new competitive environment is the ability of localities to gain an edge in some areas of high technology production. Those who can look ahead are likely to stay ahead, while those who ignore the new competition are destined to face hard times.

Every country faces a historical compulsion to herald a nationwide campaign for upgrading its educational system to meet the demands of an ever-changing world. For instance, the American psyche reverberating from the shockwave generated by the 1957 launch of the world's first artificial satellite, Sputnik, by the Soviet Union, decided to upgrade its educational systems at all levels. Americans were at that point of time wondering why such a great nation had not led the world into space, blaming America's schools, which had fallen down in producing citizens proficient in science and mathematics and able to defend democracy at home and abroad (Catherine Reef, 2009). The US institutions from that time onwards concentrated on developing core competence in their centers of higher education. Now they take pride in the fact that they have been able to create the most reputable universities in the world. The US has always been a pioneer in higher education with the largest number of top 100 universities in the world. The US dominates with 7 universities in the top ten, and a staggering 45 in the total rankings. The UK, which holds the second position, felt the need to upgrade her educational systems, back in 1980's, wherein she plunged into a period of rapid educational development by spearheading pragmatic reforms, especially in higher education.

Harvard, the Massachusetts Institute of Technology, and the University of Cambridge are currently in the top positions in the list of the top 100 universities in the world. Oxford comes fourth, up from the sixth position last year, leaving UK with nine universities in the top 100, down from 11 in 2011. The global reputation of the UK's leading universities remains strong with seven ranked in the top 100 universities in the world.

In Canada, the Ontario Government established the College Standards and Accreditation Council in 1993. The purpose of CSAC was to establish learning outcome standards for all college programmes and assess each programme to determine its standards (*Academic Transformation*, 2009).

Nations are investing heavily and restructuring their economies to create high-skill, high-paying jobs in knowledge-intensive areas such as new technologies, financial services, trade and professional and technical services. From Paris to San Diego, Bangalore to Shanghai, there is growing recognition throughout the world that economic prosperity and social well-being in a global, knowledge-driven economy require investment in knowledge resources. That is, every region must create and sustain highly educated and innovative workforce and the capacity to generate and apply new knowledge, supported through policies and investments in developing human capital, technological innovation, and entrepreneurial skill (Council on Competitiveness, 2004) *The Globalization of Higher Education*, 2008). Indeed, the impact of such restructuring of the economy of a country will be reflected in the policy changes related to the introduction of reforms in higher education.

A land of contradictions, China is the world's largest developing country. It supports the largest and, in many ways, one of the world's most effective education systems, according to Roger Goodman and David Phillips, (2003). It is expanding its higher education system faster than most other countries in the world. Striking changes have taken place since 1980's in its higher education curriculum that reflect both the personnel needs of a rapidly changing economy and rising social demand in certain popular areas. Between 1950' to early 1980's, there were very limited education opportunities in China, and only a small number of people had access to higher education. However, the curriculum, teaching materials and management systems were gradually improved to contribute to provide the talents urgently needed by the nation. Since the 1980' China has experienced a period of sustained economic growth and rapid social development. With the shift from the controlled to market economy, the industrial structure and mode of production have undergone comprehensive changes. During this period of transition, its education has also undergone comprehensive reforms involving its philosophy, system, structure, staff and curriculum Wanda Rokicka (ed), (1999). A World Bank Country Study conducted in 1997, reveals that China had initiated "a strategy to improve the internal efficiency and therefore the performance and quality of higher education institutions by (a) developing a curriculum that is both internally coherent as well as externally responsive to labour market changes; (b) enhancing teaching and research activities, while setting up processes to attract and retain qualified and experienced staff and monitoring equity issues in relation to women and minority faculty members; (c) institutionalizing quality assurance practices in order to meet agreed quality criteria, by reinforcing and extending fledgling accreditation practices, linking monetary and non-monetary incentives to good performance, and (d) instituting and sustaining structures and procedures that enables institutions to maintain levels of educational inputs (books, equipments, and other instructional materials, and facilities relevant to national norms)."

In addition, the Chinese educational policy makers supported strategies for professional development of teachers by encouraging them to qualify for further degrees through in-service programmes; developing training plans for enhancing teaching and research skills; giving the young teachers priority to attend international conferences; and providing access to publications, including theses and research articles. China, by 1985, took a bold decision to ensure quality assurance in the higher education institutions. This important step initiated in the accreditation process was known in Chinese as "ping-gu". It's interesting to note that common to all quality assurance practices are the following elements:

> "(a) the development of standards; (b) the application of those standards to a programme or institution by third parties for the purpose of assessment and enhancement; and (c) the subsequent improvement of the educational entity."

Like the Chinese objectives of accreditation of institutions in higher education, in India the institutions undergo a self-evaluation process and later invite a national level accreditation body to conduct a Peer Team visit, which basically analyzes their strengths and weaknesses. This Peer Team ranks the institution in accordance with their performance based on specific criteria decided by the national level assessment and accreditation body.

In South-East Asia, the countries like Indonesia, Thailand, Philippines, Singapore, Malaysia, Vietnam, Brunei and Cambodia have become quality-conscious in their approach to higher education. They promote academic quality for greater effectiveness and quality consistent with international standards, and have made internal quality assurance mandatory for the education administration process. Most of these countries have become members of the ASEAN Quality Accreditation Network or the Asia Pacific Quality Network or that of other international Network for Quality Assurance organizations or international agencies in Higher Education.

The basic purpose of conducting any national level assessment of the performance of higher education institutions is to improve the standard and quality of higher education. It goes beyond doubt that it is the teachers who can play an important role in enhancing the standard and quality of education in the respective institutions they serve.

"Recent studies by economists indicate that the social rate of return from investments in new industrial technology in developed countries seems to be high (20 to 30%) and that technological change in many industries and increased output of society have been based on recent academic research." (Mansfield, 1994). This study indicates the dominant role played by higher education to empower the citizens of a country to achieve higher standards of living, which is possible only if appropriate economic growth is ensured for which positive contributions from the academic community is a *sine quo non*. "A typical definition of human resources or human capital from an economist's perspective is Harbison's (1984): the numbers of persons who have the skills, education, and experience which are critical for the economic and political development of a country." Hence, to ensure proper economic development and growth, educators are expected to bring about effective changes in the education system by totally revamping the pedagogical practices and inputs by making them flexible and broad-based to meet the demands of an ever-changing economic scenario which functions in a global environment.

It is seen that in most developed and developing countries, assessment and accreditation process in higher education is rigorous and highly focused, based on explicit criteria and well-conceived methodologies. In countries like China, academic affairs are given high priority which makes them constantly improve upon the existing systems of higher education, whether it is the curriculum reform and planning or credit system or upgrade the quality of teachers or upgrade learning and research facilities.

Here is an observation by Jeffrey J. Selingo (2013) regarding the trans-pollination of educational cultures across the continents:

> "The best of American higher education remains a world leader. When I travelled with college leaders in recent years to Saudi Arabia and India, I was struck by how officials in both countries admired American universities. Saudi Arabia, by partnering with colleges here and sending thousands of students to the United States each year, wants to essentially buy the system; India wants to copy it by building its own collection of colleges. Both countries, along with China, remain behind the United States, but are catching up at a rapid clip."

The following data reveals the characteristics of international student mobility in today's global knowledge economy. In 2006, there were 2.75 million foreign students worldwide. The five major host countries were the United States, Australia, The United Kingdom, France, and Germany, which together hosted just over 50 per cent of the foreign students in the world. China and India are the two leading countries of origin of foreign students. (Kemal Guruz, 2011)

Most countries constitute university-industry consultative committees to identify the labour market needs, specialized knowledge and skills required and opportunities for placement. They recommend redesigning of courses to meet emerging requirements so as to enhance the skills of the graduates for ensuring their employability. Importance is also laid in institutions of higher learning to provide a solid foundation for students to build their future careers by enabling them to participate in workshops and seminars in career guidance, visit industrial centers and exchange ideas with the professionals in industry. Such exercises provide students basic ideas to relate their academic experience to real jobs in the labour market and motivate them to become career-oriented. The following narration will give a brief idea as to how theory and practice could be blended by having partnership between educational institution and industry.

Co-operative education is a model of academy-industry co-operation that allows students to acquire a broad-based, general education and discipline-specific work experience at the same time. The combination is popular with students, and the demand for cooperative programmes continues to grow. Co-operation is a form of continuous contextualized learning (Grosjean, 1999) that allows students to move between the classroom and the workplace contexts. Academic learning is operationalized when students undertake relevant, paid employment on a work term. Work experience is theorized when students bring their on-the-job learning back to the classroom for further analysis and reflection. In its most basic form, a co-operative programme allows students to spend a semester in the classroom to develop theoretical knowledge, followed by a semester in the workplace to implement the theory and develop skills in practical application, before returning once again to the classroom to engage in further academic study….Co-operative programmes may either be voluntary or mandatory (*Student Affairs*: *Experiencing Higher Education*, 2004).

The reforms in higher education, particularly of undergraduate education, are essential requirements not only to improve the quality of educational institutions but also to facilitate employment opportunities. Michael Tomlinson, (2013) states that employability is not just about getting a job. Conversely, just because a student is on a vocational course, it does not mean that he will automatically get employed. Employability is more than about developing attributes, techniques or experience just to enable a student to get a job, or to progress within a current career. It is about learning and the emphasis is less on "employ" and more on "ability". In essence, the emphasis is on developing critical, reflective abilities, with a view to empowering and enhancing the learner (Harvey, 2003). Our universities and colleges are expected to develop these critical abilities in students to help them to obtain jobs in their own countries or elsewhere.

In Japan, for instance, there is a remarkable close relationship between education and the economy. The fast growth of the Japanese economy for a long period has been attributed to the rich contributions made by its centers of higher education. Japan has emerged as a technological power in Asia, way ahead of other Asian countries, due to her ability to use technology up to the hilt in pedagogical practices and institutionalizing the best practices to empower the centers of high education to meet the demands of not only challenges posed by an fast emerging economy but also to develop international competitiveness.

Many advanced countries in the world have already proven a high correlation between education and economic development. In *Higher Education and National Development* (2007), a UK government report estimated that, nationally, universities generated directly and indirectly over 34.8 billion pounds of output and over 562,000 full-time equivalent jobs throughout the economy (DfES 2003). With a total income of 12.8 billion pounds, higher education is a bigger industry than advertising or air transport. In the UK and elsewhere, governments encourage closer partnerships between higher education and business, with a view to more fluent application of higher education research into the business community. Universities themselves illustrate two contrasting paradigms: the university as a detached sanctuary of science, and the university as a market-oriented enterprise (Buchbinder, 1993; Davies, 1996.). The mission, management, and consequently the knowledge generated by these two kinds will differ. (OECD, 1999).

It cannot be denied that success stories of economic development in all these countries provide compelling testimony to the fundamental and positive contributions that a modern educational system can make to empower nations in a global environment. In Singapore, the government is negotiating a change in generations by encouraging the new generation with the internet and social media, and has access to the whole world of opportunities. In Australia, the assessment of higher education institutions expects all research to be benchmarked against national and international standards.

Australian universities continue to pursue ambitious and distinctive strategies in the international education domain. The University of New South Wales (UNSW), for example, announced that it had received the approval of the Singapore Government to establish a campus in Singapore, one of only three foreign universities to be permitted to do so. The UNSW spent almost A$ 100 million to establish the campus, which opened to students in 2007. It took five years to break-even. It initially enrolled 3500 students from Singapore and nearby countries including China, India, Indonesia and received A$ 130 million in fees by 2015.

In March, 2013, the US universities decried requester as grant reductions might starve the essential funding for research. About $30 billion a year flows from Washington to universities for research and development in fields of agriculture to agro-physics, apart from other sources. It is this largesse that has enabled some of the prestigious universities in the US to reach such high standards of excellence and thereby become the envy of the world. It was thought that the cuts in grants would stifle the growth and development of all centres of higher education. But, it has to be noted that in the US, universities and colleges are able to raise huge funds from private donations like the alumni, corporations, foundations and individuals. However, if the governments do not provide appropriate budgetary provisions for the support and growth of higher education institutions, they will face devastating consequences.

If we look at the African continent, we find that, barring a few countries, it is still underdeveloped in the field of education, "By international standards Africa is the least developed region in terms of higher education and enrollments. It will be extremely difficult—perhaps even impossible—for Africa to compete effectively in a world dominated by knowledge and information unless it consciously, persistently, and vigorously overhauls its potentials and its most crucial institutions" (*African Higher Education—An International Reference Book*, edited by Damtew Tefferra and Philip G Altbach, 2003). Diambomba (1989) suggests that the key factors for the inefficiency of higher education in Africa have been inadequate links between universities and job markets, imbalances between enrolments in specific disciplines, and finally the lack of appropriate training for the skills needed in the labour market (Zaghloul Morsy, Philip G. Altbach, 1996). These observations are applicable to other countries as well that do not pay attention to this most defining component in economic development of a country. It is high time that they face the crisis in higher education boldly, and take pivotal decisions to introduce drastic changes for its improvement. Educationalists world over expect a profound change in the offing in the higher education system in such countries. It's a truism that a country that neglects education at any level will do so at its own peril.

Indian educational history dates back over 5000 years. Indian scriptures professed education as an emancipating and liberating force, a process that manifests 'perfection' already inherent in man (Marmar Mukhopadhyay, 2005). The ancient centers of higher learning, like Taxila, Nalanda, Vikramasila, Valabhi, Jagaddala, Kanchipuram, Odantapuri, etc., were the illustrious universities of India which attracted not only students from distant places but also renowned scholars from far and wide. The fame of these universities as seats of learning was mainly derived from its teachers of eminence and from their tutorial approach, which is considered in the modern times as one of the most effective ways to impart education. These centers of learning served as great intellectual and cultural centers of India which had enriched the Indian culture and society for centuries. (Kanaur V. Chandras, 1977). In 2007, three universities in India celebrated sesquicentenary of their existence. It was in 1857 that the first three modern universities were established in the country—at Bombay (now Mumbai) Calcutta (now Kolkata) and Madras (now Chennai)—following Thomas Babington Macaulay's Minute (of 2nd February 1835) and its reaffirmation in the Dispatch by Charles Woods (of 19th July, 1854) and the recommendation of a Committee (appointed on 26 January 1855) Ashby and Anderson 1966.) At present, even though there are many illustrious universities in India, they have yet to improve their quality considerably to reach international standards in their performance to be the toppers in the world. One major problem is that a large number of fresh graduates are not employable as there is a disconnect between what they have learnt and what they have to do at the workplace. The point is clarified in the works of Fred Lazin, Matt Evans and N. Jayaram (2010): The conventional system in India, confronting as it is with a systematic crisis, has not been capable of introducing any significant educational innovation or effectively implementing any educational reform….The Indian university system is extraordinarily rigid and pronouncedly resistant to change. The impetus to change does not come from within the system. When experiments or innovations are introduced from outside, they are resisted; if enforced, they are ritualized. … The lack of link between conventional courses and the job market seems to have become too apparent to students and their parents.

Universities of repute, all over the world, have been laying great emphasis on research activities, and they support such positive, decisive and prime efforts initiated by the teachers. In India, in general, there is a dearth of research output and publications. The words of Prof. V.C. Kulandai Swamy, 1991, former vice-chancellor of the Indira Gandhi National Open University, speaks volume about the necessity to develop the research potential in our universities and colleges:

"In all advanced countries basic and applied research are carried out in a large measure in educational institutions. The strength of educational institutions in research lies not so much in the expertise and the creativity of the faculty, though it is a major factor, but in the fact that the university has a successive steam of young minds, that pass through the system like a flowing stream of fresh water and the probability of one coming across flashes of genius and creative talent is very high in the university environment. However, we have in India, a situation where university research accounts for a small fraction of the total allocation for research. There is tremendous scope for further development of research potential in our universities. It needs again an enlightened research policy and the university community must provide the necessary guidance and grounds for a policy change."

In the current scenario of higher education, publications of books and journals play a dominant role in the spread of knowledge. It has been found that the cost of most of the scholarly publications is unaffordable to a large section of academicians. To surmount the problem of high cost of such publications, the Open Access Initiative provides a lot of relief to the teachers who are interested in research. The basic purpose of this academic initiative is to provide facilities for knowledge dissemination through the internet at a lesser cost. This system also facilitates open institutional repository or subject-based repository, which extends considerable opportunities to teachers as a fast growing archive for research articles. Even though this innovative practice is of great boon to the academic community, according to Leslie Chan (2012), of the close to 600 higher education institutions across India, fewer than 100 have an existing institutional repository, though many are in the planning stage.

Pooja Singh (2011) has voiced her concern about the deficiencies of the university system in India, which require substantial improvement. Some of the problems which she has raised need to be addressed by the policy makers in higher education, viz., the curricula, which have remained almost unchanged for decades; learning and creativity which are at discount in a system of assessment that places a premium on memory rather than on understanding; classes scheduled in the time table are not held and results are often declared with a time-lag of 6-12 months; the infrastructure is not only inadequate but also on the verge of collapse; the importance attached to research has eroded; the boundaries between academic disciplines have become dividing walls which prohibit the entry of new disciplines.

There are several studies conducted to highlight the importance of internationalization of higher education and improve the quality of education in universities in India. Sobhana N. (2009) has summarized her views thus: Globalization has many advantages, particularly for India, which has a large educational system and infrastructure and diverse human capabilities. D.V. Singh (2007), stressed the need for globalization of education services in the context of GATS (General Agreement on Trade in Services). Ashok Misra (2007), has also emphasized the need for globalization in higher technical education in India. R. Natarajan (2009) has highlighted the importance of globalization of engineering education which has emerged as an important contemporary issue in India. M. Adithan, B.V.A. Rao and D.P. Kothari (2009) assert that India can no longer remain in isolation with respect to its higher education, both in terms of its quality and the diversity of students passing out of the system. The quality of graduates coming out of the portals of our universities and other higher educational institutions should be considered at par with that of USA, European and other western countries. Globalization of higher education, in particular engineering education, is needed to realize it. Shaikh Saleem and Vidya Gawali (2009), have remarked that the role of higher education has aroused policy debates across the globe due to the increased recognition of higher-level skills and competence as essential to national development—especially in the context of globalization and the shift towards knowledge economies. Countries at every level of development have important national policy priorities related to higher education and need engineers and scientists to lead innovation. But the fourth largest economy in the world—India—is lagging behind in educational sector. According to Assocham Eco Pulse Study, 2008 on Comparative Study of Emerging Economies on 'Quality of Education', Russia has emerged as the frontrunner in the quality of education parameter amongst seven largest emerging economies of the world with the average GDP growth rate of 6.3 per cent. On the other hand, India has been lagging far behind in the race as it ranks at the sixth place with the score points 3.3 on the scale of 10. If we compare educational sector of India, especially higher education sector, with other countries in terms of expenditure, gross enrollment ratio, number of universities, etc., the picture is even worse. Raju Narayana Swamy (2013) has remarked that in India, there are relatively few high quality higher education institutions. These world class institutions are mainly limited to the Indian Institute of Technology (IITs), the IIMs, and few others. They enroll below one per cent of the student population in India.

Anjaney Kumar Pandey and Sanjaya Kumar Das (2009) caution us thus. The present higher education system suffers from several weaknesses, such as proliferation of substandard institutions, failure to maintain academic calendar, outdated curriculum, disparities in the quality of education and lack of adequate support for research. The marked deterioration of standards in teaching and examinations and the increasing dissatisfaction with the conduct of the university administration and elections of university authorities continue to be a matter of great concern for the last six decades. The content and quality of higher education in many areas are inadequate for our present needs and future requirements, and compare unfavourably with the average standards in other educationally advanced countries. What is worse, this large gap between the standards in our country and those in other advanced countries is widening rapidly. Unless we ensure the highest standards of teaching in our universities, our degrees will not command recognition and respect either in our own country or abroad. The average standard of our degrees still remains on the low side (Kothari Commission, 1964). The courses offered by many universities have remained archaic, rigid and irrelevant to contemporary as well as emerging needs (Gopalan, 1995). In terms of publications of scientific research in the world, India ranked eighth during 1980's, slipped to 13 during 1990's and has nosedived to 21st position in the new millennium (Srivastava, 2005). The following are some of the observations on quality of research (Rais Ahmed & Madhulka Rakesh, 2000).

- Seventy eight per cent of the supervisors felt that hardly any thesis had any intellectual contribution.
- Sixty per cent of supervisors admitted that the work was a mere repetition of known phenomenon by known methods.
- Only thirty per cent of thesis were considered good.
- Seventy per cent of students work in isolation and do not interact with other researchers doing similar work in other institutions/ universities.
- Eighty per cent of applied research is often trivial, mediocre and without any intellectual input.

It would be appropriate to air the views of Radhakrishnan Commission on University Education, (1948-49):

> "The most important and urgent reform needed in education is to transform it, to endeavor to relate it to the life, needs and aspirations of the people and thereby make it the powerful instrument of social, economic and cultural transformation necessary for the realization of the national goals. For this purpose, education should be developed so as to increase productivity, achieve social and national integration, accelerate the process of modernization and cultivate social, moral and spiritual values."

The following observation by Hemant K. Panda, (2013), explains the failure of Indian higher education system in enabling millions of youngsters to obtain employment:

> With the dwindling job opportunities in government sectors and, increasingly encouraging environment in private sectors, there is a paradigm shift in intellectual thoughts with regard to not only the

> designing of proper courses to cater to the need of the hour, but also revisiting the convent-oral course delivery system itself. Higher education in India, lately adds more than three-and–half lakh engineers and twenty- five lakh university graduates annually to the country's technical workforce, yet … about 5 million graduates remain unemployed, grossly attributed to their ill-preparedness for the market, amongst others, rendering them professionally unworthy. The efforts at the policy-making level have been inadequate to address the malady. Historically, Indian students are brilliant as per global standards, but their scholar-to-professional transition seems much lower compared to their counterparts in the developed countries.

The following comments by J.N. Chowdhary (2012), suggest that universities in India must rise to the occasion to provide academic support to enhance the employability skills of the students:

> "Higher education sector is characterized by diversity; course and student profiles are different and universities aim to develop students with distinct characteristics or attributes. Universities are required to work in developing employability skills in their students by providing academic staff with relevant support and resources, integrating these skills into curriculum and course design, providing students with work placements and exposure to professional settings and providing advice and guidance through career services."

Pawan Agarwal (2009) comments on how to build cautiously the higher education institutions in India: The country has a unique opportunity to convert demographic surplus to its economic strength. This would require the creation of a competitive environment in higher education that ensures that both public and private institutions develop and become responsive and innovative. This may require radical changes and comprehensive reforms. However, considering the nature of Indian polity and society, strategic intervention with an incremental approach would be the best way forward.

We may look into what went wrong in the performance of higher education institutions in the largest democracy in the world. The reasons are many and varied—the GER (Gross Enrolment Rate) is much below the world average as well as that of the emerging countries like Brazil, Russia and China; lack of research orientation and quality research output; dearth of high quality teachers; poor rate of accredited institutions by the National Assessment and Accreditation Council; low standard of facilities provided and inefficient administration.

If one looks into the history of university colleges in the international context of the higher education system, "the first university colleges appeared in Paris, at the end of the twelfth century. These were nothing more than modest pious foundations, serving to provide shelter to a handful of students, often in the midst of other "poor clerics". The first genuine colleges were established in Paris, and then in England, in the second half of the thirteenth century, at a time when the rate of expansion of the universities were beginning to pose serious practical problems" (Walter Ruegg, 1992). Even now some of the oldest prestigious universities like the Oxford, Cambridge, Bologna, etc., have strictly adhered to quality initiatives throughout their existence. The great qualities and strengths cherished and maintained by the old and renowned universities still enable them to maintain the splendor and glory that they have been enjoying for centuries. Those great qualities and strengths are: Highly talented teachers, diversified courses, research-orientation in their approach, maintaining high standards, incorporating technological advances and supporting the growth and development of the nation. Adopting new methods through innovation, adapting to the requirements of change and using new knowledge and skills are their mantra for success. Michael Tomlinson, (2013) comments on this great change occurring in the field of higher education thus: "The relationship between higher education, the state and the economy has been reconfigured over time. This has resulted in increasing pressures on higher education institutions to co-ordinate their activities in ways that best suit national economic imperatives."

A national level strategic planning in curriculum reform and planning, upgrading the overall quality of institutions, their teachers, libraries, laboratories, and research facilities, integrating the subjects with careers, institutionalizing the best practices in centers of higher education, assessment and accreditation of all institutions according to specific national level criteria will make education productive and serve the interests of a large section of young people. We may take for example, the significance of strategic planning in curriculum. Although the teacher's knowledge of the subject and skills in classroom management are so important, the contents of the curriculum define the limit of what will be learned and how the student will benefit from it. As a large part of old knowledge has become irrelevant in the modern times, it would not serve the society any good if we still cling on to outdated syllabus and do not take the initiative to revamp the syllabus. Another example is that the institutions hesitating to institutionalize the best practices that have emerged in their premises, regionally, nationally or internationally for some unknown reasons lag far behind.

The Ranking of Institutions

One of the key factors that typically define the success of a nation is the quality and standards maintained by its educational institutions. In this context, the governments have constituted assessment and accreditation bodies in their respective countries to oversee the institutionalization of quality assurance practices in higher education, and examine the performance of the institutions in critical areas of development. There are internationally acclaimed agencies, which based on predetermined criteria, rank them. Institutions are thus motivated to undergo a process of ranking or accreditation to enable them to prove their worth as efficient and successful organizations. The certificate of ranking or accreditation issued by a competent authority speaks for itself whether the institution possesses unique and exceptionally good standards or is yet to meet the prescribed standards. The academic community, the stakeholders, general public, and, in particular the parents and students judge the performance of an institution based on its ranking or grading.

There are several methods followed by educational authorities to rank an institution based on well-defined and clear-cut criteria. Some educational authorities even rank the institution based on its internet visibility. This criterion looks funny. But, there is a moot point to it. The details furnished by such an institution give a clear-cut picture of its academic and administrative facilities, the quality of its functioning and achievements. Some others judge on the basis of average salary of the alumni. This is also a realistic way to assess the strength of an institution. The average of salary earned by the alumni reveals the quality of the students who passed out of the institution, which in turn, reflects upon the quality of institution. Yet others decide on the basis of selection procedure of students and the quality of students noticed at the time of admission and passing out. But, those who follow the conventional methods, look into the overall curriculum, quality of teachers, classroom learning practices, teacher and student evaluation mechanism, innovative practices, success rate of students, salary of teachers, campus placements and salaries, the student-teacher ratio, research grants and support to the community. In addition, the infrastructural facilities, healthy practices and student support mechanisms of the institution are also taken into consideration.

In the Quacqarelli Symonds (QS) World University Rankings, they look into academic peer review, recruiter review, faculty-student ratio, citations per faculty, and international orientation. In the QS rankings in 2011, the University of Cambridge was ranked the top University in the world followed by Harvard University, Massachusetts Institute of Technology (MIT), Yale University, University of Oxford and others. Likewise the ratings of the Times Higher Education World University Rankings, the Shanghai Jiao Tong University Rankings, etc are relevant. In 2012, in the Times Higher Education World University Rankings, Harvard, the Massachusetts Institute of Technology, University of Cambridge, and the Oxford University are ranked as the world's topmost universities. In India, not a single university or institute of higher learning, including the premier IITs, figure on the list of 200 top-rated universities in the world. In India, three institutes, all of them Indian Institute of Technology, feature among the top 100 universities in Asia, according to the first Asia University Rankings released by the "Times Higher Education" magazine. While IIT Kharagpur is ranked 30th, IIT Bombay is 33rd and IIT Roorkee, 56th. The universities are ranked, based on 13 performance indicators in teaching, research, knowledge transfer and international outlook. The University of Tokyo secured the pole position, followed by National University of Singapore and Peking University. No Indian university has figured among the top 200 universities in the world in recent surveys even though Indian higher education system is still one of the largest in the world. In sheer numbers, too, Japan with 22 universities in the top 100 Asian institutes, Taiwan with 17, China with 15 and Korea with 14 have done much better. According to Pawan Agarwal, adviser for higher education in the Indian Planning Commission, India must develop multi-disciplinary research universities and inter-disciplinary areas to move up the ladder of ranking.

In the Times Higher Education, BRICS and Emerging Economies Rankings, 2014, the outstanding performers are the Peking University and Tsinghai University (China) followed by University of Cape Town (South Africa) National Taiwan University (Taiwan) and the Bogazici University (Turkey). The Panjab University and Indian Institute of Technology, Kharagpur (India) ranks thirteenth and thirtieth respectively. It is high time that the administrators and academics of the Indian higher education system contemplate and act seriously to produce world-class universities by concentrating on developing quality infrastructure and producing quality research output, and thereby competing with the topmost universities in the world.

In the rankings arena international institutions are pitted against each other using specific criteria, mainly based on performance indicators. The same situation prevails in a system of ranking institutions at the national level in different countries. Whether ranking is done at international or national level, its benefits are used by the premier institutions to affirm their superiority in their marketing drives to attract the best students. For many a student, ranking is a deciding factor while selecting an institution for higher studies. Rankings are useful for the academics as they can select the right institution to work in a competitive atmosphere where the ambience is of superior quality.

Ranking or accreditation of an institution is by itself a cumbersome process, very challenging and expensive. Many institutions do not volunteer to undergo any ranking or grading process as it involves a big budget. But institutions cannot afford not to participate in a process of ranking or accreditation. If perchance, they stay out of this requirement, they lose a golden opportunity to be visible in a complex and challenging environment. In the modern educational scenario, true excellence has several dimensions, including ranking, accreditation, interface with industry, excellence of teachers, contribution to the community, quality of research, among others. What attract students to a good institution are the excellence of teaching and the availability of the state-of-the-art academic facilities.

Accreditation of educational institutions has become mandatory in almost all countries. The institution is ranked on the basis of predetermined and well-defined criteria fixed by the national accreditation bodies. In some countries. it is voluntary on the part of the institution to obtain accreditation. However, within a certain period of time, as fixed by the educational authorities, the educational institution has to undergo this process to obtain ranking or accreditation certificate by an external agency. Since this is an independent review of the educational programmes of the institution which certifies that it maintains standards of quality, in the normal course, all the institutions will obtain accreditation and ranking. The accreditation body usually insists that the applicant institution fulfill seven to ten criteria to obtain the certificate of accreditation and ranking. The number of criteria changes from one country to another. Good institutions aspire for higher ranking by the accreditation body as they demonstrate their quality-consciousness endeavours. The accreditation certificate issued by the accreditation body is usually valid for five years. After which the institution will have to go for reaccreditation. In the mean time, the institution has to maintain quality of the educational programmes by appointing a 'Quality Assurance' body which will monitor the continuous quality maintenance process.

Certain important ranking criteria, like the quality of curriculum and of teaching and learning outcomes and success rates are the crucial factors which can never be compromised. These criteria stand out in guiding the prospective students to select an educational institution to undergo training. During the process of ranking the institution, more importance is given to the aforesaid criteria than to others. The teachers are to be doubly cautious regarding the pedagogical strategies devised and followed so as to provide the best learning platform. Most of the important requirements to be fulfilled, other than the teaching-learning facets of education, are to be provided by the administration.

As the success of an educational institution can be attributed to its focus on the quality of teaching and facilities provided, many institutions work hard to improve them. Also, they put more funds to improve the quality of research. Whenever an institution improves its ranking, it reflects the high quality of education imparted and maintained by it.

Since ranking of an institution speaks volume about its strengths and weaknesses, the administration has to provide all facilities to its students, without compromising on quality. The administration has to involve all the stakeholders in the process of ranking the institution by an external agency. If the institution has to live up to the expectations of the stakeholders, it has to plan effectively and execute it with a sense of purpose. For successful institutions, preparing for an accreditation or ranking process may not be that tough as for a mediocre institution. But, to a great extent, the mechanisms to be followed are one and the same for both of them. It is clear that, if an institution has strength, in the various parameters to be assessed, then those inherent strengths reveal the core competencies of the organization. The priorities of the organization will change according to the inherent strengths and achievements of the organizations.

It is advisable for all institutions to appoint a committee of experts in the institution to plan and oversee the accreditation or ranking process, first, by clearly addressing the following questions:

- What are the short term and long term objectives set to obtain accreditation or ranking?
- What is the grade chosen to obtain accreditation or ranking?
- What kind of quality has to be attained and maintained for the next five years?
- What are the strategies developed to achieve the targets?
- What kind of competencies are to be developed to attain the goals?
- What are the infrastructure facilities to be developed to achieve the goals?
- What are the methods by which adequate resources will be raised?

To start with any accreditation or rating process, the institution must first analyze its current situation and find out its strengths, weaknesses, opportunities and threats. The current institutional performance in relation to academic and extra-curricular achievements are to be evaluated. Certain critical areas, like targets and achievements, satisfaction of the teachers and students, the reputation of the institution in the community and the ranking of the institution are to be seriously considered. A SWOT analysis conducted by the institution in this regard will pinpoint the critical areas which are to be attended to by the administration on a priority basis.

The institution will have to chalk out a well-defined plan of action based on the objectives set to obtain accreditation or ranking. They are determined on the basis of the criteria of accreditation or ranking. If it is a seven-point criteria, as outlined in the accreditation document, thrust must be given to those decisive areas by the administration. A team has to function by involving all the key stakeholders in charting out the plan of action methodically and by assigning duties to all the personnel. Adequate resources are to be raised as per the budget drawn by the committee of experts.

Each department has to develop its own goals and strategies based on the overall objectives of the institution. The mission and vision statements of the organization must be reflected in the departmental mission and vision statements. It has to be borne in mind that the plan of action set by the departments has to finally enable the organization to fulfill the overall objectives set by the institution. The plans developed have to be deployed with utmost caution. While implementing them, it is always advisable to keep an eye on the critical success factors, as without fulfilling them, the overall objectives would never be achieved. All the activities, from the beginning to the end, are to be documented under this system. The committees responsible will have to review the implemented plan periodically, and if needed, corrective action will have to be taken at the appropriate level. The committees must identify the critical mismatches between the goals set and achieved. The apex committee consisting of the top leadership of the institution will have to provide the strategic direction to all other committees on an ongoing basis. In all these committees, the teachers play a vital role in the materialization of the goals.

The major problem that an institution faces while undergoing the accreditation or ranking process is the absence of a clear understanding of the process of accreditation by the constituents. In most cases, the teachers and staff do not know their responsibilities and specific roles in the fulfillment of the objectives. It is the bounden duty of the administration to provide them with a clear-cut picture of the goals, tasks, duties and responsibilities that arise in the accreditation process. As it has to be completed on a time bound basis, a dead line to complete each task has to be fixed and it has to be informed to the persons concerned. The whole system must be run with clock-wise precision. It demands excellent leadership, and highly focused team work and accountability at all levels.

No other stakeholder is as significant as the teachers in the HEI in the context of 'Reaccreditation'. More than 60 per cent marks are within the court of the teachers; and therefore, more than 60 per cent responsibility of re-accreditation lies with them. (Hence the 6th Pay Commission (India) that makes teachers real stakeholders of HEI). The total of the first three criteria 50 + 450 + 100, with respect to the colleges, comes to 600 marks out of 1000. Therefore, their role is of special significance. It is to:

(i) Improve subject knowledge, teaching skills, methods, systems to ensure students' participation in the Teaching/Learning Process.
(ii) Have honest, impartial and proper evaluation of students' performance.
(iii) Undertake research and publish papers.
(iv) Render help for the governance, administration and policy-making of the HEI.

(v) Participate in the extension work.
(vi) Maintain proper record of development of subjects and the departments.
(vii) Develop curricula and conduct remedial/bridge/add-on courses.
(viii) Conduct, participate in seminars/conferences and consultancy programmes.
(ix) Contribute to the creation and application of new knowledge.
(x) Develop systems, procedures and programmes for sustainable development and formulate strategies for knowledge management (H.V. Deshpande, 2008).

Quality assurance mechanisms have to be in harmony with global trends so that there is an international acceptance of degrees/diplomas awarded by the Indian higher education system. In this direction, Indian agencies could network with transnational and international quality assurance agencies and enter into arrangements for mutual recognition of quality assurance systems. It is desirable to make it compatible with UNESCO/OECD guidelines on the issue released the previous year (Pawan Agarwal, 2009).

The critical success factors that enable an institution to obtain accreditation or ranking are:

- A well chalked out plan of action
- A committed and talented team of teachers and staff
- Coordination and collective effort
- Efficient leadership
- Administration with a vision

Documentation: A Key Factor

In any system of accreditation or ranking, the institution has to maintain systematic documentation of all the activities, which will be used as reference material. The apex body responsible for the completion of the process of accreditation or ranking will give clear cut guidelines for the preparation of documents to each department. If the institution has been in existence for a long time, it would be proficient in maintaining such documents for accreditation or ranking. In such a situation, the existing documentation is the starting point for developing new documents. To begin with, the apex body must provide the reporting forms and give a clear idea of the specific details of information to be collected. Each document must be reviewed by the apex team to ensure its suitability and validity for accreditation or ranking. The apex body must also ensure the accuracy of the details furnished. All the documents must be formatted in a manner that allows their effective presentation to the accreditation body.

Much emphasis needs to be put on the importance of records in any system of accreditation or ranking. It is understood that all the specific records are maintained by the institution when they undergo a process of accreditation or ranking. Records are meant to provide traceability actions taken either individually or collectively by a department. Every teacher must know from the very beginning of his service the details of various records to be maintained and submitted to the authorities from time to time. Each document must have a title, which could be easily identified, a number unique to only that document, date, name and signature of the teacher or staff concerned.

In the 'Internal Quality Assurance Manual' of the institution, details of documents to be maintained by each teacher or staff and department will be given. Most institutions maintain flow diagrams which clearly pinpoint the name of the teacher or staff, description of work done, time taken for the completion of work, submission of reporting formats, review of work done, and clarifications, if any. According to the requirements of the institution, they customize such flow diagrams. Electronic document control systems are in vogue to store the documents in an access controlled database that can be routed to the appropriate authority for its efficient administration. This system facilitates better monitoring of the performance of teachers and staff on a continual basis. It also helps the top administration to review the work carried out by teachers and staff and bring about necessary changes to upgrade the quality of the institution to meet the standards of the accreditation/ ranking body. Higher authorities will be able to judge for themselves the competence of teachers and staff in fulfilling the academic and other standards. They will be able to decide how to provide adequate training for teachers and staff to upgrade their skills. These reports are of great significance for the administration not only for the purpose of obtaining accreditation or ranking, but also to ensure that the institution is maintaining quality at all levels.

Most of the institutions lay special emphasis on promoting quality consciousness and achievements. Specific targets are fixed by the competent authority to improve the quality of performance of both teachers and administration in accordance with predetermined standards. Quality management is given top priority by all leading institutions. Some of them follow the 'kaizen' or TQM or similar methods to improve them. They put in a lot of efforts to identify relevant quality parameters related to the training needs of teachers as well as administration so that the performance of their faculty members and administrative staff is of top notch quality. The 'Quality Assurance Cell' is responsible to deliver the best training opportunities to both the faculty members and administrative staff, as and when the need arises. They are also held responsible to organize effective 'Induction training' to the new faculty members and staff. It is the bounden responsibility of the Quality Assurance Cell to assist the administration to formulate policies on quality assurance and guidelines, operational policies and procedures and to share information regarding 'Quality Management' system. It is the duty of the administration to inform all the stakeholders about the decisions arrived at and the progress achieved.

The National Assessment and Accreditation Council of India has been guiding the higher education institutions in the country on internalization of the process of quality. This body has laid out specific parameters for assessing the strengths and weaknesses of institutions and aids them in their quest for excellence. This national body has tried to motivate all the institutions of higher education to develop benchmarks of excellence and to follow the best practices and measures of institutionalization of continuous improvement systems. But, most institutions hesitate to undergo this crucial assessment and accreditation method due to lack of planning and preparation and for fear of failure.

Tucker and Mantz (1978) have remarked that voluntary accreditation is one of the triumphs of higher education in the US. For decades the accreditation process was a vehicle that pulled higher education onto ascending plateaus of quality.

The American system of self-monitoring is unique among such systems in the developed nations, most of which use governmental agencies to monitor and control collegiate education. The principal instruments of accreditation to fulfill the eligibility requirements for membership are the completion of an instructional self-study; a site visit by a team of academics, who presumably have specialized knowledge of the type of institution visited; a formal, written report of that team and, when desired, an institution's response to the report; and a review of the self-study and visiting team's report, first by the professional staff and then, by the relevant commission, which finally determines the accreditation status.

The institutional self-study is increasingly the key stone of the accreditation process. Presumably, by conducting a thorough examination of every important element, an institution can detect deficiencies and make plans for improvement. This self-study provides an accreditation visiting team with an overview of the institution and serves as a chart to guide onsite enquiries. (Lewis B. Mayhew, Patrick J. Ford and Dean L. Hubbard, 1990).

In higher education, 'quality assurance' is the term which defines the institutional policies, procedures and activities that reflects the totality of performance of the institution. It provides a measure of confidence to all the stakeholders that what has been done academically is consistent with the institutional goals, mission and vision. In this context, the criteria as determined by an external body regarding the procedures to be fulfilled by an institution to obtain accreditation, and thereby safeguard the institution's interest to adhere to certain well-defined quality assurance practices are of paramount importance.

Let us examine the quality factors that are typically accorded attention in national plans in different developed countries. They invariably look into the relevance of educational contributions to the goals of national development, the number and quality of educational personnel, nationalization and localization of educational personnel, rates of student attendance and progress, staff-student ratios, the coordination of the components of educational enterprise, building and other facilities, instructional supplies and equipment, and the financing of educational operations. (*Education's Role In National Development Plans*, edited by R Murray Thomas, 1992). National Development plans lay great emphasis on education as it is the key to success of economic development.

It is imperative that a national body, like the National Assessment and Accreditation Council in India, conduct periodic assessment of different centers of higher education and determine their competencies and weaknesses, and thereby, decide whether they qualify for different levels of accreditation. It is when such national assessment accreditation bodies function effectively that all centers of higher education in a country are galvanized to pursue national educational goals. Even though it would be a herculean task to make every centre of higher education comply with specific national goals, it could enthuse a majority of them to achieve them within a reasonable period of time.

According to Indian experience, a majority of institutions in the country are adapting to the challenges thrown up by educational reforms. Upgrading the quality of higher education institutions in general; institutionalizing the best practices that have emerged locally, nationally, and to a certain extent, internationally; seeking funds for institutional development plans; asking teachers to attend training programmes to update their knowledge and skills; being aware of quality improvement initiatives; administrators becoming quality-conscious; and students becoming aware of academic needs to fit into a modern world where jobs have become specialized and closely linked with not only the knowledge but also the skills acquired—are some of the changes taking place in the higher education institutions in the country, mainly due to the impact of a national level assessment and accreditation process and educational reforms. Due to the impact of the National Assessment and Accreditation Council in India, the most auguring and encouraging outcome is an incredible and remarkable change in the mindsets of educators and administrators regarding the concept of quality. Institutions take pride in the fact that they have been graded by a national level assessment and accreditation body by undergoing a labourious process of assessment and accreditation. A culture of quality has been inculcated in their minds in this critical and evolutionary area. Those institutions which were not able to achieve the highest level in grading do their best to achieve it the next time. In the field of higher education too, the transition from an apparently laissez-fare system to a modulated system has been slow, but steady. It has been felt that higher education needs radical reforms on every single dimension imaginable, be it the quality of curriculum, or of teaching, or administration, or research. It is for certain that the patch work of reforms will not make any dent in the culture of mediocrity and complacency.

Assessment is a core element of causing quality in higher education for no other reason than it stresses improvement (Daniel T Seymour, 1992). In this context, the relevance of the vision and mission statements which convey the cardinal values pursued by the institution becomes all important. Such edifying statements can also speak about its commitment to quality and excellence.

CASE STUDY

A SUCCESS STORY

For a pretty long period, the Exton School was labeled the worst school in the region. The teachers felt ashamed to work there as it has been a 100 per cent failure most of the time whereas other schools in the locality had high percentage of results. Those parents who failed to get seats for their wards in other schools were compelled to get them at the Exton School. Most students of this school became miscreants and anti-social elements. The teachers were not at all interested in improving the situation. Even while classes were going on, some students boycotted them due to political unrest or under some other pretext. They missed classes and went to the neighboring institutions and created disturbances so as to make the management decide to postpone classes. Lady teachers were hesitant to take classes as the behaviour of the boys in each class was horrible. The institution lacked discipline. Every year admission became low and drop outs increased. As a result, some sections were abandoned. The principal called the parent-teachers meeting but, only a handful of parents turned up. Others were neither interested in the future of their wards nor in the future of the institution. Teachers became sluggish and irresponsible as they lost interest in their jobs. The good teachers managed to get transferred to other schools as they felt that nothing could be done to improve the pitiable condition of the school.

The Turn-around

A few years back, Mr. Saleh took the charges as the principal. Before he joined, his colleagues had discouraged him from taking the new assignment as they knew him to be a conscientious teacher. But for promotion, he would not have left the school where he was. Before he took charge, he had collected much information about Exton School so that he could work out some viable concrete measures to save it from further deterioration and collapse. First, he called on the District Educational Officer to seek his guidance. Then, he called a public meeting involving all concerned, including public officials, political functionaries, educational consultants, parents and teachers. In that meeting they came out with a plan of action to improve the situation step by step.

The new principal's desire to mend things was received with scorn by majority of students and public at large. Some even thought that he was pursuing a quixotic idea.

Later, the principal convened a meeting of the parents and teachers and made his plans threadbare before them. It was to be discussed at length to chalk out a practical plan of action to fulfill the objectives as decided in the public meeting to ensure qualitative improvement in the teaching and learning environment. Small committees comprising parents, teachers and municipal members were constituted, whose first task was to meet the parents at their homes so as to gain firsthand information about the students' families and involve them in the improvement of their wards by making them monitor their progress in studies at home. The parents were requested to meet the class teachers of their wards every fortnight to discuss their problems and to evaluate the progress made by them. Special classes were conducted in the evening to coach the majority of students. Parents were asked to accompany the students back home. Educational psychologists frequently addressed the students apart from regular counseling given to them. Students with deviant behaviour were put under a counsellor for as long as they needed his help. Constant monitoring of daily activities of students was religiously carried out by the class teacher and a small team of teachers which was evaluated in the end of each week. Educational scholarships were arranged by the public committee to be disbursed to the achievers and economically poor students. Some funds were kept apart to feed the students who attended special classes.

Positive changes started trickling in within two to three months after introducing improvement programmes by the new principal. They were ably supported by teachers, parents and the public. All of them noticed drastic changes in the behaviour of students, not only in their academic progress, but also in their outlook. Not a single student dropped out of the class and even the rowdy elements started paying respect to teachers and following their instructions.

All were anxiously awaiting the results of public examination as it was considered a measuring rod to assess the success or failure of the new policies and programmes. Usually, Exton School's name appeared in the 100 per cent failure section. Thanks to the efforts put in by the visionary principal and the team of hard working teachers, they gained 55 per cent pass in the first year itself. In the next few years it improved from 70 per cent to 80 per cent, and it later secured 100 per cent pass, which is still maintained.

Now, the parents in and around the town, make it a point to get seats for their children at Exton and if they fail, they grudgingly try elsewhere wondering whether their children would ever get opportunities to undergo training at a first class institution! Mr. Saleh retired from service after obtaining a President's medal for outstanding service. But even now, thanks to his efforts, the school remains number one.

☞

- What are the peculiar problems faced by this school in the beginning? Why did not the previous administrators tackle these problems?
- Suppose you were appointed as the principal in the place of Mr. Saleh, what would you have done to mend the situation? Narrate a step by step plan of action.
- What policies can administration adopt to avert such an eventuality in schools/ colleges?

13

Benchmarking and Good Practices to Follow

Chances favours the prepared mind. —Louis Pasteur

We are little men, serving great causes,
but because the cause is great,
something of that greatness
falls upon all of us. —Jawaharlal Nehru

Benchmarking: A Critical Factor

Our society is becoming more and more aware of the efficiency, accountability, competitiveness and quality of various higher education institutions. They are selective when it comes to admission of their wards in any center of higher education. There seems to be a growing anxiety amongst parents and students about the quality and performance of colleges and universities. Failures of the higher education system in a particular region can even compel students to leave a state or country in search of better educational opportunities. Outdated curriculum, lack of modern facilities, ill-equipped laboratories, ineffective teaching practices, inadequate library facilities, and failure to obtain accreditation are some of the definite reasons which create a poor image of an institution. It is in this context that benchmarking has become very important.

'Benchmarking' is a term used frequently in the accreditation process of educational institutions. It is a universally applied method to measure the performance of an institution by comparing it with the performance of a group of institutions. It means a systematic search for best practices, and once identified, to implement them to enhance the quality of the performance of the institution.

Benchmarking, according to Anthony Kelly, is a process which involves making comparisons between two units within an organization or with another organization. Using similar points of reference, benchmarking involves examining the critical activities of one institution and comparing them with the performance of another institution. The purpose of benchmarking is to improve performance and thereby to increase the effectiveness of the institution.

Benchmarking is a systematic search for innovative ideas, highly efficient teaching practices, and highly supportive systems in the learning environment.

The implementation of efficient benchmarking practices in an institution provides ample opportunities to ensure better performance. It also enables the institution to understand how other institutions which do far better follow best practices to build their strengths. The essence of benchmarking is the application of the best practices of high achievers in the field so as to gain a competitive advantage. When applied to teaching practices, it is the process of comparing the work of teachers of an institute against the best practices and outcomes in better institutions for the purpose of identifying changes that will result in higher quality performance. If benchmarking technique is effectively used in an institution, it will be able to reap good dividends by enhancing its standards. It provides insights into the functioning of successful institutions and thereby helps one institution to learn from others' competence, especially in important areas, like faculty development, methodologies of teaching, evaluation of teachers and students and healthy practices. They would decide the efficiency of the institution with regard to the achievement of its objectives.

As an increasingly popular approach to establish performance standard, processes, measurements, and objectives, 'benchmarking' helps organizations to identify standards of performance and adopt them successfully. It helps them to target problem areas, set levels of performance, and identify solutions to improve results. Best practices adding commendable value to an institute and its stakeholders are considered as the standards of quality. NAAC (India) has been using benchmarking as quality enhancement technique in the form of criterion statement to assess the level of performance in higher education. Benchmarking offers the following benefits:

- It helps organizations to make better informed decisions,
- It exposes them to innovations and breakthroughs,
- It allows them to see beyond the barriers, to embrace change, to think 'outside the box', and
- It provides them with a methodology and a game plan for accelerating, implementing and managing change (Ashwani Kumar, 2008).

Benchmarking as an instrument of positive change has revealed that the success or failure of an educational institution depends, to a large extent, on the leadership acumen of its administrators and the quality of teaching and learning. The administration will be successful in these highly important endeavors if their quality of leadership is exceptionally good. In this context, one cannot ignore the role played by the teachers in successfully implementing the benchmarking practices. While school or college leadership is a hotly debated topic among the teaching fraternity worldwide, there is a growing consensus on the nature and practice of effective school or college leadership. Benchmarking has provided better insights into the distinctive roles played by the leadership of educational institution and teachers in improving the standards of schools or colleges.

K.B. Powar (2011), asserts that if benchmarks are clearly defined, many institutions will be motivated to meet them and thereby work towards excellence in education. An individual institution can undertake internal benchmarking (in which comparison is made between different units within the institution), external benchmarking (in which comparison is made with other institutions that are seen to be competitors) and collaborative benchmarking (in which comparison is made with institutions that are seen to be potential collaborators) (J.W. Alstete, 1995).

Benchmarking opens up new opportunities for growth and development of the institution and introduces timely changes to empower teachers to meet the demands of a challenging environment. It is used by some institutions to reduce the number of dropouts by making teachers more responsible to monitor and guide weak students effectively. It is also used to support training and development of teachers so as to bring about qualitative improvement in teaching. This method is chosen to strengthen the best practices of teaching by looking both inside and outside the institution for ways to improve the quality of teachers. The most important factor to be considered for benchmarking is the effectiveness of teaching and learning criterion. It is one of the critical factors which decides the success or failure of an institution.

Educational institutions establish benchmarks to offer quality education. They adopt nationally and internationally proven best practices, benchmarks, assessment methods, accreditation systems and strategies for qualitative improvement. The policy makers in education establish effective accreditation criteria and assessment methods to bring about positive changes in the field of education at all levels. The more the importance attributed to education as a major factor for economic growth and development, the more prominence is gained by the assessment and accreditation bodies. Through these efforts, governments try to ensure that the outcome achieved by students of every country is equal in quality. Governments are also studying the feasibility of adopting successful models by integrating curriculum with the needs of industry and by ensuring quality education to meet the needs and expectations of society. Thanks to demographic changes, India is advantageously positioned in the international labour market with opportunities to the young people on a grand scale. Evidently, there is a serious gap existing between academia and industry in many countries, which could be narrowed down by establishing benchmarks decided upon by mutual consultation between the industry and academia.

A progress report from Ontario Universities, entitled "Access to Excellence" (prepared by the Council of Ontario Universities, 2001) defines an effective educational experience thus:

Extensive research indicates that certain educational experiences are viewed as "effective" by virtually all students. Common benchmarks include the levels of academic challenge, an active learning process, interactions with faculty, enriching educational experiences and resources, and a supportive campus environment.

To implement a benchmarking system effectively in an educational institution, the administration will have to decide a step by step process. In the beginning, it has to decide the scope and objectives of benchmarking and the key areas which have to be selected for the purpose of benchmarking. It has to simultaneously obtain a correct picture of the current performance of the institution in the key areas. Once it decides them, it has to identify the other institutions where comparative analysis has to be carried out by a selected team. The data collection has to be planned and the current performance gap determined by the team. Then a benchmark plan has to be developed taking into consideration the predetermined goals and objectives.

After analyzing the data, the team can recommend to the administration specific actions to improve the quality of functioning of the key areas selected for benchmarking. It is from such reports that the administration would get a clear idea whether the key areas have severe problems which prohibit the institution to perform up to the expectations of the stakeholders. In the end, it is the administration which has to implement specific actions to rectify the flaws, and monitor the progress on a time bound basis.

Benchmarking has to be carried out on an agreed upon time schedule. If the time limit is not set, the team can procrastinate over the period of study and unnecessarily delay its action and findings. One useful method is to analyze the results in the key areas of study and go back to the inputs. All data have to be quantified for the purpose of measuring and comparing so that the benchmarking process becomes foolproof, and the data collected is useful for further analysis.

A CASE STUDY

BENCHMARKING

The College of Technology is a premier institution which has maintained good standards of performance for a long time. Since its inception in 1985 as a single management organization, it has developed into one of the best institutions in management and technology subjects. In the annual meeting of the institution, the benchmarker team evaluated its performance and laid fresh programmes for development to catch up with the developments taking place in management science and technology elsewhere. The administration was quite contented with the achievements in both academic and extra-curricular activities. The overall performance was considered satisfactory.

Between 1994 and 2004, more institutions started functioning in the vicinity conducting similar programmes. Some even offered newer programmes of a higher standard. Over the same period an institution known for its remarkable performance in another country started operating in the neighboring district. Parents in this thickly populated city became choosy when they selected an institution to get admission for their wards. Since the College of Technology was a pioneer institution which maintained good results, parents preferred it to others.

In 2010, for the first time, the administration of the College of Technology had to face the shocking fact that it was not able to fill all the seats in several disciplines. Administration became panicky over this issue. They were forced to appoint a Task Force to analyze the critical problem and identify the root cause and suggest corrective measures to stem the rot. The Task Force was of the unanimous opinion that a benchmarking studies had to be conducted to compare the parameters of its success and evaluate the strengths and weaknesses of the critical success factors of the neighboring colleges. The purpose of conducting this exercise was to use benchmarking as an improvement tool to safeguard the interests of the institution at that critical juncture. The Task Force was asked to select a competent team to lead the benchmarking study, and to see that draft questionnaires related to the data were well prepared. The questionnaires were to be approved by the other institutions where the study was conducted. Only areas of mutual interest were taken up for such studies. Prior to the conduct of study, the institutions which had given consent to it had agreed upon certain conditions which all parties had to adhere to.

The College of Technology fulfilled all the preconditions related to the conduct of benchmarking study. The study was conducted for a month and reports were sent to the Task Force for their comments. The detailed study brought out the deficiencies in the system and revealed the weaknesses of the college in some of the critical areas. The gap between the college's performance and the performance of the other colleges was pointed out. There were significant negative gaps in areas like, upgrading the quality of teachers, student-teacher ratio, teaching-learning outcome, research awards and publications, involvement of teachers in the professional organizations, etc. The team clearly identified the benchmark gaps and reported the findings to the Task Force which studied at length the objective analysis and made its recommendations to the administration. They stressed the need to change the policies of the management on teacher recruitment, training, methodology of teaching, teaching and learning outcomes, student-teacher ratio, teacher performance, assessment of students, etc. It was also made clear that the college must put in more efforts to attract students and be explicit about the quality of their teaching and the type of experience they offer.

GOOD PRACTICES TO FOLLOW

Orientation is Essential

It would be appropriate to organize effective training for students in the beginning of the academic year to make them aware of: (a) the culture and healthy practices followed by the institution, (b) the opportunities for growth and development, (c) cultivating responsible behaviour and (d) contribution to the success of academic, co-curricular and extra-curricular programmes. The training programmes are to be organized to improve the ability of students to concentrate, improve listening skills and attention span. Another area of importance is to develop appropriate study skills and practice time management. One of the prominent institutions where orientation programme was organized for the newly admitted students every year, christened the orientation programme as 'Rope-in' programme. This institution is a haven of diversity hosting students from different parts of the country. The 'Rope-in' programme, which is a week long programme facilitates coalescing of the entire group into a new family to imbibe the culture of this institution whose products are accepted in any part of the industrialized world for their quality and commitment. At the end of the three-year programme the institution conducts the 'Rope out' programme when the passing out batch is given an opportunity to share the intrinsic values of the course and about their expectations and fulfillment.

It is not only the administration but also the teachers who must take the initiative to organize valuable and indispensable orientation programmes for new students. It could be organized in two or three sessions covering the important aspects of students' life in the campus. This programme helps the students to coalesce with the cultural moorings of the institution.

Encourage Students to Form Study Groups

The teachers must encourage and facilitate the formation of small study groups amongst students. The purpose of forming such study groups is to improve their learning skills and abilities. When students volunteer to form such groups, they themselves get motivated to learn the subjects with greater interest. Since there is a sense of their involvement in the learning process, the members of such small groups become good achievers. It is also found that these groups coalesce into well-knit peer groups having much influence on each other. When they face difficulties in learning an item, they meet the teacher concerned to discuss the problems and clear their doubts. The teacher has to create opportunities for the members of each group to work, share, explain and discuss the topics and see that the members are motivated to do their individual tasks. The big advantage is that the students in these small groups freely interact with one another and are always seen extending mutual help. Forming such small groups of students to encourage group study is essential if the class is large. These groups must meet the teacher at least once a week so that he attends to their queries and guides them. Since these students generally meet the teacher after discussing the problem areas within the group, they are in a better position to comprehend and appreciate the method of working out solutions to the problems.

Maintain Academic Honesty

The teachers are expected to maintain academic honesty the moment they take up teaching as a career. It is advisable for the institution to issue a circular to all new teachers about the institutional policies regarding academic honesty so that they are aware of the importance of academic integrity. Good teachers have their own values and are influenced by the strong academic culture of good institutions. The teacher must know that fraudulent, unethical and dishonest practices will not be tolerated by the institution.

The educational administrator must detect dishonest practices and take appropriate action so as to prevent them. Nowadays there is software which could be used to detect dishonest practices in academic situations. Once a teacher is caught for academic dishonesty, he should be warned and if such a behaviour is repeated, he must be removed from service.

Similarly, the institution has to enforce academic honesty among students. A commonly seen dishonesty on the part of students is cheating in the examination halls and plagiarism in preparing assignments. Like teachers, students must be given, at the time of admission, copies of the institutional policies on academic honesty so that they are fully aware of their duties. If they are caught for academic dishonesty, they should be warned then and there and corrective action must be taken so that they do not repeat similar mistakes. In all such situations, the institution has to initiate disciplinary action according to its disciplinary policies without any delay.

Be Approachable

It would be a good practice for teachers to fix appointments for all students to discuss their concerns individually. Good teachers make it a point to address the learning difficulties of weak students by giving them special appointments during the office hours. Such students are asked to stay after the classes and seek the assistance of the teacher concerned to clear their doubts or obtain personal coaching. Once the students approach the teacher and feel comfortable to speak to the teacher, then a good rapport is developed between them which is an essential requirement for the success of any programme. A teacher can influence his/her students by many a method. He/she can praise the student for his or her achievements and thereby encourage him/her to perform better. The teacher can admonish the student for misbehaviour or callous attitude, and thereby put him or her on the right path. When students pay a visit to the teacher, he must give undivided attention to them so that they would feel comfortable to speak to him. Teachers are usually found very helpful in guiding students about the details of the course of study, pattern of question papers, grading systems, facilities available and evaluation system and performance. If an appointment is fixed by the teacher and the student concerned does not turn up, the teacher has to seek a written explanation from him for his failure to report and if the explanation is not satisfactory, the teacher has to strictly deal with him.

The teachers can also contact the students on e-mail, web site or social networking site, which ever mode is preferred. This helps the teacher to convey important messages directly to the student, especially in an emergency situation.

Working Portfolios for Teachers

As soon as the teacher starts working in an institution, it is his bounden duty to maintain a 'Working Portfolio' which contains the copies of campus handbook, faculty handbook, course syllabus, calendar of events, instructional objectives, course materials, teaching strategies, methodologies, a brief summary of teaching notes and handouts, rules and procedures of grading, the titles of assignments, case studies and projects to be given, exam schedules, question papers, progress records, attendance records, notes on teaching responsibilities, etc. The teacher can include his comments on the performance of all students and make special comments on students who need special help. Copies of the minutes of the parent-teacher meetings must be kept in the portfolio. The marks of periodic tests must be entered in the prescribed form and kept in the portfolio. Details regarding research and publications, seminars and workshops attended, upgrading ICT-enabled teaching skills or any other skill, presentations made and awards won have to be separately shown. Efforts initiated to improve the quality of teaching and learning, and any worthwhile contribution made for the development of the institution must be separately mentioned. All the documents must be made available for inspection by the authorities. At the end of each term/semester, this portfolio must be updated with results of the examinations. For each term/semester, separate working portfolios have to be prepared by the teacher. The self-appraisal form has to be filled up at the end of each term and kept in the portfolio. These days electronic portfolios are in vogue which are quite convenient for teachers to create and easy to present before the authorities.

In the faculty handbook, the institution clearly defines the responsibilities of the faculty, the criteria for their recruitment, evaluation, promotion, tenure and all matters related to their service conditions. The evaluation criteria usually reflect the mission and purpose of the institution and the importance attached to various responsibilities of the faculty e g., teaching, advising, assessment, scholarship, creative activities, research, publications, professional development and community service.

This working portfolio will be referred to by the authorities during the conduct of evaluation of the teachers and during the conduct of any accreditation process.

Writing Letters of Recommendation for Students

The teachers' names are usually given as referees when the students apply for jobs or higher studies. In most cases, teachers forget to oblige, mainly due to their professional exigencies. They must know how to write an effective letter of recommendation. The teacher has to comment on the intellectual capabilities, academic achievements, attitude, creativity, communication, interpersonal and leadership skills, maturity, integrity, dependability, personal achievements and any other exceptional quality found in the student. The teacher is not expected to make any personal remarks about the student. He may state how long the student was known to him, and in what capacity. The recommendation must be honest and should not overstate the qualities of the student, both academic and extra-curricular. In some cases, the employer may ask the referee to specifically comment on certain behavioural aspects or activities of the student concerned. The teacher has to be cautious and to the point while commenting on such specific queries about the candidate as most of the employers give much importance to the teacher's remarks.

The student who mentions the name of the teacher as a referee is required to inform the teacher concerned about the purpose and seek his prior permission. It is advisable to send a copy of the letter of recommendation to the student.

Bridging the Gap between Academia and Industry

Educational institutions and industry mostly live in different glasshouses, showing scant respect for each other. In fact they are to operate for the success of each other as one is mutually dependent on the other. In many parts of the world, we find communication gap between these two important social bodies, which ultimately results in mismatch between their aspirations and achievements, and function. Frequent meaningful interactions between the academia and the industry have to take place with a view to understand the specific needs of industry and the supportive role of educational institutions to meet its demands. Academics, especially with specific research background, can act as consultants in industry to enhance the quality of their products and services. Academicians and managers must exchange their ideas to bring about changes in both the fields so that there is a clear-cut understanding of both products and services. This interface will ultimately guide the higher education institutions to remodel and revamp the curriculum to meet the demands of industry. Most of the top-notch countries in higher education have been able to build long term sustainable models of collaborative partnerships with industry. A sizeable number of research projects are funded by industry in such countries. With mutual trust, respect and realistic expectations, both the entities can definitely take up collaborative projects to improve the quality of life and also enjoy the fruits of labour.

Teacher-trainers and other professional trainers can work in educational institutions as well as in industry so that they would cement the gap between the academic and industry interests with respect to their employability. If fresh graduates are to be gainfully employed, their knowledge and skills must necessarily match with the requirement of the workplace. Executives from industries can be invited to deliver talks in the campuses and facilitate closer interaction between the industries and academic institutions. Research projects in the higher education institutions can be funded by industries and joint research projects can be carried out by making use of the facilities available in industries and research departments at higher education centers. The quality of curriculum can be enriched by incorporating the inputs from the industry. The importance of industry in the new economic scenario is well known. It is its sustainable development that ensures economic progress for humanity. The business corporations can play a vital role in empowering higher education institutions by instituting research fellowships in the universities and colleges as part of industry-academia collaboration. Higher education institutions can also plan and conduct many useful value-added courses by interacting with industry at different levels. Both industry and academia can collaborate on technology transfer partnerships which would be beneficial for both the entities to upgrade their standards.

The drawback of the Indian higher education system has been highlighted by K.N. Panikkar and M. Bhaskaran Nair (2012): Education in India turns out degree-holders with poor skills for employability or even self-employment. It has been reported that about 70 per cent of our educated youth are not engaged in meaningful employment because of the absence of required skill. The skill deficit is even more acute in professional courses where a large number is left out without any suitable employment. A nation cannot afford the wastage of such vast human resource. Creating suitable employment opportunities is one of the major challenges in the years to come. Of late, the crisis in higher education has become so serious that the national attention is getting more and more focused on quality expansion, infrastructure and public-private partnership in this field. Today the system seems to be under tremendous pressure to bring about radical reforms in conformity with international standard.

In the absence of any pragmatic industry-academia collaboration, it would be very difficult to prepare students for careers in their respective disciplines. The need of the hour is an integration of subjects with careers. In this new age, the academic charisma and industrial prowess have to be blended to create a nation with immense opportunities which will fully utilize its inherent potentials and strengths to grow, and thereby provide the much needed support to the young people to lead a decent and comfortable life.

Universities have an impact on technology diffusion, and thereby contribute to national and regional competitiveness through mechanisms such as consultation and clinical activities, contract research, joint ventures with business firms and participation in consortia aimed at solving generic industrial problem. By encouraging the development of consortia, institutes and joint ventures, joint funding helps universities to be in closer contact with market dynamics. Universities are not good at setting priorities for applications-oriented research (*Rethinking the Future of the University*, 1998).

Universities have to build closer ties with industry. The executives of these organizations can serve on advisory boards or special committees for the purpose of updating the other organization about the on-going changes and propose necessary changes to meet the demands of each other. For a country like India, it is high time that the government and policy makers initiate a closer link between academia and industry, which would be one of the best ways to provide greater opportunities to the younger generation. About 65 per cent of the population in India is below the age of 35. The country has to turn the youth-power to its enormous advantage through effective planning.

Importance of Extension Services in Educational Institutions

An educational institution must enable students to become civic-minded, socially conscious and patriotic citizens who would volunteer to meet the social needs of the community in which they live. It cannot exist as a cloistered entity, cocooned in a self-made island without responding to the basic needs of its society. In the twenty-first century, nations need the services of the younger generation to engage themselves in nation-building exercises or national reconstruction programmes on a priority basis. Such exposure will transform them into responsible and committed patriotic citizens. World over, educational institutions are now obligated to develop clear strategies for community extension programmes. They are also required to designate responsibilities for community extension service at their respective institutions.

An educational institution, with the guidance of specifically trained teachers to undertake social projects through volunteerism, has to play a pivotal role in the conduct of essential extension service programmes in the community after assessing its requirements. These programmes have to be integrated with the extra-curricular programmes of the institution for which specific hours are to be allocated. Once a student successfully completes, after productively spending a specified number of hours on a part of a project identified by the institution, he or she could be awarded academic credit for the work done. All students must be made aware of its value.

Aim of Organizing Extension Services Programmes

The purpose of conducting the extension programmes is to bring about positive changes in the mental attitude of students about commitment to societal needs.

Once they are involved in a community development project, they come to grip with the stark realities of life of fellow citizens and also come to know about the possibilities to improve their standard. The experience they gain from such projects transforms them into more service-minded citizens and foster in them love for the nation. In addition, they are able to learn important skills, both hard and soft, which would necessarily make them well-equipped to integrate their theoretical knowledge with practical orientation. When students are involved mentally and physically in a project, they master critical organizational and leadership skills, and to a certain extent, learn some technical skills too, which they may not have mastered in a classroom situation. They are also exposed to certain management skills while engaged in these projects.

In a community development project, students interact directly with the people of the locality, the public officials, the representatives of the organizations which are collaborating with the institution—to be precise, with people from all walks of life. This rare and unique opportunity definitely enriches the organizational skills and leadership qualities of students. They practice communication, negotiation, decision making and technical skills, and gain competence in the key areas of human development. If the project director could also obtain a report of the activities completed by every student, the participants learn the art of writing reports effectively. Moreover, any kind of community life undergone by the student enhances his confidence level to take up more challenging projects. This method of learning by doing boosts his morale considerably and renders him the necessary skills to tackle social problems, thereby, building competence, to be a better leader later.

Potentials of Extension Service Programmes

When teachers and students put their heads together to find solutions to a community problem by engaging themselves as a team, the resultant synergy is a remarkable achievement for the institution, which is highly appreciated by the community. In some countries, social service or community extension service is enthusiastically promoted by the government or local bodies involving students in schools and colleges.

Some institutions seek the assistance of social organizations or local administration which are actively involved in social projects so that such collaborative endeavors result in the efficient execution of the project. The sharing of expertise by the collaborating organization helps students to learn more about the technicalities of executing a project successfully. There are many governmental and non-governmental organizations which extend their expertise and funds to execute community development projects. The educational institution can find such organizations operating in their region, and jointly decide the appropriate project to be taken up.

As part of community extension services, an institution can put to use its teaching expertise or its learning resources. The institutions can establish advisory boards with memberships of public bodies so that they are able to identify the exact needs of the community and devise better programmes after obtaining feedback from the public bodies on the suitability and efficacy of the conduct of the extension programmes in the locality.

There are lots of projects available for an educational institution to execute. The important criteria to be looked into by an institution are to assess the benefit of such projects from the point of view of the community and the institution. They must also prepare a feasible roadmap for the successful implementation of the project, including its financial viability. Students must be involved in all the stages of planning the community development project as part of extension service rendered by the institution. A team has to be set up by clearly demarcating their duties and responsibilities. Students must be nominated in different positions so that they feel responsible and accountable for the success or failure of the project. Tasks are to be assigned to each and every participant, who are to report, on a daily basis, the progress achieved, which should be evaluated daily. Those participants who have done well must be appreciated by the head of the team, that too, on a daily basis. The participants must be able to enjoy community life and participate in cultural activities at the end of the day. A committee of teachers should monitor the progress of the work and its chairman should report to the administration of the institution periodically on all developments and progress achieved. Press communiqués could be released by the institution to create public awareness of the project executed.

A Variety of Projects to be Undertaken

Institutions can undertake housing projects for the economically disadvantaged people, projects for the handicapped, including the blind, environmental projects, literacy projects, palliative care projects, laying recreation parks, career guidance projects, cancer care projects, disaster relief projects, AIDS awareness projects, child health projects, laying roads projects, humanitarian aid projects, medical camps, 'Keep the City Clean' projects, Special Olympics projects, training camps at different levels and for different purposes, 'Green the Campus' projects, avenue plantation projects, conducting of socio-economic surveys—the list is endless.

The institution can undertake a project after conducting a survey in the locality and prioritize, according to the urgency of the situation, the most essential, but feasible project. Before implementing a social project, systematic and comprehensive planning has to take place by involving the teachers, students, representatives of the collaborating organizations and experts in the field.

14

Accreditation—Challenges and Problems

Long is the road from
conception to completion. —Moliere

Importance of Accreditation of Educational Institutions

All educational institutions are expected to obtain accreditation within a fixed period of time from the competent authority. The institutions are to follow rigorously effective and sustainable curricular practices to highlight the quality and result-oriented teaching practices, which is one of the key areas to be assessed by any accreditation body. Starting with the systematic implementation of curriculum formulated by universities in India, the institution can improve upon the mechanisms to fulfill all the common criteria determined by the National Assessment and Accreditation Council in India. Maybe, in one stretch an institution may not be able to fulfill all the requirements as set out by the Council. If we examine the criteria fixed by such bodies, we can understand the kind of efforts to be put into by the respective institutions to serve the students of different abilities and backgrounds. The institution has to introduce interactive instructional techniques through the use of different types of methodologies of teaching which include group discussion, case study, buzz group, project, seminar, etc., and application of ICT-enabled teaching to engage students in intellectual pursuits of higher order. To fulfill the requirements of these criteria, the institution must continuously evaluate the performance of its teachers so as to ascertain their professional qualities to meet the academic goals and raise the standards of the institution. Simultaneously, students are to be continuously assessed for their learning skills. The focus of this criterion is captured in the following criterion statements issued in general by most of the assessment and accreditation bodies in the world.

Important Criteria

I. The institution has a transparent admission process.
II. The programmes of teaching and learning cater to individual differences of students.

III. The institution facilitates the effective conduct of teaching-learning processes.
IV. The institution has provision to use the ICT to enhance teaching process.
V. The institution has a well-conceived plan to monitor the progress of students continuously.
VI. The institution has an effective mechanism to recruit adequate qualified faculty.
VII. The evaluation processes of students are reliable and valid.
VIII. The institution has an open and participative mechanism for the evaluation of teaching and promoting work satisfaction of the teachers.
IX. The teachers have opportunities for continued academic growth and professional development.
X. The institution has sustainable good practices in teaching, learning and evaluation to achieve academic excellence.

The best practices in curriculum aspects as prescribed by accreditation bodies underlie the significance of the role played by teachers in ensuring academic excellence. They are a must for the sustained development of any educational institution which would like to maintain benchmarks of excellence and function successfully and consistently in a competitive environment.

The overriding purpose of assessment and accreditation is to ensure quality in all spheres of higher education. "Quality is hard work. It requires a commitment to excellence, a dedication to leadership, and a willingness to change," says Jerome S. Arcaro, the author of, '*Quality in Education*'. We believe that there is logic behind useful educational evaluation, which leads to well-grounded practice for individuals, organization and society. This logic is based on the criterion that an educational system is to serve the needs of society and add value to stakeholders (Roger Kaufman, *et al.*, 2006). Evaluation is broadly concerned with some kind of assessment of the value of efforts and reforms (*Evaluating Educational Reforms*, edited by Peder Haug, 2001). Basically assessment is a strategy for evaluating the performance of an organization in relation to the expectations of its constituencies, and the organization's mission and vision. Quality improvement involves developing plans and strategies, working to reduce gaps, and institutionalizing changes into the normal work process of the organization (Brent D. Ruben, 1995). Quality assurance should be comprehensive and examine inputs, processes, and outputs (Barnett, 1987; Church, 1988). The concern for quality is because of the need for accountability to society.

According to K.B. Powar (2011), till the end of September, 2010, the National Assessment and Accreditation Council in India had accredited 159 universities and 4,171 colleges. Amongst the accredited universities, 60 (37.7%) were placed in A Grade, 95 (59.7%) in B Grade and 4 (2.6%) in C Grade. Category-wise, the best performance was that of deemed universities (55.3% in A Grade), followed by central universities (44.7% in A Grade), with the state universities (29.4% in A Grade) trailing in the third place. Shyamasundar (2010) is apprehensive about the performance of the institutions in higher education in India. He states that unfortunately, the quality of education imparted in different academic institutions in India is highly variable....Overall, the situation is that of islands of excellence in a sea of mediocrity. He argues that there is an urgent need to improve the quality of education. He also points out that the high incidence of unemployment amongst university graduates in India is because of the lack of relevance of education imparted by our universities and colleges. Our higher education institutions are not relevant to the needs of the society. An extreme view is that the 'average graduate', at least in the liberal arts, is not employable. There appears to be a mismatch between what is taught in our academic institutions and what is required by industry, business, administration, various professions and the society-at-large. The universities will have to address the question of relevance by updating their curricula following dialogue with different constituents of society, development of proper infrastructure, and close co-ordination with the 'users'. Jayaram (2004) has drawn attention to the fact that the lack of a link between the conventional courses and the job market has now become apparent to both students and discerning parents. There is also awareness that in most of our colleges, the standard of education is low, with practically no attention paid by teachers and administration to the teaching-learning process.

These matters are of great concern to the higher education system in India as in all these areas of significance, our institutions are trailing behind other international institutions. Moreover, a majority of Indian institutions have compromised on quality, and are not delivering quality education to a large number of students.

If we peruse the guidelines of the accreditation bodies in education all over the world, we will be able to appreciate their implications and nuances because they insist on consistent improvement of quality of education. In the US, the standards for accreditation are considered to be 'an articulation by the higher education community of what a college or university must do in order to deserve public trust. They also function as framework for institutional development and self-evaluation'. In some countries, the authorities take steps to penalize the erring institutions who do not fulfill the basic requirements as set forth in the guidelines to obtain accreditation within a stipulated period of time.

The different dimensions of quality in higher education are as follows:

- Academic Quality
  - Instruction
  - Research
  - Services/Outreach
- Administrative Quality
  - Processes
  - Systems
  - Procedures
  - Information Flows
- Relationship Quality
  - Relationships with public/consumers and one another
  - Interpersonal sensitivity and skill
  - Co-operation and Collaboration
  - Service Orientation

Source: Adopted from "*Quality in Higher Education*", Brent D. Ruben, 1995.

In different types of accreditation systems, emphasis is given to different criteria, depending on the accreditation authority's policies and priorities. Some studies, such as those concerned with performance indicators, concentrate on institutional inputs and outputs (e.g., Cave *et al.*, 1988; Johnes and Taylor, 1990.) Others examine processes, sometimes assessing the feasibility or otherwise of bringing to bear on university practices ideas drawn from total quality management in industry (e.g., Barnett, 1992; Ellis, 1993, Green, 1994; Sinclair Goodlad, 1995).

Most situations delve deep into the criteria related to the curriculum design and structure. The modules and courses within a programme are clearly identified. The academic depth of each module and course is analyzed and so are the mix, structure and level of core, elective and basic modules. Then, they check whether the selected modules really satisfy the range and depth of knowledge required and whether their contents have been developed to ensure minimal overlap. The delivery methodology of programme modules, assessment methodology and the progression routes are verified. The accreditation body also finds out whether transferable skills have been identified and student-centered activities and opportunities as expected of the specific requirements of the curriculum are available.

Instructional design is another key area of concern which justifies the impact of teaching and learning. Instructional design involves organizing and using tools of the mind and of learning to improve the conduct of education and training. According to Gagne and Briggs (1974), the purpose of the systematic design approach is "to encourage setting objectives, and provide a way to know when they are met. The process combined with a growing body of learning theory provides a set of tools that allow us to maximize individual learning potential."

The process of teaching and learning are given utmost importance in any assessment criteria. Regarding, the areas related to teaching, learning and assessment, they check, in detail, the methodologies used for each module and its effectiveness, including the clarity of instructional objectives, resources used, and the time spent for planning, development of the contents and pace of the programme. The learning strategy followed, student support mechanisms adopted and the assessment requirements are the other important areas examined. Records of assessment carried out are verified. Student-feedback on the quality of teaching is analyzed. In some cases, the inspection/peer team observes the teacher handling a class and even put questions to the students to verify their knowledge in the subject concerned. "Evaluation and accountability are inextricably linked. Both have the potential for organizational renewal through insights into organizational and group performance" (Douglas B Reeves, 2009). Academic standards are determined and/or evidenced by the level of academic preparation of the student body, the college curriculum, teaching methods, expectations for learning or grading standard, and achievement levels of graduates. Assessment of students' outcome is important if institutional quality is to be judged partly on the basis of the effectiveness of a programme in assisting student learning (*The Quest for Quality*, 1990).

Another crucial area examined is that of the availability of learning resources in the institution. All the physical resources, including library, workshops, IT and other laboratories are to be inspected. It is to be verified whether students are provided with open access and independent learning materials in the library. The role of staff, their training levels and the accommodation provided for classrooms, libraries, laboratories, workshops and IT labs are also to be examined.

Regarding the student support and guidance requirements, the peer committee of the accreditation body will find out whether a strategy to provide meaningful support and guidance to students is in vogue at the institution. The arrangements made for facilitating students' admission, induction and progression is to be verified. It is checked whether students have access to the institution's administration/academic facilities for the development of their soft skills, and social, and physical skills. The tutorial system and counseling facilities are checked. The service provided by the liaison staff is evaluated. The career development programmes and the effectiveness of such programmes is evaluated. On student progression and achievement, the peer committee looks into the strategy, policy and procedures of the institution in assessment, grading and credit rating. The details of student entry, intended outcome of programmes, the progression rates and non-completion rates are identified. Transfers in and out of the programme are noted.

Since quality assurance is an ongoing activity in all educational institutions, the strategies, policies, procedures and systems followed by the institution for improving quality and maintaining standards are examined in detail. The views of the teachers and staff are sought on the operational aspects of the institution regarding quality assurance practices and systems of quality control. The appraisal reports on teacher and staff performance and the details of training and other professional development programmes attended by them are checked. Research and consultation and associated academic enrichment facilities are other areas of concern.

The teachers are to be made aware of the requirements to be fulfilled to obtain accreditation. They are to be given responsibilities to manage 'Quality Assurance' cells and comply with the demands of such internal bodies. They are to be made aware of the self-assessment and performance appraisal systems followed by the institution. They are to be motivated constantly to achieve the targets specified as the key performance indicators. The importance of maintaining appropriate documents to substantiate the work completed in each area of activity by teachers must also be clearly communicated.

The purpose of accreditation, in the final analysis, is to help the institution understand the assessment results in order to improve further. In most cases, the institutions undergo this process with lot of dedication and commitment, but fail to do self-introspection when the results come. During the conduct of the assessment, the peer group, on the final day, share their experience with the institution and suggest better methods and practices to enhance the quality of education. In the report they make clear-cut suggestions for improvement. Whether the accreditation process was a success or failure, it is the bounden duty of the institution to pay attention to its suggestions. The whole assessment process may be viewed as a well-intended exercise carried out to support the development of the institution to set benchmarks of excellence in all aspects of teaching and learning. But, the impact of assessment and accreditation depends on how frequently and in what manner all the stakeholders make use of its results to rectify the weaknesses, and develop and strengthen the core competence of the institution.

The following are common barriers in achieving quality in education initiated through a process of assessment and accreditation by an External Agency:

1. An institution which has never undergone any assessment of its performance by an outside agency will in the beginning show signs of reluctance and give excuses to avoid such assessment for fear of exposure to its inherent weaknesses and failures.

2. Some institutions feel that such assessment by external agencies is a kind of unwarranted intrusion in their 'secluded existence'.
3. Some feel it is a sheer waste of time and resources of the institution which is already cash strapped even to provide the routine facilities.
4. Some feel that this kind of assessment by external agencies might lead to a simmering conflict between the various departments, and also at times between the institution and the outside agency.
5. They fear the imposition of new measures to control the institution which compels them to follow a strict regime of quality-oriented practices, which may be repugnant to teachers and other staff.
6. The entire teaching community and staff may not understand, appreciate, and feel the importance of quality assurance. In such circumstances, those who are not committed turn a deaf ear to such proposals for change and development.
7. In most cases, the teachers may dislike more work thrust upon them as part of the duties assigned in connection with the assessment and accreditation process.
8. Some even fear retribution by administration if they do not rise up to their expectations to contribute effectively for the fulfillment of the criteria laid out by the assessment and accreditation body.
9. Some teachers might criticize even the very intentions of the assessment and accreditation bodies as sheer nonsense as they consider themselves superior to other academics.
10. Some detest such assessment programmes as they are inherently averse to any kind of quality initiative.

Before deciding upon inviting an assessment and accreditation agency to its campus, the college or university administration may first initiate the conduct of orientation sessions for the teachers, students and staff to create awareness about the need, purpose, benefits accruing from such proactive exercises, the commitment required, resources to be made available and efforts to be put in by all the stake holders. During such interactive sessions, the administrators including teachers, may clarify the doubts raised and convince the sceptics about the pros and cons of such academic and administrative exercises.

Another challenge, which is of a life-threatening nature for the higher educational institutions, is the high level of competition in this field from international players or from local institutions which maintain international standards in education. The world has become one global village. We live among determined, well-educated and strongly motivated competitors. If the colleges and universities do not maintain high quality in their performance, the competitors in the field would take over the place of the poor performers. As we all know, "history is not kind to idlers."

Relevance of Quality Assurance Cells in Educational Institutions

The Quality Assurance Cell is basically a quality management technique which concentrates on maintaining quality in all the departments of the institution by actively involving both administration and teachers in the decision-making process associated with developing benchmarks of excellence. It operates at all levels of the organization, especially at the top administrative level and at the departmental level. It sets the goals for the institution regarding assurance of quality in its functioning for each academic year. It meets periodically to discuss, analyze and find solutions to all problems related to quality assurance. A team sets the goals for each department after carrying out an in-depth SWOT analysis. The targets are set by joint consultation with the teachers and administration which focuses on collaborative efforts of all the stakeholders of the institution. It analyzes the drawbacks of the prevailing system and suggests changes to be incorporated to bring out better results. If effective methodology of teaching is needed to improve the system, then, the Quality Assurance Cell may recommend conducting faculty development programmes for the teachers in this crucial area. Once it is implemented, the Quality Assurance Cell has to collect feedback regarding the performance of the teachers who were assigned to undergo such training and assess whether any qualitative improvement in performance has been achieved.

The teacher who becomes the leader of a Quality Assurance Cell may be the head of a department or a senior teacher or any other teacher who has the will, competence and passion to achieve the targets by motivating the entire stakeholders of an institution. The coordinator of the Quality Assurance Cell is assisted by a team of teachers and the administrative personnel. The leader of the group must be conversant with the 'Quality Assurance' process and strategies as an expert consultant and should be an effective motivator and communicator.

According to the National Assessment and Accreditation Council, in India, the Internal Quality Assurance Cell has to be established as a post-accreditation quality sustenance measure. Since quality enhancement is a continuous process, the Internal Quality Assurance Cell, will become a part of the institution's system and work towards realizing the goals of quality enhancement and sustenance. The prime task of the Internal Quality Assurance Cell is to develop a system for conscious, consistent and catalytic improvement in the performance of the institution.

A CASE STUDY

ACCREDITATION—CHALLENGES, PROBLEMS AND FULFILLMENT

The Sahara College of Science and Arts was one of the reputed colleges in the locality with a dozen departments which consistently produced good results. Being a pretty old institution, in general, only a few of its teachers took pains to know about the history of the college and their own departments. Basically, they knew about the founder's perspective as included in the mission statement of the institution.

When instructions reached the college from the higher authorities to take steps to obtain national level accreditation, the principal, with the guidance of the college council, constituted a committee with a nodal officer in charge to fulfill the requirements for accreditation.

The college council, which is a high power committee in a college comprising the heads of all the departments with principal as its chairman, discussed at length the modalities and strategies to be followed to obtain accreditation. The committee constituted for the purpose with the nodal officer as its chairman started functioning. Their major task was to collect the self study report from each department. Unfortunately, they were not able to do so.

For some time, the administration was quite concerned with the slow progress of work. Later, everybody almost forgot the responsibility to obtain accreditation and the project had a natural death. The college council did make several attempts to revive the activities of the committee, but failed in its efforts. The problems that the college faced were mainly due to the perception related to the concept of accreditation itself. The purpose of obtaining accreditation was not made clear and those responsible were not motivated to carry out the work which needed expertise, dedication and sacrifice. The stakeholders of the institution were not convinced about the need for obtaining accreditation. They thought if they underwent a detailed and cumbersome process of accreditation, they would be forced to elicit information from various sources, consolidate reports after collecting data and prepare the self-study report. This work, they knew would consume much time and overburden them, and might affect teaching. Some of them asked for extension of time to submit the departmental self-study reports. Others did not pay heed to the suggestions from the committee specially constituted for the purpose of submitting the final reports to the accreditation authorities as they faced teething problems and lack of interest from other members of the departments. As some had mentally rejected the proposal to go for accreditation because they considered the whole activity as imposed from the higher echelons in the education sector with a plan to control the system, they too backed out. Resistance to change was but a natural outcome.

In such a large institution, each department was an island by itself and they did not appreciate intervention from others, whether it was for a good cause like institutional accreditation or for enhancement of the quality of the departments. Some departments were snobbish as they considered themselves as superior to others, because they had over the period of time developed high-achievement.

In the end, the principal convened a meeting of the college council to review the progress of the work. He had to face the stark reality that nothing serious was done and very little progress had been made by most of the departments. So, they were forced to shelve the project and remained silent for some time.

Meanwhile the government authorities and the university evinced interest in accreditation and issued orders to pursue the accreditation process seriously. The principal convened a meeting during the following academic year after the university examinations and vacation were over. The former nodal officer resigned, and a new person was given an opportunity to be in his saddle. Even though he knew it was a herculean task, he took up the new assignment with a lot of hope and confidence to do something creditable for that reputed institution. Of course, he was lucky to obtain the unstinted cooperation from his colleagues from almost all the departments. Fortunately, those departments which had turned a deaf ear to the assessment and accreditation process previously, supported the cause eventually with some qualms. Meetings, both formal and informal, were called to discuss the problems they faced and solutions were worked out. Since no one had any prior experience in this field, very often they were all stumbling in darkness. Meanwhile, the new nodal officer carried out some research, and in this connection, visited some premier institutions in the country where they had undergone the accreditation process successfully. These visits made it possible for him to set up a clear-cut roadmap to fulfill the objectives of assessment and accreditation with the support of the newly constituted committee. A bunch of members of the team visited each department and guided them to prepare their self-study reports. Simultaneously, another team prepared the institutional self-study report with necessary justifications and documentary proof. Thanks to this highly motivated team, the whole exercise was completed with a great sense of satisfaction within a short time.

In between, the university convened a meeting of all the colleges under its jurisdiction to review the progress of work done by the individual colleges to obtain accreditation. The principal deputed the nodal officer to represent the college. At that meeting, after the address of the vice chancellor, during the discussion those colleges which had already prepared the self-study reports and were ready to submit them to the accreditation body were asked to address the meeting. The nodal officer from Sahara College of Arts and Science, stated that the institution was ready to submit the self-study report within three months. His announcement was followed by a long silence as not a single college had prepared the assessment and accreditation report. For them it was a totally new experience. After that meeting, the nodal officer told the principal and members of the committee about their commitment to prepare all the reports in time and submit them to the concerned Comittee to expedite and finalize the reports from all departments.

As most of the faculty members had been serving the institution almost for their entire career, the nodal officer and the committee fondly hoped that it would not be difficult to prepare the self-study reports. However, problems erupted from some corners. In one of the departments, they were all getting ready to organize a series of national seminars, and could not concentrate much on the preparation of the self-study report. In another department, things were moving at a snail's pace as the responsible members were apparently non-cooperative. The active members of the team approached them several times, but of no avail. The time for final preparations was nearing. Another major setback which they confronted was the retirement of the dean who was mentally prepared to assist them to prepare that department's self-study report, but could not do much. Some of the departments felt too overburdened with such administrative tasks. In one of the departments, the dean was on a foreign tour. Surprisingly, some of the departments were running from pillar to post to dig out their history and desperately convened meetings of the alumni. Another blow came from a new department, which literally stalled the proceedings by not giving the details of the profile of the department.

However, the team concentrated on the main task, and collected most of the details to be furnished by all departments. The college administration supported the nodal officer and the committee to collect information about the profile of the institution.

Some of the departments were reluctant to do the paper work as they were not used to do so. As they required factual reports from all, many of them pleaded lack of knowledge about the matters concerned. For the new committee, time was running out and they felt desperate.

Some comments from the departments were as follows:

> "We need not report that we do not know anything about the past achievements of the department. Who knows when this department was established and about its past achievements? There are no documents kept in the department stating anything important about its past performance or history, and we are not to be blamed for it."
>
> "The preparation of the self study report is a time consuming and really challenging task, and we do not understand its implications."
>
> "This institution is already a renowned college with lots of achievements. We do not understand why such an institution with admiring credentials needs to go for accreditation?
>
> "We are only academics. Why should we bother about these new systems?"

Against all these odds, the team prepared the final report and submitted it to the authority for accreditation.

Questions to Ponder Over:

- ➢ Recommend a course of action to get all the departments involved in the process of accreditation in the very beginning itself.
- ➢ Recommend solutions to the problems raised by the departments.
- ➢ Is institutional accreditation a necessary evil?
- ➢ Is resistance to change a major issue in this context?
- ➢ Monitoring the effectiveness of decisions put into action is an essential factor that would decide the success or failure of a project—Comment on this statement.
- ➢ Do you think that an accreditation process would enhance the qualities of an institution? If the answer is YES, provide justification.

15
Strengthening Work Culture

Nations have passed away and left no traces,
And history gives the naked cause of it-
One single simple reason in all cases;
They fell because their peoples were not fit. —Rudyard Kipling

Importance of Organizational Culture in Educational Institutions

Organizational culture is defined as a cognitive framework consisting of attitudes, values, behavioural norms and expectations shared by the members of an organization. It refers to a system of shared values held by the members of an organization that differentiates it from other organizations. The system of shared meaning denotes certain major characteristics which the organization cherishes and values.

According to Robert G Owens, organizational culture is the body of solutions to external and internal problems that has worked consistently for a group and that is therefore taught to new members as the correct way to perceive, think about, and feel in relation to them. This culture develops over a period of time, and, in the process of developing, acquires significantly deep meaning. Therefore, culture can be defined as shared philosophies, ideologies, values, assumption, beliefs, expectations, attitudes, and norms that knit a community together. Cultural differences between various institutions are the off-shoots of the individual institution's basic ideologies, values, assumptions, beliefs, expectations and attitudes.

Organizational culture means the collective cognition that is reflected in the traditions and habits of an institution. The moment we enter the premises of an institution, howsoever overwhelmed we are by the grandeur of its building, we are affected by its culture. The vision statements communicate the cardinal values of the institution. It is a rallying force behind its cultural evolution. When we interact with its stake holders, we come to know about the exceptional qualities of its people. Those who run it—whether they are teachers, staff or students, spontaneously reflect its culture. The visitors feel how a distinct culture represents the life force of that organization. Illustrious institutions are characterized by a set of noble and lasting values passed on to generations of students who, indeed, take pride in them. It is needless to state that a student who undergoes studies in a renowned institution acquires certain cardinal values of life through a process of acculturation, or socialization, which is the hallmark of that institution. They put him in good stead throughout his life. Indeed, good schools, colleges and universities shape the destiny of their students in a great way. Those products bear the stamp of excellence of their alma mater wherever they go.

In any organization, its core values differentiate it from others. An educational institution is no exception to this basic concept. The core organizational values to be inculcated and cherished by an educational organization in relation to teaching are: the value placed on the teachers, openness in communication, sensitivity to the needs of students, encourage the teachers to contribute new ideas for the development of the institution, willingness to adopt changes by both administration and teachers, development of a congenial atmosphere and creation of a collaborative and supportive mechanism for personal growth and development of teachers.

Role of Culture in the Institutions

The cultural values nourished and nurtured by an educational institution goes a long way to mould its cultural edifice. They have a great effect on the entire entity and its ethos permeates through the society in which it exists for a pretty long period. Basically, culture signifies the very soul and inner strengths of the organization. It clarifies and reinforces standards of behaviour for all the members of the organization which includes students. The culture of an organization is so important that it acts as a guide to mould and shape one's behaviour and provide stability to it.

Richard J. Light (2001) asserts that campuses really have unique culture. When asked if he could explain why faculty members at some colleges seem to care deeply about the effectiveness of their teaching, while colleagues at other similar colleges clearly care less, a distinguished anthropologist responded, "It is in the air." When pressed harder, he said, "I think it is a combination of history, faculty values, leadership, and student expectations."

From the behaviour of students of a campus one can easily judge the quality of the school or college they belong to. Culture of an institution always reminds people of what their institution is all about. Everyone knows about the impact of good schooling on students. Culture establishes a sense of identity. It is this culture of an institution which binds the students to its alma mater till the end. The role played by the culture of an educational institution in its evolution and projection is very vital. It is the responsibility of teachers and administration to create an impressive and unique culture which is reflected in its core values and dominant perceptions, and etched in the minds of all the members of the institution for ever. For instance, a culture of accountability on the part of administration and teachers makes a good institution great.

According to the management pundits, there are seven identifiable characteristics which encapsulate the quintessence of the culture of any organization. They are as follows:

1. *Innovation and risk taking*: It means the degree to which the teachers are encouraged to be innovative and take risks. The teachers who work in such an environment become proactive and change-oriented. They opt for introducing newer teaching methodologies and aids and thereby bring about drastic positive changes in the institution. Such institutions, in the end, become the leaders in this competitive field. In the process they take risks which may be considered by the run of the mill institutions as merely taking chances.
2. *Attention to detail*: It means the degree to which teachers are expected to exhibit precision, analysis, and attention to details in their performance. In the institution which promotes pragmatic approach to raise the standards of performance of its teachers, it seeks minute data about them based on predetermined performance criteria. This criterion is circulated amongst the teachers beforehand to alert them about the need to comply with the requirements.
3. *Outcome orientation*: It means the degree to which management focuses on results rather than on the processes followed to attain these results. The organization in such circumstances invariably concentrates on the targets to be achieved by the teachers, as it is those results which ultimately grade the institution as an outstanding institution or a just a mediocre one.
4. *People orientation*: It implies the degree to which management decisions rely on the implication of the effect of results on people within the organization. The more the effect of good results on the teachers, the better the progress of the institution as a centre of excellence. The organization with a better orientation will primarily appreciate the impact of good teaching practices.
5. *Team orientation*: It refers to the degree to which teaching activities are facilitated with the active involvement of groups rather than individuals. The thrust is given to group initiative and participation in decision making. In successful institutions the administration delegates the authority to middle level management consisting of senior teachers who in turn manages the department or a cluster of

classes by forming compatible groups. It is these teams that deliver the expected results through their combined effort.

6. *Aggressiveness*: It refers to the degree to which the teachers are aggressive and competitive rather than lackadaisical and lazy. The aggressive nature of teachers to achieve the goals and a competitive spirit to face the challenges of the institution with a positive mental attitude determine how an institution is rated in the society. An institution where teachers lack initiative and drive to maintain or surpass previous records of achievements, soon becomes the least preferred institution in that locality.
7. *Stability*: It refers to the degree to which the institutional activities put emphasis upon maintaining the status quo instead of achieving growth. In an era of keen competition, those organizations which strive hard to achieve growth find it difficult to maintain status quo. This challenging situation can make or mar the future of the institution.

To understand the culture of the institution one has to determine the shared understanding of the teachers in respect of these characteristics. If the organization has a composite culture with a blend of all these typical characteristics, it will be a successful institution.

Organizational culture denotes a common perception held by teachers and all other stakeholders. If the organization culture encompasses innovation, a risk-bearing attitude, goal and member orientation, aggressiveness and stability, its overall impact is optimistic and pro active. The result of such positive qualities naturally brings satisfaction and higher productivity.

In any educational institution, the composite organizational culture is affected by the influence of a dominant culture which expresses the core values shared by a majority of teachers. It is the evolution of this dominant culture that finally decides the charted course of that institution. The core values of this dominant culture reflect the aspirations, expectations and achievements of the institution.

These days a new culture of learning is also evolving. Thanks to the contribution of Douglas Thomas and John Seely Brown in their book, "*A New Culture of Learning*", we are able to understand the impact of changes in the learning process. They exhort us to rethink about learning and strive for ways to amplify it and make it scalable, mainly due to the fact that "the world is changing faster than ever and our skill sets have a shorter and shorter life." Simultaneously, as our access to information is unparalleled in the modern times, we are able to make use of 'peer mentoring'. Teachers have to become aware of the incredible power of the new cultures of learning, tap new resources, especially the peer to peer learning.

To ensure smooth and effective organizational change, an institution must not skip any of the following important steps.

Steps for Effective Organizational Change

- Establishing a sense of urgency.
- Forming a powerful guiding coalition.
- Creating a vision.
- Communicating the vision.
- Empowering and motivating others to act according to the vision.
- Planning and creating short term wins.
- Consolidating improvement and bringing out more changes.
- Institutionalizing new quality approaches for growth and development.

Key Factors that Decide the Educational Environment of an Institution

The following are the key areas of administration that make an institution stand out from the ordinary. Maybe, it takes years of perseverance and strong commitment to make an impact in the internal and external environment of an institution and create goodwill and reputation. Ultimately, the educational environment of any institution is moulded by the impact and influence of these factors.

1. The vision, mission and objectives of the institution;
2. Its culture and values;
3. The culture and values of its personnel;
4. The structure of the Organization, Authority, Responsibility and Roles;
5. Institutional governance;
6. Compliance of rules and regulations of the State;
7. Transparency in dealings;
8. The curriculum of the educational programmes offered;
9. Quality of teaching and quality assurance strategies;
10. Quality of service provided by the administration;
11. Fairness in dealing with staff;
12. System of monitoring, guiding, reporting and controlling its activities.

It is the educational environment of an institution that makes it distinct and unique. All the key factors mentioned above have to be considered seriously by both administrators and teachers in the making of an institution. It is a long drawn out process which requires total dedication from all corners.

CASE STUDY

THE AFTERMATH OF A SHIFT IN THE ORGANIZATIONAL VALUES AND POLICIES

The Brighton College was one of the leading private colleges in the district for quite a long period. From its inception, thirty years back, it enjoyed a long standing reputation with creditable achievements. Of late, the standards had fallen and most of the parents were disgusted with its performance. The downturn started almost four years back when a new set of administrators were appointed from the field of business in the place of the old academic-based administrators. As a major shift in the policy, the new administrators who wanted to run the institution almost like a business, set growth targets in enrollment of students, so that they could make more profits. They were not much interested in the academic process. The principal was forced to admit students irrespective of their qualities, which resulted in the admission of a large number of mediocre and poor quality students. The sole aim was to fillup maximum number of seats. Earlier, the institution followed a policy of admitting students on merit, which resulted in leaving several seats vacant. During the current year, administration had met the growth target and reached its peak intake, but, in the process was constrained to compromise much on quality and merit.

The teachers found it hard to handle the classes as planned as many students were not interested in studies. They were whiling away their time in the campus and had created a lot of disciplinary problems, which in a sense resulted in diverting the attention of teachers from the academic priorities. Some students behaved unruly in the classrooms, which affected the general discipline of the institution. Though the institution had the highest number of intake of students in its history, it had a severe backlash on its credentials because its reputation for quality and high level of performance had undergone a down swing. The failure on the part of the new administrators to understand the serious implications of bypassing the long term admission policies of the previous administration became a matter of great concern for both parents and students.

Some of the parents opined, "The administration should not have digressed from the core organizational values to make a fast buck." "The administration should have retained the old guards instead of bringing in the new administrators who had more of commercial interest in them and lacked sound educational background." "They should have made use of ICT enabled teaching so as to manage the large number of students in the classrooms." "A time has come for bifurcation of the institution while restructuring the whole organization for better administration."

Some parents were considering shifting their children to better institutions. It was an uphill task as it was very difficult to obtain admission in good institutions after the first year of study. During the last meeting of administrators, a serious conflict arose between them. Some of them had started realizing the consequences of the blunder committed by them in compromising with quality and diluting the importance of the admission criteria. They suggested appointing a consultancy to analyze the problem and suggest strategies and ways and means to tide over the current critical problem.

With the reputation of the institution at stake, and the pressing need for reaccreditation in the offing, the administration became panicky, and majority of them regretted such turn of critical events. The morale and motivation of both teachers and staff touched its lowest ebb, and they too blamed the new administrative policies for the disaster. Meanwhile, the institution started facing stiff competition from other players in the field who were quality conscious in their operations.

Questions to Ponder Over:

- Do you think that the new administration followed a wrong policy by changing its long term policy of admission by merit?
- As the new administration faces a sizeable challenge in plotting a new course that would guarantee growth as well as quality, what would be your recommendations?
- Should higher education be made selective, and admission made open to students with the right aptitude and quality only?
- In your opinion, will the Brighton College collapse after few more years of functioning had the administration followed the same strategy in admission? If, YES, what would be your recommendations to save the institution from its downfall?
- You may construct a recommendation as to what the administration should do to make a turn around and follow a new vision for growth with quality.

16

Major Concerns of Education Institutions

When you have exhausted all possibilities,
Remember this: you haven't. —Thomas Edison

Student-Teacher Ratio

Student-teacher ratio refers to the number of teachers in a school or college with respect to the number of students in each class in the institution. If the ratio is high, then the number of students in each class will be high and vice versa. Several studies have been conducted to find the affects of both low and high ratios, mainly to find the effects of the size of the class and students' achievement.

It is found that due to more individualized attention given to students in smaller classes, they perform better in all aspects of learning. The graduation rates are high and they outperform the students who study in larger classes. Moreover, there are fewer drop-outs and the percentage of success rate is high. In smaller classes, students build better relationships with their classmates and the teacher when compared to the students who attend large classes. They are also more engaged in their classroom activities. Teachers also find it easier to organize classroom learning activities effectively. For the teacher, classroom management becomes easier and efficient and more quality instructional time is used to make learning effective.

In smaller classes, students are more responsible and their self-esteem levels are high. They are more considerate, concerned and harmonious in their behaviour. As they nurture a positive attachment to the institution, they willingly extend co-operation to the developmental programmes. It is found from studies that there is a positive impact of smaller classes on learning effectiveness. The personal attention given to each student substantially reduces the boredom that students face in large classes.

It has been noticed that many institutions turn education into an individualized process by preferring smaller classrooms. Indeed, this paradigm shift is a bi-product of the digital revolution. The infinite possibilities of the digital world has been explored and exploited in modern classrooms. Whether this kind of increased individualization of students at the expense of positive social habits would create psychological problems for the young generation is a question to be examined by sociologists and psychologists. In our experience, when the ratio is low, the teacher's productivity increases, which results in increasing the student's achievement and success rate, and it simultaneously reduces behavioural problems in the classrooms. The recommended ratio is 1: 25 at secondary and under-graduate level and 1:10 at the post-graduate level.

The Teacher-Student Relationship

The teacher-student relationship is the most enduring relationship, which makes their life more meaningful. The respect earned by a teacher is something special and it continues for ever. We may recall an incident which illustrates the beauty of their relationship. The author was watching two kids playing on the beach. As most kids do on a beach, both of them ventured into building a sand-castle by the sea shore. It was beautifully completed with gusto and in team spirit. If looked like a marvelous piece of fine-tuned architecture. They were so elated that they hugged each other to celebrate the big feat. All of a sudden a big wave came, knocked down the sand-castle and reduced it into a heap of sand. The author expected both of them to burst into tears, devastated by the cruel blow dealt by the waves. Instead, they ran in all gaiety, holding their hands, up and down the beach. They forgot the tragedy they had suffered, and settled on another part of the beach, unmindful of the catastrophe, and built another beautiful sand-castle. Their expression of faith and confidence conveyed a lesson. What ultimately stand out in a relationship are—faith, trust and mutual respect. In life, we may build castles after castles by spending our time, energy and resources, but if those structures are built without the strong foundations of faith, trust and mutual respect, they all crumble into pieces. Only those relationships which are based on faith, trust and mutual respect endure till the end. All other relationships are knocked down by forces known and unknown to us.

A teacher has to possess qualities which make a student comfortable in the class. He can always encourage, inspire, and also forgive a student. The students do have immense faith in their teachers. They trust them and have the greatest respect for them. A teacher is a surrogate parent who constantly builds confidence in the minds of students and shows them the right way to live. It is these qualities which make the teacher-student relationship ennobling and everlasting.

Stability of Tenure of Personnel

We are reminded of one of the greatest gurus of management, Henri Fayol, whose contribution to the theory and practice of management is monumental.

In one of the fourteen principles of administration, he has delineated the importance of stability of tenure of personnel, indicating that a long term tenure of personnel makes an organization healthy. According to Henri Fayol, high turnover of personnel, can damage morale and efficiency. It is expected that organizations follow policies that ensure long term tenure of their personnel.

Similarly, in educational institutions, the administration must ensure the stability of tenure of teachers as they are the main pillars of the organization who guarantee the quality of education. It has been noticed that high teacher turnover drags the institution's grades lower. In institutions where there is the prevalence of abnormally high teacher turnover rates, the grading is lower. The negative impact of such policies of educational administrators is that, it severely affects the growth and development of the institution. If the teacher turnout is more than 20 to 30 per cent, then it demands serious study of the situation. Such high percentages in turnout would point a finger at the inefficiency of administration to tackle the basic problems leading to teacher turnover.

There is a strong correlation between teacher turnover and quality of education. The reasons for teacher turnover in individual institutions must be analyzed by a team of experts and their recommendations must be adopted by the institution to rectify the serious malady. Whether it is the salary structure, working conditions, heavy work load or any other reason, the institution has to take immediate steps to motivate the teachers to continue in their service. Teacher turnover is a matter of great concern. If it continues unabated, the rating of the institution would fall drastically, which in turn, would affect its credibility.

Leadership

An institution requires administrators and teachers who have a clear vision for the future of the institution, and can articulate this vision to all the stakeholders. Such leaders can elevate the spirits and inspire the team of teachers and groups of students to achieve their goals. They should be able to enlist support of all the stakeholders to develop a collaborative institutional culture focused on effective teaching and learning. They should possess the competence to plan, organize, staff, motivate, communicate, coordinate, report and control, and, thereby achieve the objectives, meet the standards and assume responsibility for effective administration through collaborative efforts. It should be their top priority to work together to implement a shared vision and mission which they have developed through collaborative efforts. Moreover, they should be able to promote continuous and sustainable development of the institution. But, many educational institutions lack proper and effective leadership at the administrative and academic levels, which results in their poor performance whereas good institutions with effective leadership practices perform better.

The success or failure of an institution depends mainly on the quality and style of leadership at the higher echelons of administration as well as of teachers. What the leadership attempts to achieve is the realization of the overall objectives of the institution. It is a combination of a group of major objectives. It is the duty of the leadership, consisting of both administrators and teachers, to constantly motivate and move their respective teams or groups to action and thereby fulfill the overall objectives of the institution. But the overriding ambition must be to transform the institution into a centre of excellence by developing its core competence as stated in its vision/mission statements. It has been found that some outstanding institutions follow the practice of expanding their vision and establish new goals as demanded by the emerging situations. Some successful institutions, which build on their inner strengths and capabilities, maintain certain enviable strategic positions and eventually evolve themselves as leaders in their field. Rome was not built in a day. It takes years of persistent positive actions to build a class institution. It is a labourious task which calls for sacrifices and strong determination from administration and teachers. Institutions can follow different styles of leadership which are—the autocratic, the democratic and the laissez-faire. In the autocratic style of leadership, the leader himself decides everything and strictly enforces his decision. In the democratic style of leadership, which adopts a consensus method of decision making, the leader sits with the team, they discuss the matter and mutually arrive at a decision which is implemented. In the laissez-faire style of leadership, it is a free for all as nobody bothers about the consequences of any decision. The last style of leadership is completely unacceptable as it can trigger chaos and confusion.

Of the many theories of leadership, the one which suits an educational institution is the Contingency Theory of Leadership proposed by Fred Fiedler. He identifies two main leadership styles. One is the relationship motivated-leadership which obtains satisfaction from good personal relationships. It is more concerned with what the group feels and encourages contribution of ideas from all the members. The other, is the Task-motivated leadership, which is always more concerned with the successful completion of tasks assigned to the team. They give clear-cut orders and ask the group to follow standardized procedures. He states that both the styles can be effective in appropriate contexts. He prescribes a contingency approach to leadership and rejects the proposition that there is one best style which is suitable in all situations.

This widely publicized theory holds good in institutions as it contains relationship between leadership style and the favourableness of the situation. Situational favourableness is attributed to three empirically derived dimensions, which are as follows:

1. The leader-member relationship, which is the most critical variable in determining that the situation is favourable.
2. The degree of task structure, which is the second most important input that makes the situation favourable.
3. The leader's position power obtained through formal authority, which is the third most critical dimension of the situation.

Situations are considered to be favourable to the leader if all the three dimensions mentioned above are high. If not, a situation is unfavourable to the leader.

Teachers who aspire to become proficient in leadership qualities are nowadays offered plenty of opportunities to undergo courses and specialized training to build leadership competence. Teachers who aspire to become education-administrators make use of such opportunities.

Lessons from geese are a conventional, but convincing illustration from nature about the relevance of effective leadership.

The geese in formation can be seen honking from behind to encourage those upfront to keep up their speed. This honk is positive, encouraging and helpful for the entire team. When the lead goose gets tired, it rotates back into the formation and another goose flies at the leading position. As geese flap their wings, they create uplift for the birds following. As they fly in a 'V' formation, the whole flock adds greater flying range than if any goose were to fly alone. Whenever a goose falls out of the formation, it immediately feels the drag and resistance of flying single, and speedily gets back to the formation to take advantage of the lifting power of the goose just in front. If a goose falls sick, one or two geese drop out of the formation and follow the sick one until it is able to fly again, and join a new formation.

As leaders, teachers are to follow a proactive and transformative leadership style of the 'geese' and build a highly focused and collaborative team.

CASE STUDY

THE NEW PRINCIPAL

Years back the Bright School had a principal who was very strict, and often behaved like a terror. The very sight of him made the staff and students shudder. As far as possible, they tried to avoid him. The teachers were horrified when he came to their classes or peeped. The students moved in stark silence when they saw the principal at a distance. He was a stickler to rules and never bent it to please anyone. He was able to command respect and obedience. The students attended the classes on time and the teachers were punctual. He never convened a teachers meeting, but frequently sent memos and notices to the teachers to get things done. A real task master, indeed. His style of leadership was that of an autocrat and he rejoiced in his achievements. The results were fairly good. The discipline was up to the mark. Parents had immense faith in him as any chance for indiscipline would be nipped in the bud with severe punishment. Not a single student ventured to create any ugly scene in the institution. Absenteeism amongst the teachers was not at all an issue, as nobody dared to take unnecessary leave. The teachers used to say—"whatever is the nature of the principal, the institution had no problems and things went on smoothly as long as they did their duties well."

However, this principal was transferred by the management as they wanted to appoint a task master in their new institution. Another principal joined who knew the ways of his predecessor. He suggested he was making the functioning of the institution democratic. Within a few days of his assuming office, he convened a meeting of teachers and made it threadbare that he would follow a policy of open discussions and democratic ways of decision making. He assigned some new duties to the teachers and appointed new committees to oversee the functioning of newly constituted bodies to improve the academic atmosphere of the institution. He requested the teachers to lend him support to bring about the intended changes. Surprisingly, only a handful of teachers paid heed to his suggestions, but never completed the tasks assigned to them. Some even summarily rejected the proposals put forward by the principal. A senior teacher commented, "There is no need for these changes as things went on well without these new programmes." Later, when the principal convened meetings, the attitude of the teachers became negative and non-cooperative. Some teachers boycotted the meeting by giving ostensible reasons. The teachers as a whole became irresponsible and neglected their duties.

☞

- Discuss this case and find out the central problem faced by the institution.
- Should the former principal be reappointed and the new incumbent transferred?
- Have you come across such situations in your institution?
- Do you approve the leadership styles of both the principals?
- If you were the principal, which style would you choose to set things right in both the situations?

A Conflict between the Staff and Teachers

Line and staff is a concept used in management parlance. There is no doubt that in an educational institution, the employees who are directly connected with the realization of the objectives of the organization are the teachers. The staff is the administrative staff of the institution that provides assistance to teachers and others for its regular functioning. They act as a link between the principal and the teachers. The staff feels they are superior to the teachers as they deal with all the administrative affairs and are closer to the State Boards or Universities. The teachers, on the other hand, feel they are more competent to deal with matters related to the main objective of the institution, and hence they are superior to the staff. Since both believe that they are superior to each other, they have some suspicion about the other; they fear that the other is sabotaging their prospects. They lack confidence in each other, and occasional tiffs arise between them. It results in a lot of misunderstanding, which contaminates the atmosphere in the organization.

In educational institutions when there is a conspicuous rift between the line and the staff, the principal can patch up these differences, and bring out harmony in the organization. The different departments are the operating wings of an educational institution and are responsible for accomplishing its objectives. The staff communicates the decisions of the institution or higher authorities through the principal to the various departments. They may act as advisors on certain technical matters after going through the rules and regulations which the institution has to follow in letter and spirit. In reality, there is no need for a conflict between line and staff as such. Even though they represent two different hierarchies of the organization, they complement each other's work so as to achieve the overall objectives of the organization. Both of them are equally responsible for the growth and development of the institution.

Need for In-Service Training for Teachers in the Higher Education Institutions

(i) Fresh master's degree holders with scant training opportunities are not conversant with many fundamental requirements of a teacher when they embark on this challenging and demanding career.
(ii) Most of them try to imitate their own teachers without knowing the pains taken by them to reach high standards of performance over the years.
(iii) They are not exposed to important areas in education, viz., educational psychology, curriculum design and development, teaching strategies, course administration, classroom management, effective tutoring, setting goals for individual students, education technology, evaluation methods, performance appraisal, research methodology, and accreditation.
(iv) They sometimes lack maturity, self-control and discipline.
(v) They may lack stress management skills and communication skills.
(vi) Some of them are unaware of or not familiar with the modern ICT-enabled teaching practices.

In-Service Training programmes for the new teachers in the following areas can put them in good stead and help them to improve their efficiency:

- Educational Psychology
- Curriculum Design and Development

- Curriculum Administration
- ICT Systems in Education
- Course Administration and Management
- Micro Teaching and Teaching Skills
- Communication Skills
- Teaching Methodologies and Tools and Aids to Teaching
- Evaluation Techniques and Grading Systems
- Quality Teaching and Learning
- Reflective Teaching
- Staff Administration
- Learning Styles
- Student Engagement in Learning
- Curricular Outcome Orientation
- Group Instructional Feedback
- Research Methodology
- Positive Disciplinary Skills
- Managing Stress
- Student Care
- Coping with Change
- Time Management
- Assertiveness
- Professional Development
- Research and Publications
- Membership in Professional bodies
- Emotional Intelligence
- Team Teaching
- Peer Evaluation
- Self Assessment
- Performance Appraisal
- Internal Quality Assurance
- Enterprise Resource Planning (ERP) Solutions
- Accreditation
- Extension Services
- Healthy Practices
- Collaborative Programmes
- Consultancy
- Interface with Parents and Alumni
- Interface with Industry

Faculty mentoring, which is carried out by senior and experienced teachers in an institution, is an ideal method by which the new faculty member undergoes a faculty development training programme within the four walls of the institution, and thereby gain confidence in handling various facets of teaching effectively. According to Anup K. Singh (2013), faculty mentoring is probably one of the best strategies of faculty development, especially for the new faculty. The objectives of faculty mentoring are as follows:

- Familiarization of new faculty with the institution;
- Their acculturation in the academic culture;
- Career progression and career counseling;
- Competence building and instructional effectiveness;
- Course design and development;
- Student care and mentoring;
- Research, proposal writing and publication;
- Institutional service and extension work; and
- Personal development and networking.

It is also suggested that an Induction Training Programme be conducted by the institution for the benefit of the new teachers. Universities and colleges can regularly organize workshops and seminars to highlight the latest trends and advances in various subjects and educational technology. Apart from these programmes, the institutions can conduct 'Faculty Development Programme' after understanding the performance-deficiencies of the faculty and to offer guidance to teachers in methodologies of teaching.

The academic staff is the backbone of an educational institution. To foster effective learning and to get the best out of the teaching profession, a code of professional conduct would necessarily create a strong sense of commitment to teaching. In this context, suggestions of Peter McCaffery (2010), about the code of professional conduct for academic staff, as given below, could be used as guidelines.

Academic staff is expected to commit itself to:

1. Doing things on time.
2. Being punctual, courteous, caring.
3. Being available.
4. Taking responsibility for supporting and guiding students' learning.
5. Being properly prepared, including knowing how to use teaching and learning facilities.
6. Preparing materials of quality on time.
7. Continuing own learning.
8. Engaging in intellectual work (scholarly activity; research).
9. Evaluating learning as a means of evaluating teaching.
10. Being aware of the vision and values of the university.

The university can establish a common professional standard which it may expect all academic staff to adhere to, irrespective of status–a basic minimum standard of performance by which to gauge academic conduct and practice.

In modern times, many universities maintain their own Academic Staff Colleges who conduct orientation programmes and specialized faculty development training programmes on a continual basis. Such faculty development programmes are of much practical use and benefit the teaching community to a great extent.

The Academic Staff College

The concept of Academic Staff College was developed over the years in India. Starting from the Kothari Commission report and later, the National Policy on Education, special emphasis has been laid on in-service training programmes for the teachers in higher education. In 1987, the University Grants Commission renamed the Academic Staff Orientation Scheme as Academic Staff Colleges for the purpose of providing adequate opportunities for the professional development of teachers. The Academic Staff Colleges have become nodal institutions established in the universities as autonomous entities and designated within the university to ensure the professional development of teachers. It is funded by the University Grants Commission. Participation of teachers in the in-service training programmes has been made mandatory for their career advancement.

According to K.B. Powar (2011), the Academic Staff Colleges, now numbering 57, are responsible for providing specially-designed orientation programmes covering teaching pedagogy and general awareness, and also refresher courses that update the university teachers in recent developments in their fields.

As the goal of the Academic Staff Colleges is to contribute positively to enhance the quality of higher education by drastically improving the competence of teachers, newer and more effective programmes which are of high standards, but which also meet the local needs, are to be designed by involving experts in academics and administration. A 'Training Impact Evaluation' can be conducted periodically to assess the effectiveness of the in-service programmes organized by the Academic Staff Colleges in all the universities. Evaluation of such training programmes can mainly be undertaken to assess the impact of training on the participants with specific reference to their learning, preparedness to make use of the knowledge and skills gained, and changes introduced by them in the methodology of teaching and in the effective use of technology in the classrooms, and the impact of training on student performance.

Effective Teacher Recognition Programmes

Teachers are to be highly honoured and recognized for their invaluable contribution in building good educational institutions, and thereby building a strong and vibrant nation. Most of the institutions give awards and have special recognition programmes in their schools and colleges to reward their best teachers annually. They enhance the employees self-esteem by sending out a strong message that the organization cares for them. The teachers in such institutions know that they would be recognized for their outstanding contributions by the administration. It motivates them to put in more efforts to improve their performance. Those teachers who are selected for such recognition, usually by a panel of judges, become the role models in their profession, and may qualify for state or national awards later. In some institutions, it is found that they institute Teaching Excellence Award, Teaching Innovation Award, Young Teacher Award and the Teacher of the Month Award. Long term service awards for the senior teachers can also be introduced. Most of the countries recognize the services of the most proficient teachers at the state or national level. The principles which guide the administration while instituting teacher awards are that everyone must feel valued for his work; it should be true and spontaneous valued for his work.

Such recognition awards which focus on individual achievements are powerful tools to sustain teachers' motivation and help them to promote their professional growth. It not only provides a clear-cut message from administration to the winners of such prestigious awards about their accomplishments, but also acts as great morale booster to them. They encourage them to become more committed and dedicated and encourage others to follow suit.

On honouring teachers, here is a solid justification which can be emulated by all societies: When our society fully values teaching, it will incorporate rituals of regard that will teach everyone, especially students, to recognize and respect teachers. A major transformation in education will happen when teachers of all levels receive regard they deserve. When they are revered, admired profoundly and respectfully, their ability to teach is enhanced as is the ability of students to learn (bell hooks, 2010).

While instituting teacher recognition awards, the organization has to circulate in advance criteria for them so that the teachers would know about the conditions to be fulfilled. If the criteria are not made known to teachers beforehand, they might have doubts about the fairness in judgments. There are many awardees in each society who have been held in high esteem for their unparalleled contributions. The spectacular contributions made by them are remembered for ever by generations of teachers and the society.

Enhancing Quality Education (Conclusion)

Not gold, but only man,
can make a nation great and strong.

You never get a second chance to make a good first impression.

Our Gratitude to Teachers

The four G's which make our life satisfying and wholesome are:

- God
- Geniality
- Generosity
- Gratitude

By gratitude one means the quality of being thankful, of showing appreciation for something. Students must express deep gratitude to their teachers for the invaluable service rendered by them in transforming their life into a life of joy and achievement so that they could explore the potentials to grow, develop and excel as full-fledged human beings with fine virtues and rich qualities of life. Gratitude is the expression of a good heart who thanks the giver of wisdom by expressing it in one's humble way. While expressing our gratitude, let us not forget that the highest appreciation is not the expression of words, but in words, but to live by what one is grateful of. Gratitude creates happiness, exudes confidence and builds an everlasting relationship. In the words of John Milton, "gratitude bestows reverence, allowing us to encounter everyday epiphanies, those transcendent moments of awe that change forever how we experience life and the world."

As gratitude makes sense of our past, brings peace for the day and creates a vision for tomorrow, it does not have any bounds. In the ancient books of knowledge in India, a teacher is known as a '*guru*', which means a person who enlightens the disciple by removing darkness and brings the light of wisdom abundantly to him. The disciples, in those days, were ready for self-sacrifice and self-restraint. They followed the gurus in all humility and obeisance as their first and foremost priority was to acquire knowledge through the arduous way, showing utmost respect to the guru.

The New Learning Environment

Times have changed. Learning environment has become sophisticated and a fast acquisition of knowledge, even from a virtual centre of education, without even seeing the guru directly (but, seeing the guru through an internet-interface network) has become the order of the day. Even then, a guru is a guru, the enlightened teacher who is a giver of knowledge and information, be it the hi-tech era or the Stone Age. It is the paramount duty of a student to show utmost respect to the teacher and always feel obliged to the giver of knowledge.

Our case for New Learning is grounded in a 'new basics' of education applicable anywhere in the world. They consist of knowledge competence, and sensibilities necessitated by changing technology, culture and economy in our times. Paradoxically, however, such a global approach is necessary, not only because teachers and learners face the same dilemmas all around the world, but because one of the key dilemmas of the New Learning, is diversity itself—amongst learners and between the settings in which learning occurs (Mary Kalantzis and Bill Cope, 2008). According to Jerome Bruner, "the first objective of any act of learning, over and beyond the pleasure it may give, is that it should serve us in the future. Learning should not only take us somewhere, it should allow us later to go further more easily". Educational systems change slowly because they tend to be hierarchical command and control systems, rather than devolved-power adaptive systems. Teachers and lecturers are neither given the power nor the means to improve the nature and quality of the teaching/learning process through technology (Elton, 1999).

As knowledge-driven organizations, colleges and universities should be greatly affected by rapid advances in information technology–computers, telecommunications, networks. In the past several decades, computers have evolved into powerful information systems with high-speed connectivity to other systems throughout the world. Rapidly evolving technologies are dramatically changing the way we collect, manipulate, transmit, and use information. The faculty of the twenty-first century may be asked to adapt to a new role as designers of learning experiences, processes, and environments. Today's students learn primarily on their own through solitary reading, writing, and problem-solving. Tomorrow's faculty may need to develop collective learning experiences in which students work together and learn together, with the faculty member acting as a consultant or a coach. The faculty member will be less concerned with identifying and then transmitting intellectual content and more focused on inspiring, motivating, and managing an active learning environment for students. It will require a major change in graduate education, since few of today's faculty members have learned these skills. One can easily identify similar profound changes occurring in the other roles of the university. The process of creating new knowledge–is evolving rapidly away from the solitary scholar to teams of scholars, spanning disciplines, institutions, and even national boundaries. (James J. Duderstadt, 1999).

Educational curriculum is of great significance in understanding and appreciating the culture of a country during a particular period in the history of human civilization. The *Handbook of Research in Curriculum* (1992) explains the importance of curriculum thus: A curriculum is, after all, a selection of certain elements of a society's culture. Accordingly, when we know what areas of knowledge and belief have been consigned to schools for deliberate inculcation, it can help us understand what was consciously, or even unconsciously, valued in that society in particular periods. Hence, it is the paramount duty of teachers to diligently apply their minds when they are entrusted with the great task of designing a curriculum.

Technology changes what people do. More importantly, technology changes what people can do. People can teach and learn with it (Jonassen, 2006; Lowyck and Ellen, 2004; Spector and Anderson, 2000). Even though the effects of technological evolution are promising, some writers are sceptical about its over-bearing influence. For instance, Joel Spring writes in '*Education Networks*', (2012), that "there is also the factor of human resistance to technological advances. Some people may hate the idea of learning online in contrast to the social interaction of face-to-face instruction. Others might love online instruction because it frees them from the classroom." There is a word of caution in "*Learning without Boundaries*", (1994), that technology as such does not automatically enhance the transferability of educational materials and systems.

The view of education as a moral development in humanity can be associated with the vision of 'learning to be' recognized in a UNESCO endeavour in the early 1970's (Faureet *et al.*). "The aim of development is the complete fulfillment of man, in all the richness of his personality, the complexity of his forms of expression and his various commitments—as an individual, member of a family and of a community, citizen and producer, inventor of techniques and creative dreamer."

This was later developed by UNESCO in the Delors Report (1996). Individual development, which begins at birth and continues throughout life, is a dialectical process which starts with knowing oneself and then opens out to relationships with others. In that sense, education is, above all, an inner journey whose stages correspond to those of the continuing maturing of the personality (*Teachers as Learners*, edited by Ora Kwo, 2010). It is this goal of education as formulated by UNESCO which has to be appreciated and understood in its fullness by the teacher who engages in an intellectual quest for excellence with a missionary zeal.

The following words of Andy Hargreaves about teaching in the knowledge society are all the more relevant in the present context:

> "Teaching is a paradoxical profession. Of all the jobs that are or aspire to be professions, only teaching is expected to create the human skills and capacities that will enable individuals and organizations to survive and succeed in today's knowledge society. Teachers, more than anyone, are expected to build learning communities, create the knowledge society, and develop the capacities for innovation, flexibility and commitment to change that are essential to economic prosperity."

The twenty-first century unfolds a lot of promises to the teaching community and the students as reflected in the book, '*A New World of Knowledge*' (1999): Education in all sectors is being transformed to prepare today's students to work in a world that will be undergoing a wide-ranging process of integration and globalization at many levels….In fact, the greatest expectations at present focus on teaching and introducing what could be considered a truly international education.

Teaching today is an increasingly complex work, requiring the highest standard of professional practice to perform it well (Hargreaves and Goodson, 1996). It is the core profession, the key agent of change in today's knowledge society (Thomas R. Guskey, 2000). But even though that the teacher occupies a key position in the society as a catalyst for change, in reality, the teaching profession is undergoing turbulence as felt by a majority of them. The problem faced by the teaching community has been highlighted by Philip G. Altbach, (1998), thus: In most countries, the professoriate has found itself under great pressure in recent years. Demands of accountability, increased bureaucratization of institutions, fiscal constraints in many countries, and an increasingly diverse student body have all challenged the professoriate.

To the teacher, one would like to pass on a message through the words of Lou Anne Johnson, the author of the bestselling book that inspired the movie, *Dangerous Minds*: "Twenty (or even forty) years from now you may not remember your students, but they will remember you. They may not remember the lessons you taught them, and they may have forgotten your face, but they will remember quite clearly the way you made them feel about themselves. They will remember your criticisms and your compliments—often word for word."

The main drivers for the teaching profession are curriculum, quality assurance, resources availability, and the requirements of the assessment process. Teachers who take professional pride in the essence of teaching—enabling a learner to reach their learning potentials—will also be driven by their insights into learner needs, and the desire to make their subject loved and understood by others (Diana Laurillard, 2008). Curt Dudley-Marling and

Penny A Freppon, 2001, give substantial guidance to how a teacher must function. "The teacher's development clearly shows a strong sense of social justice and the understanding that teaching is a moral endeavour. Such attributes of good teaching have been described by Ayers (1993) and Graves (2001) whose research works show that, as in all professional practices, teaching requires energy and dedication. They become self-sustaining when it is supported by:

- Teachers who are principled people;
- Teachers who have a strong sense of responsibility for student learning and motivation;
- Teachers who search for their own strengths;
- Teachers who long for enjoyable interactions with students and have an abiding passion for them (Ayers, 1993).

Who can make our higher education institutions centers of excellence and meet the demands of an ever-changing world, where it is clear that, a highly educated population is the key to economic competitiveness and social well-being? Clayton M. Christensen and Henry J. Eyring (2011) insist that ideally, the faculty members, administrators, and alumni who best appreciate the totality of the university's contributions to society will, in the spirit of self-regulation, play a leading role in revitalizing their beloved institutions. They have the capacity to determine their own fate and in so doing take the indispensable university to new heights.... Much as the identity of a living organism is reflected in its every cell, the identity of a university can be found in the structure of departments and in the relationships between faculty and administrators.

Higher Education in a State of Flux

In *The Role of Higher Education in Achieving a Sustainable Society*, Tony Cortese (1992) writes:

> "Higher education institutions bear a profound moral responsibility to increase the awareness, knowledge, skills and values needed to create a just and sustainable future. These institutions have the mandate and potential to develop the intellectual and conceptual framework for achieving this goal. They must play a strong role in education, research, policy development, information exchange and community outreach and support... They have the unique freedom to develop new ideas, comment on society, and engage in bold experimentation, as well as contribute to the creation of new knowledge" (Peter Blaze Corcoran and Arjen E.J. Wals, 2004)

The central purposes of a university, according to David Horowitz, "are the pursuit of truth, the discovery of new knowledge through scholarship and research, the study and reasoned criticism of intellectual and cultural traditions, the teaching and general development of students to help them to become creative individuals and productive citizens of a pluralistic democracy, and the transmission of knowledge and learning to a society at large." For centuries the university has been widely considered to be separate from the society in which it operates. The term 'ivory tower' has been used to characterize this separation, suggesting an unsullied environment above the problems and temptations of everyday life. Our institutions cultivate this image in a physical sense, often surrounded with brick walls and wrought-iron gates (*Higher Education in a Changing Economy*, edited by Katherine H. Hanson, *et al.*, 1990). The broader objectives of university education is outlined in the book, *The University: International Expectations*, edited by F. King Alexander and Kern Alexander: "University education should be seen as the primary advanced means to develop the intellect, expand the horizons of knowledge, and prepare youths for a life of contribution and sacrifice in building a democratic society based on virtue." Indeed, universities can become social engines of growth for an economy, if they come forward and accept their responsibilities to keep abreast of the changes taking place in higher education in the national and global environments and play an active role to stimulate and ensure a balanced economic development through their timely and well-conceived educational strategies for growth and development.

In modern times higher education has become a growth industry, as it undoubtedly stimulates economic growth. For this reason, it is all the more important for nations to bestow proper attention and care for the effective development of higher education institutions. It is both an opportunity and a responsibility for nations, as higher education creates employment opportunities and at the same time enhances its responsibility to support the growth and development of institutions of quality. Peter McCaffery, (2010), asserts that globalization and the knowledge society have also generated far-reaching implications for higher education through the way in which they have transformed the nature of our daily working lives. In today's education-driven economy the message is loud and clear: 'if you don't learn, you won't earn'. And, if, you want to prosper, then–given that there are no more 'jobs for life'– you will have to commit yourself to 'life long learning' in order to maintain 'life time earning'. Thus, whether one likes it or not, higher education has become–and is almost certain to remain–a growth industry.

One of the main problems faced by the present day universities and large colleges is the very pyramidical structure from which it functions, more like government departments, with air-tight compartmentalized hierarchies, controlling the institution from different corners, which are all centers of authority. They dictate their terms very often rather to stifle the growth and development of the institution. These tall organizational structures with many layers of administration, metamorphose themselves eventually into bureaucratic white elephants and tighten their grip by a centrifugal system of power and authority mechanism. This is a complex situation, and it is very difficult to wriggle out of this intricate web of authority and power. In modern times, most of the business corporations have opted out of this age-old system and preferred smaller organizations with independent administration and freedom to decide its operations and style of functioning. Decentralization and devolution of power have become the order of the day, as they enable the institution to make efficient decision-making, much faster than in a large and highly centralized institution. Maybe, this is one major reason why higher educational institutions all over the world are clamoring for autonomy. It is a truism that the administrators and teachers can be empowered effectively in a more decentralized institution. Flat organizations are preferred as they tend to be more adaptable to changes and they facilitate greater and faster communication between the administration, teachers and staff. In *Managing Colleges and Universities*, edited by Allan M. Hoffman, Randal W. Summers, (2000), the need of the hour is stated in unequivocal terms: "What is needed is a new kind of organization, one that responds faster and is more flexible."

About the ill effects of bureaucratization of the universities, the author of '*Rethinking the Future of the University*', (1998) comments:

> "The bureaucratization of the university is well known to all in it: the endless meetings, new forms to fill out, complicated social issues to address—or avoid. All these have greatly reduced the amount of time that can be profitably spent on what really matters to most academics: research, and teaching."

What plagues Indian universities has been pointed out by Mahendra Sodha, Moradhwaj Verma and Reena Srivastava, (2008): "The routine running of the university and firefighting constitute the main pre-occupation of the university management; this leaves little time for long range thinking, let alone for formulation of a shared vision and corresponding plan of action. It is true that most of the universities have a statutory body for educational research and planning, but the body has no academic support; the faculties of education and management have in general no interest in the area of higher education and make negligible contribution to the development of the university at large… The absence of a challenging, contemporary and employment-oriented syllabus is the biggest impediment in the serious pursuit of scholarship by students. With a comprehensive library and internet search, personal knowledge of the faculty and participation of prospective employers it should be possible, to formulate such a syllabus, but the exercise is rarely undertaken."

Relevance of higher education has become a matter of great concern for academics and policymakers. M. Ramanathan (2008), reminds us of its relevance thus: "In a rapidly changing social and natural environment, higher education is called upon to play a varied and complex role in development. Relevance is a key factor in this regard and this term has been used to refer to the fit or the match between what higher education institutions do and what society expects of them. This concerns the role and place of higher education in society, but it also covers access and participation, teaching and learning, the research function of the universities, the responsibility of higher education to other sectors of society, the world of work and the community service function of higher education." Factors affecting relevance in higher education are:

- population growth and population education,
- globalization, regionalization and sub-regionalization,
- rapid scientific progress,
- access and participation,
- increased cultural sensitivity and pressure for democracy,
- the need to cater to more diverse clienteles and changing labour market needs,
- new instructional methods resulting from the application of ICT,
- funding constraints and privatization, and
- reorganization of systems and diversification of structures.

Important challenges include constructive partnerships between government and institutional leadership, demonstrating the impact of higher education in development, correcting provision imbalances on the national/ regional/ sub-regional levels (including rural/urban provision), promoting institutional diversification as well as innovative curriculum and pedagogy, preserving cultural identities, advancing knowledge through research, and linkages to the whole education system.

Relevance of Quality Enhancement in the Emerging Education Scenario

> Meeting the Challenges of Higher Education in the New 'Voyage of Discovery': the Impact of Changes, and the Future of Higher Education

Higher education institutions are expected to improve their quality and excel in their performance, especially in the crucial area of advancement of knowledge. In the words of John Bowden and Ference Marton (2004), "the idea of improvement has been a quest of universities since their beginning; it is the cornerstone of what a university is about when it talks of advancing knowledge. To make improvement, it is necessary to be aware of the current status of the knowledge process or outcome that is being improved. This implies evaluation of some kind, either implicit or explicit. It also implies some follow-up which makes use of the outcomes of evaluation in undertaking research and modifying existing practices, with the expectation that this will lead to improvement." Higher education institutions are also bounden to update the syllabi and redesign the curriculum of the various courses that they offer, as they are supposed to prepare the younger generation for handling situations in the future in their workplaces. The more updated the syllabi, the more useful it becomes for the student to adjust themselves to new realities in their workplace. To be more realistic, to get the best results of a well-planned educational system, the primary, secondary, higher secondary and higher education systems have to be integrated laying emphasis on a well-conceived national goals of education, the future educational requirements of young people and meeting the national and global standards in education.

M.S. Kurhade (2008) comments on quality education: Quality education is to equip an individual with knowledge and wisdom as well. It is true that it is a long, tedious process and takes years of perseverance and focus to reach this stage. We have to ensure that quality is not only sustained but also nurtured. Therefore, we should know that quality is not a programme but a process, and not an instant cure....Overall quality of colleges is much related to the following elements:

- Interface between colleges and industry.
- Available employment opportunities.
- Preparation of students for any task in life.
- Use of electronic learning technologies.
- Professional development programme.
- Infrastructure and college organization.

The university's potential lies in the cultivation of rigorous scholarship, leading to ever-deeper understanding in many fields, and thus, as a long-term by-product, to profound benefits to the society (Janice Newson, Claire Polster, 2010). Universities are now regarded as indispensable to more practical activities than were ever conceived before as requiring systematic knowledge, and hence, the need for higher education for the acquisition of that knowledge (*The Calling of Education*, 1997). But, are the universities as citadels of higher education paying attention to the needs of the society in which they exist? Jaroslav Pelikan (1992) asserts that one of the most besetting vices of the university, and yet at the same time one of its most charming characteristics, has always been its quaint tendency to look inward and ignore the context of the society within which it lives and without which it could not exist.

The issues facing the university are very clear: an emphasis on access and participation leading to increased diversification of the student body; the requirement that research should have demonstrable user-relevance and thereby be seen to impact upon policy and practice; the need for higher education to support economic regeneration at a local and national levels; and the significance of global markets freed by the new technologies and the technological apparatus of distance learning. These policy trends have a profound influence on the ways in which institution of higher education conceive of the methods and ways in which learning operates (*A Profession in Crisis*, 2004). As universities and large colleges are monolithic establishments with an archaic and antiquated system of administration and practices, it is difficult to redeem them from the systemic problems which they have been facing for a long time. The universities apparently continue to survive amidst complex situations. What is alarming is that the system of democratic governance followed by a large number of universities around the world has been totally mired in bureaucracy. Sadly enough, most of these centers of higher learning have remained steadfast in their inefficiency and mediocrity. However, a silver lining has been noticed, though quite infrequently, that whenever such large institutions are led by illustrious academics who are endowed with charismatic leadership qualities, erudition and efficiency, things go on well. They do their best to introduce innovative changes to improve the educational system which results in providing fresh opportunities to the student community to grow and excel. Those stalwarts in the realm of higher education have introduced best methods, practices and quality initiatives to strengthen the standards of the institutions and have done remarkable service for the cause of higher education. In fact, the efforts of such luminaries in the world of academics have contributed to the development of higher education institutions, and assured its robust growth and qualitative improvement.

Universities, in general, whether they meet the aspirations of the society in which they exist or not, have survived most of the formidable challenges. How they manage to outsmart the society's compulsions and priorities has been analyzed by Philip G., Altbach, (1998): Universities, as organizations, have two large advantages. For one, they have shown over centuries of history that they have great staying power. Even when revolutionaries and emperors abolished them, they have come bouncing back. For the second, universities have adapted to every passing age, and they are now showing anew that they can construct the means of renewing and, transforming themselves to become adaptable organizations."

University administrators, similar to corporate executives, often search for best practices and apply total quality management (TQM). Such a change may come from the top of the institution and occur after considerable attention to direction and design (Manuel London, 1995).

Education is not only expected to address the challenge of changing skill and knowledge requirements; but also to provide solutions to remove poverty and prejudice, as well as to enable social justice, cohesive sociality, job skills, scientific discoveries, wealth creation, personal fulfillment and self realization (Mary Kalantzis and Bill Cope, 2008).

The National Policy on Education, India, (1986), visualizes education to be:

- A process of empowerment which is to promote the development of knowledge, skills and values (Education for Development), and
- An instrument of social change that provides means for upward economic and social mobility through enhancement of qualifications (Education for Equality).

There is a convincing idea circulating in different parts of the world, which has been expressed candidly by Jeffrey D. Sachs (2011): "We should recognize that the knowledge of science and technology is a public good that should be promoted actively by the government alongside the private sector. Markets alone will not create the twenty-first century knowledge society."

Universities and colleges are to be funded adequately in accordance with a time bound schedule by the governments as such public funding will benefit millions of young people to undergo higher education at a reasonable or lesser cost and enable them to get jobs, and thereby ensure social justice and economic growth. The main justification for public funding of the institutions of higher education is that it protects our younger generation from economic deprivation and insecurity. It is the fundamental duty of governments to provide equal opportunities to the underprivileged and marginalized sections of the society so that they improve their quality of life. Governments must target the weaker sections of the society, in particular, and encourage, motivate and provide financial assistance or scholarships to them to undergo education at the higher levels because significant talents are lost every year for want of proper education to the underprivileged. Also, the administration of universities and colleges should be handed over to committed academics with proven competent leadership acumen, as they, with their rich experience and intellectual acuity, would be more capable to run them with the right vision and thereby, promote quality teaching and research effectively. Majority of academics who became administrators of universities and colleges have proven their mettle as excellent and meritorious functionaries at the helm of affairs. Such renowned academics have been able to introduce innovative strategies to empower teachers and administrators and to stand up to the challenges of higher education in a complex global environment.

The major challenge that universities and colleges face today is from the internationalization of higher education. It has been observed in

'*Internationalizing Higher Education*' (2005), that internationalization is high on the agenda of national governments, and institutions of higher education (de Wit, 1999). According to Knight (2003), internationalization at the institutional level is defined as the process of integrating an international, intercultural global dimension into the purpose, functions or delivery of post-secondary education. These days internationalization of higher education is a permanent feature of all universities and colleges world over. The views of Roger Goodman and David Phillips (2003), provide better insights into the impact of globalization on education:

> "Globalization has become a major factor in motivating countries to reform their education systems and in their choice of specific reforms. They are concerned about the loss of jobs in traditional industries and recognize that competitiveness will depend increasingly on a highly skilled workforce that can meet the demands of knowledge and high technology industry."

With the perceived value of higher education increasingly tied to potential lifetime earnings, students face pressure at home and high school to figure out what they want to do with the rest of their lives and then pickup a major in college that will lead them to a job (Jeffrey J. Selingo, 2013). Colleges and universities may have to restructure the courses and redesign the curriculum so as to make the transition into the working world easy. It is high time that the universities and colleges think and act to bring about radical changes in their functioning by prioritizing the actual requirements of students so that they are able to make use of their knowledge and skills productively in the workplace without being put to too much stress. In this context, the suggestions of Donald Kennedy (1997) are timely and pertinent:

> "The commanding feature of this process of redesigning the university will be the reclamation of its central mission. It is, after all, society's agent for cultural transmission and cultural change. It works by the thoughtful, participatory transfer of knowledge and excitement from one generation to the next. Accordingly, its improvement must entail putting students and their needs first. Once that is done, the rest falls into place: the complex challenges posed by intellectual property rights, the tension between teaching and research, the ethical problems in faculty-student relationships, professional misconduct issues, the need for creative thinking about undergraduate education reform—indeed, all the manifold difficulties so prominent in the growing public mistrust of our academic institutions. Placing students first is a simple design principle, but it has great power."

Amritha Maheswari (2012) argues in favour of strengthening the research capabilities of Indian universities in the following words:

> "Interdisciplinary and cross-disciplinary research perspectives are the corner stone of the present day research and should take roots in the culture of our universities where individual departments largely operate as islands without connectivity to other. Identified problems which engage faculty in interdisciplinary research should therefore become significant in our university system. Interface between the university and the industry ought to be a dominant feature in the functioning of our universities as our universities are sustaining themselves on largely academic research supported by internal funding through research grants. The R&D cultures can facelift the research profile of our university system."

The future prospects of higher education would be bright and encouraging if the system could produce quality degree-holders who are able to survive and succeed in competitive environments facing the complex political, sociological, technological, business and environmental challenges. In an economy driven by knowledge and innovation, in a world of opportunities and risks, and in diverse workplaces, the youth are exposed to greater challenges of the modern world. The panacea is a vibrant system of higher education with universities and colleges adapting to the changes and teachers and administrators enhancing their qualities to meet the real challenges posed by a dynamic environment. Once education is put on the centre stage of policy decisions taken by a government, it can become the driving force to transform the economy into a self-sustaining one so as to build a wealthy and welfare state. In the words of Colin Brock, "Education has massive potential for good in terms of maximizing the capacity of human population to relate positively to each other in the interest of mutual well-being." One should think of the most crucial factor that would shape the destiny of nations. Clark Kerr, 1995, reminds us of the vital role played by the product of a university—knowledge, in transforming nations into economic and social powerhouses: The basic reality, for the university, is the widespread recognition that new knowledge is the most important factor in economic and social growth. We perceive that the university's invisible product, knowledge, may be the most powerful single element in our culture, affecting the rise and fall of professions and even of social classes, of regions and even of nations. He continues to state that, because of this fundamental reality, the university is called upon to produce knowledge as never before—for civic and regional purposes, for national purposes, and even for no purpose at all beyond the realization that most knowledge comes to serve mankind. And it is also being called upon to transmit knowledge to an unprecedented proportion of the population.

We can pin our hopes on the survival of traditional universities in the future as well, as they too have strong core competencies by which they can face the imminent threat of digitalization of educational practices. It has been clearly stated in '*The University, International Expectations*' (2002), as follows:

> "Some observers have suggested that traditional universities will in the new century give way to virtual universities located in cyber-space. I do not see such an extreme change occurring. The heritage and reputation so exemplified by the colleges at Oxford and Cambridge, combined with the strength of quality institutions around the globe, argue against that happening. Still, we should aim neither too high, with out-of-this-world expectations about what the new technology can accomplish, or so low that we miss the opportunity to improve education (David W. Olien).

It is difficult to wind up writing a book on teaching and administration as it is a live subject with great potentials for improvement. In the twenty-first century, breathtaking innovations are taking place on a large scale in the realm of teaching and administration of educational institutions. On the one hand teachers themselves are becoming more and more creative and resourceful and on the other, technology is expanding beyond recognition and innovative practices are increasingly used in educational institutions. Students too are becoming more and more responsive, responsible and tech savvy. The courses of study and the course wares have undergone a seachange. At the same time, the onslaught of virtual systems of education and distance education programmes are engulfing the emerging scenario of education, which will further be impacted by internationalization of higher education. Indeed, it is a challenging, and hopefully, a promising situation for the younger generation.

It is an indisputable fact that due to the preponderance of computer-enabled gadgets, the presentation skills of teachers have improved by leaps and bounds. Technology, if used intelligently, can create a world of opportunities to teach and learn well. As it moves forward, it poses many daunting tasks for the educators all over the world. In the emerging situation, teachers are expected to keep up with these technological changes which directly impact the tools and methodologies used in the classrooms. Technology also affords the teachers opportunity to improvise new tools and methodology to a great extent, and get the best or optimum results. Another advantage of technology is that teachers can upload the notes in the institution's website and interact with students. But, as time passes by, like obsolete knowledge, obsolete technology will also become a burden on the education system. When it happens, the policy makers in the field of education must come to the rescue of the system, and take appropriate and timely action.

The impact of this new technology has come more quickly and been more obvious in sectors other than higher education. The magnitude of change that confronts colleges and universities is immense. The potential reach of the new technology seems almost without limits. Whatever the ultimate impact, technology has already changed higher education institutions—the way we organize ourselves, our policies, our culture, the way faculties operate, the way we work, and those we serve. And this transformation will continue well into the next century (*Challenges Facing Higher Education at the Millennium*, 1999).

A great potential which is provided to teachers also by the internet is to develop networked academic communities, which enhances the scope for professional development of teachers. As observed by Manuel Ortega and Jose Bravo, "Networked technologies have the potential to change educational practices, by providing teachers and students with an expanded scope and quality of content, activities and resources." These technologies, in turn, not only enhance the quality of the teaching profession but also improve the core competence of the institutions of higher education.

Carl A. Raschke (2003) has noted how the new knowledge space would look like, which is as follows:

This new space is what we may refer to generically as 'postmodern knowledge space' which is a sort of multi-model, hypertextual 'hyperspace'. It is an illimitable space laid out through a network of signifying relations that are at the same time a texture of 'contextualities', a web of ligatures and differences. The hyper-university with its new pedagogy of hyper-learning is the charter school for the exploration of this knowledge space.....Exploring the internet will then become the voyage of discovery it was envisioned to be a decade ago. The way in which internet has become the central conduit for communication among scholars themselves testifies to these possibilities.... The space of the postmodern university is an unbounded knowledge space."

In the words of Eric Schmidt and Jared Cohen (2013), the co-authors of, "*The New Digital Age*," "the most important pillar behind innovation and opportunity—education—will see tremendous positive change in the coming decades as rising connectivity reshapes traditional routines and offers new paths for learning. Most students will be highly technologically literate, as schools continue to integrate technology into lesson plans and, in some cases, replace traditional lessons with more interactive workshops. Education will be a more flexible experience, adapting itself to children's learning styles and pace, instead of the other way around."

Higher education will witness further drastic and remarkable changes as knowledge expands and skills diversify. These changes, though formidable and demanding, are going to present greater opportunities for introducing timely and pragmatic reforms in the qualitative improvement of institutions, in the form of new faculty roles, professional development of teachers, need to design and develop newer courses along with innovation and a more global perspective in curriculum, developing research-based knowledge, the preponderance of ICT-enabled education, application of indigenous knowledge and practices, upgrading of facilities and infrastructure, women's education, vocational education, learning new languages, online education, enrollment of students in hi-tech courses, placement and training, collaboration with international centers of higher education, and industry-academia collaboration. These crucial changes will play a dominant role in facilitating a continuous process of development in higher education and substantially raise the quality of experiences for students. In turn, education will become a catalyst for growth and development of the economy of each and every country. As the task of discovery and knowledge production has long been paramount to the vision of universities and colleges in this new era, we hope that the knowledge emerging from research in the various centers of higher education will lead to new products, services and applications that will result in the material progress of countries all over the world.

The following trends are apparent from various possible scenarios for the future of higher education:

- Student participation will continue to expand and will in most cases be evident from growth in the size of higher education systems.
- Women will be the majority in the student population.
- The mix of the student population will be more varied, with greater numbers of international students, older students, and those studying part-time, etc.
- The social base in higher education will probably continue to broaden, along with uncertainty about how this will affect inequalities of educational opportunities between social groups (*Higher Education to 2030*, 2008).

Except for the mix of the student population, where it is expected that greater numbers of foreign students, older students and part-time students would be attending educational programmes in some countries, all the other trends forecast are seemingly applicable to a large majority of countries.

Most academics agree that the reach of technology in the field of education will be extensive, remarkable and unparalleled. In this connection, the words of caution from R.W. Burniske and Lowell Monke, the authors of "*Breaking Down The Digital Walls*" is pertinent: "If telecommunication helps us dream of that "brave new world," fashioning better people, societies, and institutions, then we will have to celebrate. However, technology cannot accomplish such things on its own; it needs the human spirit and imagination." However, there is ample room for optimism, as echoed in the words of Christopher Driver, who, early as in 1972, had predicted that "ultimately, I believe, the computer is bound to "explode" the university in a new sense, by helping it to extend learning facilities into the student's home."

One important concern of institutions in higher education now is the nature and facilities of modern libraries. Already our existing libraries have started undergoing the process of converting themselves into the bookless, digitalized libraries. As posed by Russell Francis, (2010) "should we respond to fund-raising appeals for new libraries? Or should we convert existing libraries into more dining spaces and coffee areas where students' web-supported projective identities must be tested? Without doubt these are implications for how universities organize their physical resources to play their part in supporting students' learning."

Teaching and scholarship are entwined and interdependent. Teaching without scholarship will not serve its purpose. In this connection, the words of Pat Hutchings and Lee S. Shulman (*The Scholarship of Teaching*) are worth noting:

The scholarship of teaching draws synthetically from the other scholarships. It begins with scholarly teaching itself. It is a special case of scholarship of application and engagement, and frequently entails the discovery of new findings and principles. At its best, it creates new meanings through integrating across other inquiries, negotiating understanding theory and practice. Where discovery, engagement, and application intersect, there you will find teaching among the scholarships (*Learning from Change*, 2000)

Now-a-days a lot of training is imparted either in institutions or at Staff Training Colleges for the benefit of the teacher. But, is the training transforming the teacher into a versatile teacher? Has he been able to understand the intricacies of teaching so as to learn the methods by which he can become an accomplished teacher? Alexander Meiklejoh's concern about the aftermath of most of the training programmes is worth noting: "One of the greatest failures of our contemporary training of teachers is that they become mere technicians. They do not learn the beliefs and motives and values for the sake of which the classroom exists." To be successful, a teacher must possess the essential qualities of a resourceful teacher, the right pedagogical skills, a good grounding in the subjects and have a great passion to excel. In this field, nothing becomes successful if the teacher lacks the initiative and drive to fulfill the tasks assigned both methodically and pragmatically. In teaching, the most common failing, is teacher's negative attitude to teaching. Such a teacher should quit the job as he is unfit to be a teacher. Persons who do not posses flair for teaching are a burden on the institution. It would be difficult to train them who are generally indifferent and have a negative mindset. A discontented teacher eventually becomes a big liability to the institution. Teachers who are incapable of maintaining the expected standards and producing good results are also a liability to the system. When a person selects teaching as a profession, he has to think twice about his suitability to be a part and parcel of this ennobling profession which demands continuous preparation, planning, and self-evaluation. Teachers are primarily engaged in a very responsible job of shaping students and thereby, building the future of a nation. If they fail, the nation fails. Similarly, administration that should set examples to excel in all phases of the development of an educational institution must rise to the occasion and enable it to advance and keep pace with the times. An old tribal wisdom is clear on what a teacher who is unsuccessful should do: When you discover you are riding a dead horse, the best thing you can do is to dismount and leave. This applies to inefficient administrators as well.

Here is a valuable message from Brent D Ruben, which may motivate the teachers, administrators and staff to be proud of their positions and to become responsible to the respective institutions where they work:

"Perhaps the most important task facing all of us—faculty, administration, and staff—is to continually remind ourselves of the vital role we play as full-time ambassadors for our institutions in each and every interaction with the students, parents, alumni, and the public. Every conversation we have presents an opportunity for us to play a significant personal role in helping to enrich the understanding and support for the purposes and aspirations of our college or university, and higher education in general."

Before we conclude, all the distinguished colleagues of the profession, are reminded once again, that the purpose of education is to prepare students to be intellectually alert, morally upright, physically strong, aesthetically sensitive, socially committed and economically self-reliant. The mission is all the more challenging as time passes by. Indeed, teachers will ever be considered the happiest among all professionals. However, they will ever remain unsung heroes, but the world knows it is they who transform the world into a better place to live in. Let learning become a life-long passion for all of us. "Motivation for learning throughout the life span must become more common, expected by the society, and supported by the programmes that add quality to life" (Paris S. Strom and Robert D. Strom, 2011). The problem with the twenty-first century has been highlighted by Alvin Toffler: "The illiterate of the twenty-first century will not be those who cannot read and write, but those who cannot learn, unlearn, and relearn."

We would like to sum up by quoting the meaningful and timely words of one of the greatest innovators of our times, Steve Jobbs (1955-2011), the co-founder of Apple Inc.:

> "Your time is limited, so don't waste it living someone else's life. Don't be trapped by dogma—which is living with the results of other people's thinking. Don't let the noise of other's opinions drown out your own inner voice. And, most important—have the courage to follow your heart and intuition. They somehow already know what you truly want to become. Everything else is secondary."

References

Access to Excellence–A Progress Report from Ontario Universities, Council of Ontario Universities, 2001.

Achieving Performance Excellence in University Administration, Manuel London, Praeger Publishers, 1995.

Adithan, M., B.V.A. Rao, D.P. Kothari (2009), Internationalization of Higher Education in Universities in India, *University News*, Vol. 47, No. 39, Association of Indian Universities.

Agarwal, Pawan (2009), *Indian Higher Education Envisioning the Future*, SAGE Publication India Pvt., Ltd.

Alan, Brinkley, Esam EL-Fakahany, Betty Dessants, *et al.*, (2011), *The Chicago Handbook For Teachers—A Practical Guide to the College Classroom*, The University of Chicago Press.

Albert, E. Sloman (1964), *A University in the Making*, Oxford University Press.

Alexander, F. King and Kern Alexander (ed.) (2002), *The University: International Expectations*, McGill-Queen's University Press.

Alexander, Jonathan (2006), *Digital Youth*, Hamton Press Inc.

Altbach, Philip G. (1998), *Comparative Higher Education*, Ablex Publishing Corporation.

Andres, Lesley and Finola Finlay (eds.) (2004), *Student Affairs: Experiencing Higher Education*, U.B.C. Press.

Angelo, Thomas A., K. Patricia Cross (1993), *Classroom Assessment Techniques: A Handbook for College Teachers*, Jossey-Bass.

Anne, Lou (2011), *Teaching Outside the Box*, Johnson-Jossey-Bass.

Ashby, Eric (1969), *The Academic Professor*, British Academy.

Bain, Ken (2004), *What the Best College Teachers Do*, Harvard University Press.

Banner, Jr. James M. and Cannon, Harold C. (1999), *The Elements of Learning*, Yale University Press.

Barbules, Nicholas C., Thomas A. Callister, Jr. (2000), *Watch IT The Risks and Promises of Info-Technologies for Education*, Westview.

Barron, Ann E. and Gary W. Orwig (1997), *New Technologies for Education*, Libraries Unlimited, Inc.

Beach, Charles M. (ed.), *et al.* (2005), *Higher Education in Canada*, McGill-Queens' University Press.

Benson, Barbara P. (2009), *Meet Standards, Motivate Students, and Still Enjoy Teaching*, Corwin Press.

Bereiter, Carl, (2002), Education and Mind in the Knowledge Age, Lawrence Erlbaum Associates.

Bergquist, William H., Steven R. Phillips (1979), *A Handbook for Faculty Development*, Council for the Advancement of Small Colleges.

Black, J. Stewart and Hal B. Gregersen, (2004), *Leading Strategic Change*, Prentice Hall.

Bond, Sheryl and Jean-Pierre Lemasson (1999), *A New World of Knowledge*, International Development Research Center.

Bottery, Mike (2004), *The Challenges of Educational Leadership*, Paul Chapman Publishing.

Bourner, Tom (ed.) (2000), *New Directions in Professional Higher Education*, SRHE and, Oxford University Press.

Bowden, John and Ference Marton (2004), *The University of Learning*, Routledge Falmer.

Brent D., Ruben (1995), *Quality in Higher Education*, Transaction Publishers.

Bridges, David, Palmira Juceviciene, *et al*., (2007), *Higher Education and National Development*, Routledge.

Brock, Colin (2011), *Education as a Global Concern*, Continuum International Publishing Group.

Brock, Colin and Lorraine Pe Symaco (2011), *Education in South East Asia*, Edited, Oxford Studies in Comparative Education, Symposium Books.

Brophy, Jere (2007), *Using Video in Teacher Education*, Elsevier.

Brophy, Jere (ed.) (2001), *Subject-Specific Instructional Methods and Activities*, Elsevier Science Limited.

Brophy, Jere and Stefinee Pinnegar (2005), Learning from Research on Teaching: Perspective, Methodology, and Representation, *Advances in Research on Teaching*—Vol. 2, Elsevier.

Budd, John M. (2009), *Higher Education's Purpose*, University Press of America.

Burniske, R.W. and Lowell Monke (2001), *Breaking Down the Digital Walls*, State University of New York Press.

Chandras, Kanaur V. (1977), *Four Thousand Years of Indian Education: A Short History of the Hindu, Buddhist, and Moslem Periods*, R&E Research Associates Inc.

Chiazzese, G., M. Allegra, A. Chifari and S. Ottaviano (eds.), *Methods and Technologies for Learning*, Italian National Research Council, Institute for Educational Technology, WITpress.

China: Higher Education Reform (World Bank Country Study), 1997.

Chowdhary, J.N. (2012), Quality Assurance in Higher Technical and Management Education, *University News*, Vol. 50, No. 10, Association of Indian Universities.

Christensen, Clayton M. and A. Hansen (1994), *Teaching and Case Method-Barnes*, Harvard Business School Press.

Christensen, Clayton M. and Henry J. Eyring, (2011), *The Innovative University—Changing the DNA of Higher Education from the Inside Out,* Jossey-Bass.

Cleveland, Bernard F. (1984), *Master Teaching Techniques*, The Connecting Link Press.

Collins, Janet (2002), *Manifesto for Learning*, Joe Harkin and Melanie Nind, Continuum.

Cookson, Peter W., Jr., Alan R. Sadovnik, and Susan F. Semel (eds.) (1992), *International Handbook of Educational Reform*, Greenwood Press.

Coppola, Eileen M., (2004), *Powering up: Learning to Teach Well with Technology*, Teachers College Press.

Corcoran, Peter Blaze and Arjen E.J. Wals (eds.) (2004), *Higher Education and the Challenge of Sustainability*, Kluwer Academic Publishers.

Craft Alma (ed.) (1992), *Quality Assurance in Higher Education*, The Falmer Press.

Crane, Beverley E. (2000), *Teaching with the Internet*, Neal-Schuman Publishers Inc.

Creemers, Bert. P.M. and Leonidas Kyriakides (2008), *The Dynamics of Educational Effectiveness*, Routledge.

Cummings, William K., (2003), *The Institution of Education*, Symposium Books.

DeNeef, A. Leigh and Craufurd D. Goodwin (eds.) (1995), *The Academics Handbook*, Duke University Press.

Deshpande, H.V. (2008), Role of the Stakeholders in Re-Accreditation, *University News*, Vol. 46, No. 46, Association of Indian Universities.

DeZure, Deborah (ed.), *Learning from Change*, Stylus Publishing LLC.

Driver, Christopher (1972), *The Exploding University*, The Bobbs-Merrill Company Inc.

Elaine, Martin (1999), *Changing Academic Work*, the Society for Research into Higher Education and Open University Press.

Fenwick, W. English (2008), *Anatomy of Professional Practice*, Rowan & Littlefield Education.

Fenwick, W. English (2008), *The Art of Educational Leadership*, SAGE Publications.

Frain, John (1993), *The Changing Culture of a College*, The Falmer Press.

Francis, Russell (2010), *The Decentring of the Traditional University*, Routledge.

French, Sidney J. (1954), *Accent on Teaching*, Edited Harper Brothers.

Freppon, Penny A. (2001), *What It Takes to be a Teacher*, Curt Dudley-Marling, Heinemann.

Gabbard, David A. (ed.), (2000), *Knowledge and Power in the Global Economy*, Lawrence Erlbaum Associates, Publishers.

Gage, N.L., David C. Berliner (1991), *Educational Psychology*, Houghton Mifflin Co.

Gilbert, Ian (2011), *Why DO I Need A Teacher When I've Got Google*, Routledge.

Goleman, Daniel (1995), *Emotional Intelligence*, Random House.

Goodlad, Sinclair, (1995), *The Quest for Quality*, The Society for Research into Higher Education and Open University Press.

Goodman, Roger and David Phillips (2003), *Can the Japanese Change Their Education System?* Oxford Studies in Comparative Education Series.

Goodwin, William L. and Herbert J. Klausmeier (1975), *Facilitating Student Learning*, Harper & Row, Publisher.

Gorman, Richard M. and Charles E. (1974), *The Psychology of Classroom Learning*, Merrill Publishing Co.

Green, Jane (2011), *Education, Professionalism and the Quest for Accountability*, Routledge.

Grosby, Steven (ed.) (1997), *The Calling of Education*, University of Chicago Press.

Guruz, Kemal (2011), *Higher Education and International Student Mobility in the Global Knowledge Economy*, State University of New York Press.

Guskey, Thomas R. Corwin Press (2000), *Evaluating Professional Development*, Inc., A Sage Publication Co.

Hackbarth, Steven (1996), *The Educational Technology Handbook*, Educational Technology Publications.

Hanson, Katherine H., *et al*., (eds.) (1990), *Higher Education in a Changing Economy*, Macmillan Publishing House.

Hargreaves, Andy (2003). *Teaching in the Knowledge Society*, Teacher College Press.

Hassard, Jack (2005), *The Art of Teaching Science*, Oxford University Press.

Haug, Peder, Thomas A. Schwandt (2001), *Evaluating Educational Reforms*, Information Age Publishing Inc.

Haydon, Graham (2006), *Values in Education*, Continuum.

Hayes, Dennis (ed.), 2004, *The Routledge Falmer Guide to Key Debates in Education.*

Hermanowicz, Joseph C. (ed.) (2011), *The American Academic Profession*, The Johns Hopkins University Press.

Hersey, Paul and Kenneth Blanchard, *Management of Organizational Behaviour.*

Higher Education to 2030, OECD, 2008.

Highet, Gilbert (1950), *The Art of Teaching*, Vintage Books.

Hilton, Margaret (ed.) (2002), *Enhancing Undergraduate Learning with IT*, National Academy Press.

Hirsch, Werner Z. and Luce E. Weber (1999), *Challenges Facing Higher Education at the Millennium*, American Council of Education and the Oryx Press.

Hoffman, Allan M. and Randal W. Summers (2000), *Managing Colleges and Universities*, Bergin & Garvey.

Holbeche, Linda (2010), *HR Leadership*, Butterworth-Heinemann, Oxford.

Hooks, Bell (2010), *Teaching Critical Thinking*, Routledge.

Hoy, Wayne K. and Cecil G. Miskel (1992), *Educational Leadership and Reform*, Edited, Information Age Publishing.

Huston, Therese (2009), *Teaching What You Don't Know*, Harvard University Press.

Jackson, Philip W. (ed.) (1992), *Handbook of Research in Curriculum*, Macmillan Publishing Co.

James, W. Hall, (1991), *Access through Innovation*, American Council of Education and Macmillan Publishing House.

Jaques and Salmon, (2007), *Learning in Groups*, Routledge.

Jeffrey, David Lyle and Dominic Manganiello (eds.) (1998), *Rethinking: The Future of the University*, University of Ottawa Press.

Johnson, Dewey E. (2002), Prentice Hall of India.

Jones, Anthony S.; Lawrence W. Bagford and Edward A., Wallen (1979), *Strategies for Teaching*, The Scarecrow Press Inc.

Joseph, Sarath Babu, When internationalization rules, Education Plus, *The Hindu*, Feb., 27, 2012.

Journal of Instructional Design, American Council on Education, Macmillan Publishing Co., 1989.

Joyce, Bruce, Marsha Weil, Emily Calhoun (2011), *Models of Teaching*, PHI Learning Pvt., Ltd.

Kafai, Yasmin B., *et al.* (2004), International Conference of the Learning Sciences, Lawrence Erlbaum Associates.

Kaku, Michio (2011), *Physics of the Future*, Anchor Books.

Kalantzis, Mary (2008), *New Learning*, Bill Cope, Cambridge University Press.

Kaufman, Roger (2006), *Practical Evaluation for Educators*, Corwin Press—A Sage Publications Company.

Kendall, Jane C., John S. Duley, Thomas C. Little, Jane S. and Permaul, Sharon Robin (1986), *Strengthening Experiential Education within Your Institute*, National Society for Internships and Experiential Education.

Kennedy, Donald (1997), *Academic Duty*, Harvard University Press.

Kerr, Clark (1995), *The Uses of the University*, Harvard University Press.

Ketteridge, Steve (2002), *The Effective Academic*, Kogan Page Limited.

Klapper, Paul (1920), *College Teaching*, Edited World Book Company.

Klatt, Bruce (1999), *The Ultimate Training Workshop Handbook*, McGraw Hill.

Koehler, Virginia Richardson, *et al.* (1987), *Educator's Handbook: A Research Perspective*, Longman.

Kohlberg, L., (1984), *The Psychology of Moral Development*, Harper Collins.

Krumsvik, Rune (2009), *Learning in the Network Society and the Digitized School*, Nova Science Publishes Inc.

Kumar, Ashwani (2008), Some Quality Issues in Higher Education, *University News*, Vol. 46, No. 46, Association of Indian Universities.

Kurhade, M.S. (2008), A Pathway to Quality Education, *University News*, Vol. 46, No. 46, Association of Indian Universities.

Kwo, Ora (2010) (ed.), *Teachers as Learners*, Comparative Education Research Centre, Springer.

Laurent, A. Daloz (2012), *Mentor Guiding the Journey of Adult Learners*, Jossey-Bass.

Laurillard, Diana (2008), Digital Technologies and their role in achieving our ambitions for education, Institute of Education, University of London.

Lazin, Fred, Matt Evans, N. Jayaram (ed.) (2010), *Higher Education and Equality of Opportunities*, Lexington Books.

Lefrancois, Guy R. (2000), *Psychology for Teaching*, Wadsworth.

Light, Richard J. (2001), *Making The Most of College*, Harvard University Press.

Lofty, John S. (2006), *Quiet Wisdom*, Peterlang.

Luthans, Fred and Irwin (1998), *Organization Behaviour*, McGraw Hill.

Lynton, Rolf P. (2008), *Training for Development*, Udai Pareek, Visstar Publications.

Mahadevan, G., In defense of Open Access Systems, Education Plus, *The Hindu*, Dec., 31, 2012.

Maheshwari, Amrita (2012), Crucial Role and Relevance of Higher Education Research, *University News*, Vol. 50, No. 51, Association of Indian Universities.

Marmar, Mukhopadhyay (2005), *Total Quality Management in Education*, Sage Publications India Pvt., Ltd.

Martinez, Mario C. and Mimi Wolverton (2009), *Innovative Strategy Making in Higher Education*, Information Age Publishing Inc.

Maxwell, John C. (2004), *Winning with People*, Thomas Nelson.

Mayhew, Lewis B., Patrick J. Ford, Dean L. Hubbard (1990), *The Quest for Quality*, Jossey-Bass Publishers.

McAlpine, Lynn and Gerlese Akerlind (2010), *Becoming an Academic: International Perspectives*, Palgrave Macmillan,.

McCaffery, Peter (2010), *The Higher Education Manager's Handbook*, Routledge.

McLean, Monica (2006), *Pedagogy and the University*, Continuum.

McNergney, Robert F. Joanne M. Herbert (2001), *Foundations of Education: The Challenge of Professional Practice*, Allyn and Bacon.

Melinda, Mangin, Sara Ray Stoelinga (2008), *Effective Teacher Leadership*, Edited Teachers College Press.

Melko Matthew (1998), *A Professor's Work*, University Press of America Inc.

Merideth, Eunice M., Corwin Press, (2007), *Leadership Strategies for Teachers*, Sage Publications India Pvt. Ltd.

Milano, Michael (1998), *Designing Powerful Training*, Diane Ullius, Jossey-Bass.

Milward, Peter (2006), *What is a University*, Shepheard-Walwyn Ltd.

Moller, Leslie, Jason Bond Huett, Dourglas M. Harvey (2009), *Learning and Instructional Technologies for the Twenty-first Century*, Springer.

Morsy, Zaghloul and Philip G. Altbach (1996), *Higher Education in an International Perspective*, Garland Publishing, Inc.

Mourlas, Constantinos, *et al.*, (2009), *Cognitive and Emotional Processes in Web-Based Education*: Integrating Human Factors and Personalization, Info Science Reference, Hershey.

Muijs, Daniel, David Reynolds, (2001), *Effective Teaching*, Sage Publications.

Newson, Janice, Claire Polster (2010), *Academic Challenges*, Canadian Scholar's Press Inc.

Nikolopoulou, Anastasia Taisha Abraham, Farid Mirbagheri (2010), *Education for Sustainable Development*, Edited, Sage Publications India Pvt., Ltd.

Nilson, Linda B. (2010), *Teaching at Its Best (A Research-Based Resource for College Instructors)*, Jossey-Bass.

Nimus, Nihil, Robert Boice (2000), *Advice for New Faculty Members*, Allyn and Bacon.

Ninnes, Peter and Meeri Hellsten (eds.) (2005), *Internationalizing Higher Education*, Springer.

Norman, D.A. (1980), *What Goes On in the Mind of the Learner*, Jossey-Bass.

Norris, Nigel (2008), *Curriculum and the Teacher*, Edited by Routledge.

Norton, Arthur O. (1909), *Readings in The History of Education Mediaeval Universities*, Published by Harvard University.

O'Connell, Sir Bernard (2005), *Creating an Outstanding College*, Nelson Thornes Limited.

Orlich, Donald C. Robert J. Harder, Richard C. Callahan, Michael S. Trevisan, Abbie H. Brown, Wadsworth (2010), *Teaching Strategies*.

Ortega, Manuel and Jose Bravo (2000), *Computer and Education in the Twenty-first Century*, Kluwer Academic Publishers.

Owens, Robert G. (1970), *Organization Behaviour in Education*, Prentice Hall.

Palmer, Stuart (1998), *The Universities Today*, University Press of America.

Panda, Hemant K. (2013), Higher Education: Time for a Paradigm Shift, *University News*, Vol. 51, No. 09, Association of Indian Universities.

Pandey, Anjaney Kumar, Sanjaya Kumar Das (2009), Hallmarking the Higher Education: An Imperative Need in Globalization, *University News*, Vol. 47, No. 39, Association of Indian Universities.

Panikkar, K.N., M. Bhaskaran Nair (2012), *Globalization and Higher Education in India*, Pearson.

Pelikan, Jaroslav (1992), *The Idea of the University*, Yale University Press.

Pittinsky, Matthew Serbin (2003), *The Wired Tower: Perspective on the Impact of the Internet on Higher Education*, Pearson Education Inc.

Pollard, Andrew, (2006), *Reflective Teaching*, Continuum.

Powar, K.B. (2011), *Indian Higher Education Revisited*, Vikas Publishing House, Pvt. Ltd.

Ramanathan, M. (2008), Relevance in Higher education, *University News*, Vol. 46, No. 46, Association of Indian Universities.

Ranjana, Bhatia (2011), Enhancing Teaching: Learning with Technology, *University News*, Vol. 49, No. 31, Association of Indian Universities.

Raschke, Carl A. (2003), *The Digital Revolution and the Coming of the Postmodern University*, Routledge-Falmer.

Reeves, Douglas B. (2009), *Assessing Educational Leaders*, Corwin Press.

Reis, Richard M. (2012), *Tomorrow's Professor*, John Wiley & Sons.

Robert, P., Engvall (1997), *The Professionalization of Teaching*, University Press of America, Inc.

Rogers, Jenny (2007), Adults Learning, Open University Press.

Ruben, Brent D. (2004), *Pursuing Excellence in Higher Education*, Jossey-Bass.

Ruegg, Walter (1992), *A History of the University in Europe*, Cambridge University Press, 1992.

Sachs, Jeffrey D. (2011), *The Price of Civilization*, Random House.

Sahoo, Sarat Kumar, Pratima Pradhan, Empowering Teachers for Institutional Development, *University News*, Vol. 49, No. 01, Association of Indian Universities, 2011.

Saleem, Shaikh, Gawali, Vidya (2009), Does India Need Foreign Universities, *University News*, Vol. 47, No. 39, Association of Indian Universities.

Schmidt, Eric and Jared Cohen, (2013), *The New Digital Age Reshaping: The Future of People, Nations and Business*, Alfred A. Knopf,.

Schutz, Paul A. (2007), Reinhard Pekrun, *Emotion in Education*, Elsevier.

Sean, Kelly (2012) *Assessing Teacher Quality*, Teachers College Press.

Seidel, Robert J. and Paul R. Chatelier (eds.) (1994), *Learning Without Boundaries*, Plenum Press.

Seidel, Robert J. and Paul R. Chatelier, Jennifer A. Moon (eds.) (2006), *Learning Journals*, Routledge.

Seymour, Daniel J. (1992), *Causing Quality in Higher Education*, Macmillan Publishing Company.

Shils, Edward (1997), *The Order of Learning*, Transaction Publishers.

Singh, Anup (2013), Mentoring New Faculty for Student Success in Higher Education, *University News*, Vol. 51, No. 26, Association of Indian Universities.

Singh, Pooja (2011), Pitroda Commission on Quality of Higher Education: Reasons for Concern and Recommendations of Concern, *University News*, Vol. 49, No. 34, Association of Indian Universities.

Sodha, Mahendra, Moradhwaj Verma, Reena Srivastava (2008), Some Options for Progress of Indian Higher Education System, *University News*, Vol. 46, No. 46, Association of Indian Universities.

Spring, Joel (2012), *Education Networks*, Routledge.

Strike, Kenneth A., Pamela A. Moss (2003), *Ethics and College Student Life*, Prentice Hall.

Strom, Paris S. and Robert D. Strom (2011), *Adult Learning and Relationships*, Information Age Publishing, Inc.

Stronge, James H. (2006), *Evaluating Teaching*, Corwin Press, Sage Publications.

Swamy, Raju Narayana (2013), Envisioning the Internationalization of Higher Education in India, *University News*, Vol. 51, No. 09, Association of Indian Universities.

Swamy, V.C. Kulandai (1991), Academic Leadership—The Desideratum, Government of Pondicherry.

Tatto, Maria Teresa and David N. Plank (ed.) (2007), *The Dynamics of Global Teaching Reforms*, Symposium Books.

Tefferna, Damtew and Philip G. Altbach (2003), *African Higher Education, An International Reference Handbook*, Edited by Bloomington Indianapolis.

Thelin, John R. (1982), *Higher Education and Its Useful Past*, Schenkman Publishing Company Inc.

Thomas, R. Murray (1992), *Education's Role in National Development Plans*, Edited, Praeger Publishers.

Vygotsky, L.S. (1997), *Educational Psychology*, St Lucie Press.

Walter, W. McMahon, (2009), *Higher Learning, Greater Good*, The John Hopkins University Press.

Warren, Bennis (2009), *On Becoming a Leader*, Basic Books.

Wassermann, Selma (1994), *Introduction to Case Method Teaching*, Teachers College Press.

Weber, Lucye and James J. Duderstadt (ed.) (2008), *The Globalization of Higher Education*, Economica Ltd.

Wechrich, Heinz and Harold Koontz (2002), *Management*, Tata McGraw Hill Publishing Company.

Weiss, Renee E. (2000), *Principles of Effective Teaching in the Online Classroom*, Jossey-Bass.

William H., Krieger (1998), *Continuing Professional Education in Transition*, Edited, Young, Publishing Company.

World Guide to Higher Education (1996), UNESCO Publishing.

Zachary, Karabell (1998), *What's College For*? Basic Books.

Zachary, Lois J. (2000), *The Mentor's Guide*, Jossey-Bass.

Index